LAST CHANCE
TEXACO

LAST CHANCE TEXACO

Chronicles of an American Troubadour

RICKIE LEE JONES

Grove Press

New York

FIRST EDITION

Published simultaneously in Canada
Printed in Canada

This title was set in 11.5-pt. Abobe Caslon Pro by Alpha Design & Composition of Pittsfield, NH.

First Grove Atlantic hardcover edition: April 2021

Library of Congress Cataloging-in-Publication data is available for this title.

ISBN 978-0-8021-2712-9
eISBN 978-0-8021-8880-9

Grove Press
an imprint of Grove Atlantic
154 West 14th Street
New York, NY 10011

Distributed by Publishers Group West

groveatlantic.com

21 22 23 24   10 9 8 7 6 5 4 3 2 1

This book is dedicated to my family
On whatever stage they call their own

CONTENTS

DRIVER'S SEAT

THE WAY BACK SEAT

LAST CHANCE
TEXACO

PROLOGUE

Frank "Peg Leg" Jones

H ere are the histories of my parents and siblings whose often tragically shaped lives feed my music and personality. Here are the stories of my friends and lovers, co-writers and producers, and those demons and angels who wage a constant battle for my soul. There were cave dwellers, Southern hoodoo, urban jails, and some of the most opulent hotels in the world. I've traveled to these places via my thumb and VW bug and a few times, the Concorde supersonic jet. I've lived volumes as a young girl long before I was famous and here I share the largeness of events I experienced through my younger eyes.

I sense a natural language being whispered that is shared by all of us. After all these decades, life remains stubbornly mysterious. In dreams I sometimes understand the symbols, but then I wake up and they're gone. A puff of ink that will not stick to this reality. What was I hearing? What were they saying? Was it music? Surely I heard *something*. After all these decades, life remains stubbornly mysterious.

Music shapes us and fundamentally changes us. Once we have listened we do not stop. We do not ever recover from music. We will return again and again to the radio, the record store, the bedroom where girls listen to records all day.

Performing is a religious experience for me. You can never know what I feel, only what you feel. My secret courage is my magic. You are doused with my strange water of emotion as you witness this courage, and that is my true performance. It sounds like music but something is being passed between us. Something personal.

I have come to believe that I am moving in the right direction, following a path more than forging the way. My performances center around that belief. I am propelled forward by seemingly random events linked together by the fact that eventually I end up in better circumstances than when I began. Sure, bad things happen but if I keep pushing to become my best self, I am brought from the pain into a brighter passage. That instinct—to believe in my heart—always delivers me. I go where *she* is going. I'm with *Her*.

INTRODUCTION
A PRELUDE TO GRAVITY

I named this book "Last Chance Texaco" because I spent most of my life in cars, vans, and buses. Back seats, shotgun, and driving myself. From these vantage points I watched life approach and recede. As time went by I was always running away from and moving to new life, but once I finally got there I could never lay down roots. For me, it seems, life is the vehicle and not the destination.

The meaning of "Last Chance Texaco" is simple. It is the light in the distance that never goes out, refuge for the tired traveler on a dark road. "You can trust your car to the man who wears the star" sang the old commercial—an important backstory people today may not know—"The big bright Texaco star!" I used the familiar signposts and lingo of my generation to build the lyrics of "Texaco," and in fact most of my early songs make reference to obscure Americana nearly forgotten today. When my young life seemed to be nose-diving into the desert sands of Hollywood, going nowhere fast, I raised that Texaco star like a pirate flag and overtook my future against all odds. The man with the star is as much Christ as he is a lover or a stranger in a gas station, whomever it is you need to put your trust in tonight. "Last Chance Texaco" remains a kind of living spirit to me. A whisper of belief in impossibilities.

When I was twenty-three years old I drove around L.A. with Tom Waits. We'd cruise along Highway 1 in his new 1963 Thunderbird. With my blonde hair flying out the window and both of us sweating in the summer sun, the alcohol seeped from our pores and the sex smell still soaked our clothes and our hair. We liked our smell. We did not bathe as often as we might have. We were in love and I for one was not interested in washing any of that off. By the end of summer we were exchanging song ideas. We were also exchanging something deeper. Each other.

Tom had two tattoos on his bicep. He liked to don the vintage accoutrements of masculinity: sailor hats and Bernardo's pointed shoes. The more he tried to conceal his tenderness, the more he revealed a chafed and childlike nature. I adored him. He was my king. In bed he was the greatest performing lion in the world. I mean to say that Tom was never not performing.

Then quite suddenly, in November we were no longer seeing each other.

I spent the fall driving around with Lowell George, the charismatic guitarist from Little Feat, a local hero who kept his little feet "in the street" as it were. He found me there in my squalid basement encampment and we went drivin' around in his Range Rover, seated high above the street studying various motels and apartments where he had spent time with Linda and Vicki and Bonnie too. He showed me the hotel I would live in one day—the Chateau Marmont—and we sat in the living rooms of managers who would load him up with drugs for the chance to put his signature on paper. He flirted with them all like a child flirts with the devil, toying with their furious drugged-up machinations and escaping, like a child called home by his mother, just before he signed his soul away. Lowell seemed unconcerned about his own mortality. The play was the thing, and that boy could play the guitar.

In bed Lowell was a fat man in a bathtub. I mean to say that something about him was in another room, laughing, singing to himself. He was a handsome man, unhealthy, kind to a fault.

By June we did not speak much anymore. He'd tried to obtain the publishing rights to "Easy Money" and Warner Brothers intervened. It left a very bad taste on both our tongues. I learned that lesson out of the gate; when push comes to shove, money trumps friendship.

The next summer I drove around with Dr. John. It was a very different car, a station wagon used to take his kids to school and bring groceries home to his wife, Libby. He had been married a couple times and had a number of "sprouts." He also had a ghost he kept with him, a thing that followed him, watched from behind the curtains in the hotel rooms and the plastic-backed chairs in the diners we visited. I mean to say it was his addiction.

By the end of summer, he left his companion with me and I drove alone for the rest of the year.

Then Sal Bernardi picked me up in a car with broken windows and cardboard to keep the cold out. He drove like Mr. Magoo. "Road hog," cried the New York City cabbies as he careened his "vehicle" down Fifth Avenue toward the Village one snowy December evening in 1978. He was wearing his pajamas and a stocking cap. Sal was always so punk rock. He wrote a melody too tender and too complex to be understood by the alley cats he was inclined to throw his songs at.

The apex of my love life corresponds to my career success, and unfortunately my success corresponded with my drug use. My drug career was short-lived—three years from 1980 to 1983. I quit and headed to France. But the damage was done.

I did drugs like I did everything else. On fire, with no back door. I escaped, of course, and I carried my heart out in a birdcage. But she was burned, and she cried so loud, casting wild notes over water and cloud. Freed of such beauty, she waited to be freed of her sorrow. Maybe that is the picture I see. I turned it into poetry, what else could I do?

By the following spring, Waits and I were back together. I remember driving down La Brea Avenue from the airport. Tom and Chuck liked to pick me up at the airport. There was plenty of traffic so when "Chuck E's in Love" came on the car radios it echoed across the stoplights and the exhaust pipes. Tectonic plates of culture and music were colliding around us. The three of us, me riding in the middle, were the last Neanderthals, the holdouts of the Tropicana Motel. Once Tom and I moved in together, a way of life ended. Eskimos began migrating south and all the mammoths died away.

*   *   *

My 1957 Lincoln got mangled that summer by Chuck E. and Mark Vaughan who went joyriding while I was on tour. When Tom and I broke up, Tom ditched his Cadillac in self-storage and I left my roughed-up Lincoln with a nurse up north. She worked at the hospital where I nearly died from a heart infection.

I quit driving around with people then. I rented cars and lived in hotels. For a long time I looked over my shoulder thinking there was someone behind me. Just the shade of the demon. I was sober but something was following me.

A collage of images from my Chicago infancy is forever glued to my music. I see rickety wooden fire escapes and recall holding my sister's hand in an alleyway. I know the smell of dime store lunch counters where Mother and I ate pie in thick coats of cigarette smoke. The carbon monoxide fumes and air brake screech of the city buses we took. Most of all, I remember Riverview Park where terrifying rides and bright lights and loud calliopes enchanted me. Speeding carousels with huge wooden horses I was too small to mount, a perpetual state of fear and longing that became the backdrop for so many songs.

I must have been lost more than once on that fairway, as Mom stood in line for tickets. Outside the bright spotlight I wandered toward the dark sea of an unlit backstage where monsters slept. I was drawn to the darkness and terror. No matter how much a ride frightened me, I begged to go on it again and again.

We left Chicago in 1959 when I was four years old. I grew up in the Arizona of the 1960s. Phoenix was a quiet place in the endless desert, and the radio was our only means of touching the larger world. The Phoenix I knew, ancient and unchanged, is gone now.

My family took such a long trip across America that I felt as if I had always lived in the back seat of our 1959 Pontiac. My big brother Danny and I kicked, poked, and tickled each other in a blender of games that turned the long minutes into long hours. Once I kicked my brother right in the balls and he tore into me like a tornado. I didn't really know what was down there. He kicked me too. It hurt, but catching the attention of the front-seat referee was not allowed. If Mom said Danny was too rough he might not play with me, so I had to pretend I was not hurt. We were shaping rules not only for hurting each other, but for whom we might be as adults.

On that magical tour into the U.S.A., we saw stalactites in New Mexico, and in Yellowstone National Park we encountered bears rummaging through the garbage like homeless Russian astronauts in fur coats. They were as alien to me as if they had dropped from the sky. I knew them as the cartoon Yogi ("smarter than the average bear"), but in person they were hungry as hell. They came up to our car and demanded food and suddenly I was terrified. "Hurry, roll up the window," with Mom and Danny laughing. They were always laughing at danger. I couldn't understand why they didn't take these things seriously. Finally, our road trip ended in Pomona on my uncle Bob's doorstep.

America was succumbing to an expanding postwar pressure of social symmetry: be alike, fall in line. In California my family became the idealized version of itself. We had a collie dog just like Lassie and my brother had a raccoon cap like Davy Crockett. We were Walt Disney's America. Mother wore gloves and Father had a crew cut.

Trying to fit into the Protestant world around them and win the good graces of my Protestant grandmother, my parents baptized me Presbyterian and we attended Presbyterian services. All the rest of my family remained Catholic. It was a terrible source of friction and in spite of everything we tried, the Joneses remained unwelcome in Grandmother's Temple City. There was an argument and we hit the road, coming to a stop in our new home in the Arizona desert.

The shy desert, a chalky remainder of countless millions of years of other living things. Animals who raised their young on these unforgiving rocks, only to lay down their burden and wait. The skeletons of their lives are the dirt of our cactus gardens. We too will become fossilized pages in some unimaginable future. Well, maybe imaginable: "Look, can you see my fossilized arm—under the Xazzcandra Prelapse? I think it is turning pink again."

There is a little girl down there we need to talk to. Can you see her? I wonder, do you think she can hear me singing? What's she doing with that frog?

THE BACK SEAT

CHAPTER 1

What Were the Skies like When You Were Little?

"Oh the skies were beautiful, pink and yellow and blue . . ."

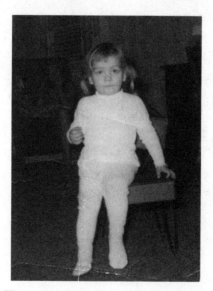

Three-year-old Rickie and big sister Janet

Down along the end of the street was a well, a concrete circle about five feet in diameter. There you could find all manner of water-loving creatures, drawn from the desert to the shade. Tadpoles swam with tiny mosquito larvae. I was carrying a frog I found in the mud.

In the desert, shade means the difference between life and death. Wherever there is shade there are fairies. I knew this instinctively but my father told me all about fairies: "Watch for them out of the corner of your eye. In the dappled light fairies can be seen as they take form, and if you are very still you may see them darting across the limb of a tree."

Studying the drop down to the bottom of the well, I saw that it was only about ten feet. I let the frog slip from my hands into the well and said:

"Water there."

"You can swim down there."

"Be out of the sun."

When I returned later and saw the frog dead, I looked up from that well and I was sore inside. I had killed a thing. I was inconsolable. There was nowhere to run away from this feeling.

That experiment was nothing like what I expected. Now I knew. People could cause terrible harm, and even I could hurt an innocent thing. That it was an accident made no difference to me or the frog. "I'm sorry, I wish I had not put you down there. I wish I could take it back." It was here by the well I made up my first song. The song made its home in me and I kept it there. I sang:

> *I wish, I wish,*
> *That wishes would come true,*
> *And then, I know,*
> *That it would be alright.*

God's little scientists want to know how things work, and sometimes quite by accident, they find out the hard way. I was forging roads between my imagination and the world before me. The real frog died but I saved it in my first song. Out here, in fairy kingdoms, anything seemed possible.

I wandered the neighborhood with my invisible friends, inspecting everything I came across. I was often frozen in some daydream when an invisible horse galloped down the street in a storm of wild fury, only to find me waiting and fearless. A trembling velvet muzzle pressed against my hand, the horse's gesture of acceptance and trust. Only I understood and could tame its wild heart.

I hollered out loud to my invisible horse to the consternation of my sister and brother who watched me in bewilderment.

The garbage men often ate their lunch in the shade at the edge of our backyard, parking on the dirt road that ran along the farmer's field next to our house. One morning my mother sent me out with a pitcher of water for the men. Standing some feet away, I began to sing, pretending not to notice they were watching. A couple of the guys clapped their hands, the oleander bush cheered. I bowed, and Mother called me into the house.

My very first performance I was three years old, a snowflake in a ballet recital of "Bambi." Bowing low at the end of our dance I heard the audience's applause and took it personally. I remained bowing long after the other snowflakes had melted and left the stage. The dance teacher had to escort me off but the audience was delighted and the die was cast. I liked it up there.

What I really wanted most was to play the piano. Pidgey Muncie lived three doors down and she had a piano.

Pidgey was my age, shy and sweet, plump like her mother. Pidgey could not have visitors once her father came home from work but I would stay until the very last moment to play that little spinet piano. I sounded out the notes to the Doublemint commercial and Pidgey and her mom taught me "Heart and Soul." They were terrified that I'd still be there when Mr. Muncie came home so they unceremoniously escorted me out the back door.

Mr. Muncie was the most terrifying man I'd ever met. He was short and stocky with a crew cut. An ex-Marine and currently a very angry man. Then one morning I was playing in the backyard when I saw Mr. Muncie digging a hole in the farmer's field. He had a bag in his hand that he put into the hole and buried. I ran in and told my mother. "Mr. Muncie buried something in the field!"

She was doubtful of what I had seen, but she called Mrs. Muncie, who said:

"Yes, the dog had puppies today. He just took them out there and buried them alive."

Buried them? What? Alive?

"We have to go dig them up."

"They are dead now, Rickie. We cannot go get them."

I felt panicked. How could we sit there as little innocent babies were dying? We must bring them back to life.

Pidgey's dog died a few days later. I felt she died of a broken heart from watching her babies taken from her. My mother told me she died because there were no puppies to drink her milk. I quit going to poor Pidgey Muncie's house. I now knew that there were terrible people in the world, people who hurt innocent things, people who were also daddies, or uncles, or neighbors.

My brother had gotten a red bicycle for his eleventh birthday. I was allowed to ride his bike, if I was able to do so. Unable to reach the seat, I balanced on the ungainly apparatus and rode the five houses to the end of our street, then navigated the wide turn and returned to Mother and Danny. I had passed the test and was admitted to the grown-up world of bicycle riders. It wasn't that hard, really.

One morning I asked my mother if I could ride Danny's bike.

"Yes, but only to the corner and make sure I can see you."

I rode round and round in circles at the end of our street. A car came suddenly and stopped right in front of me. It was followed by a second car that screeched to a stop. A redheaded boy jumped out of the first car but then a bigger man in the second car caught up to him. He was swearing as he moved toward the redheaded boy, who seemed to be crying, "I'm sorry, I'm sorry."

"Son of a bitch, you son of a bitch, goddamn."

"I'm sorry," the boy was crying.

I felt bad for the redheaded boy because he was so afraid, he seemed so sad.

The seat was too high for me to stop the bike without falling, so I rode around in circles watching the men until I could place the pedal in just the right position and gently fall over. I set the bike on the sidewalk and moved carefully toward the cars and the yelling.

The big man looked into the back seat, right over the shoulder of the redheaded boy he had pushed up against the window. Now tears of rage as the man's fist caught the boy in his jaw, and he threw him down by his shirt as he wept. I was frightened but I approached the car to look into the back-seat window. There was a little girl lying there, a very little girl, maybe two or three. She was lying down on her back.

I cannot remember anything else. My mind—or fairies maybe—lifted that picture and flew it away on the wings of mourning doves. I don't remember what I saw. Did I see blood? The child seemed languid, stunned. Did I make that up? I petted her, I spoke to her, but I don't know what I saw in the back seat.

Pidgey and I had met this redheaded boy before. He was the little girl's babysitter and seventeen-year-old cousin. We'd been to her yard to play. I remembered that he was very protective and would not let us play with her. It was noticeable, so we spoke of it as we left the house.

To leave that little girl's house we had to cross a fairy ditch. A shaded patch behind her house that filled me with dread. Something told me there was danger there, and it shaped the warning into a pulse, a feeling, a thrill. Perhaps something had already happened there. Or perhaps I felt echoes of time to come, calling to time happening now. Or maybe it was what I now know, that pedophiles are all around lining up to claim the innocent.

Back on the street, people were drawn by the furious shouting of the father. They broke up the fight and pulled him off the redheaded rapist. The father went looking for the babysitter after he discovered his little girl missing but he found them too late. He pursued the boy in a dangerous car chase through town right up to the dead end where I was riding my brother's bike around in circles on a warm and sunny Phoenix morning.

A lady asked me what was happening. "I saw it all," I said. She told a policeman and he said, "We will come to interview you later on." Oh, I felt so important, so grown-up.

The sun had set by the time the officer came. I was safe in my old footie pajamas, wiggling my toes as I watched my mother talk with the policeman. He was standing on the other side of the screen door.

"Yes, Rickie Lee is here, but she doesn't know what rape is. She's only five years old."

"Yes I do!" I called from behind.

The officer veered around my mother to address me. "Tell me what it is." I stepped up to the screen. "It's when someone beats someone up really bad." The officer nodded and said, "We will be in touch if we need your testimony." He said to my mother, "I don't think they'll ask her to testify. She's innocent, no reason for her to know anything like this."

My mother closed the door and we all sat down to watch television. Daddy was home that night. He passed out Eskimo Pies. My dad loved Eskimo Pies. I was safe that night, and in spite of the obvious, all that was cruel and ugly seemed far away from our doorstep.

The very first week of school, I was excited and engaged. Then the art teacher said I did not need the special apron my mom bought with pockets for pencils and paintbrushes. She embarrassed me in front of the other kids and she didn't seem to like me. Perhaps that was enough to change my mind, sow a seed of self-doubt. Starting school was too much for me. I started getting boils and headaches. I was very young to start school, that first year they had to drag me screaming down the corridor. Yet I loved playing horses on the playground, and I loved Stevie Barnes.

I was always pretending I was a horse, no matter where I was. At school I spent my recess minutes galloping past all the other children. One day another little girl started running with me. Soon I transformed all the girls in my grade into a herd of horses, and we ran around whinnying and galloping. By the end of that week of roundups, I couldn't wait to get to school.

That's when I met Stevie Barnes. Stevie and the other boys chased those wild horses like rodeo cowboys. Stevie would catch my braids and I would gallop away, making a three-beat sound of hooves, my hands hitting my hips and my feet running in a two-beat ba-dump. In my childhood I never ran without making that sound. Pa ba-dump, Pa ba-dump, Pa ba-dump.

If Stevie Barnes ever kissed me, and I hope he did, I wiped it off like spit even though I was very pleased and proud to be Stevie's horse.

If there were another book of my life, a different version of myself, it would be one where I grow up with Stevie Barnes and he marries Rickie Lee, his green-eyed mare and childhood sweetheart. I would grow up a good girl and a confident child, pleasing my parents and balancing everything so as not to be too much of anything—too much trouble, too much joy, too much body, too much soul. I would be contained, and all of Rickie Lee and Stevie's children would be happy grazing in the valley of the sun.

My first and second grade at Ocotillo School were the only years I was a confident and happy child. My mother led the Singin' Swingin' Blue Birds troop (Camp Fire Girls) to a triumphant live performance at the father-daughter banquet. One meeting we crafted wooden bluebirds. I still have most of mine. By the end of the second grade those halcyon days ended with a haircut and a move to a new school district. I don't know which was harder, the loss of my friends or the spectacle of my braids lying on the salon floor. Either way, childhood was abruptly and forever altered, and not for the better.

Chapter 2

Juke Box Fury

My mother, Bettye, and my nieces

My mother was raised in orphanages around Mansfield, Ohio. Her parents, James and Rhelda, were unable to care for her. The Glens were a clan who ran full on at life and just kept going.

My maternal grandfather, James Glen, was the youngest boy in a family of women and a doughboy in World War I. He survived the terrible Battle of Argonne, in France, where mustard gas was used on soldiers. Family lore claims he was badly damaged by the gassing, and for the rest of his brief life he drifted, jobless. I don't know how he felt about his children. There was only one encounter between James and my mother. There are no pictures of him. He died of tuberculosis while my mother was still a teenager, and I do not know if anyone came to his funeral.

James Glen returned from the blown-up fields of France and against his family's wishes, married a teenage girl, Rhelda "Peggy" Rudder. Together they made four children in rapid succession: Don, Fritz, Jimmy, and Betty Jane, my mother. Peggy was Dutch and French, her people were poor. Peggy's mother, Ora Issey Spice, had no hand to lend her wayward daughter, and no husband to bring in money. I recall the story of the great grandfather who bought one of the first automobiles in the county and crashed it trying to avoid a rearing horse and buggy. His Airedale dog, dismayed and confused, would not let anyone get to the dead man in the driver's seat and had to be shot by the sheriff.

Other than her remarkably musical name, Ora Issey Spice was absent from bedtime stories but she did have a brother named "Hangman" whom mother spoke of from time to time. "Did he hang people, Mama?" Nope. Just a nickname (I hope). Uncle Hangman was a diabetic who had to shoot himself up with an old blunt needle that would hardly penetrate his skin. He was too poor to afford a new needle.

Grandmother Spice's family were pioneers, turn-of-the-twentieth-century Americans who "combed their teeth with a wagon wheel." Born in the late 1800s, my great-relatives worked their way across this young country. They had no running water, no electricity. Funny, it wasn't much more than a hundred years ago they were all just kids. Now they are weeds in the wind, a trickle down your back.

Life is a locomotive, and as long as you watch it from a distance it takes a long time to go by. Ride that train and you'll be gone in the blink of an eye, the landscape moving with you.

"Night Train"

By the time Grandma Peggy was twenty years old she had three children and was fending for herself while Grandpa Jim was camping out in the fields of Ohio. He lived as he did back in France, sleeping under trees and building campfires. He never fully returned from the war. In one of those fields near a farm that had just been robbed of some chickens, the sheriff found Grandfather roasting a bird under the stars. The judge sentenced him to a year in prison for stealing chickens, and while Jim was in prison, Peggy gave birth to their fourth child, a blue-eyed girl named Betty Jane. My mama.

With James Glen in jail, Richland County officials took a personal interest in the Glen children. They removed all three sons from Peggy's custody, but for the next few years Peggy managed to elude the authorities and keep her baby girl. She'd already lost her boys and her husband—she was not letting go of her daughter for anybody.

Baby Betty was sleeping in Peggy's bedroom when the social worker came to take her away to the orphanage with her brothers. The social worker had official papers and a police officer with her as she pounded on the front door. Peggy hurried to the bedroom and gathered up my mother and climbed out the window. Peggy went a-running as fast as she could through the cornfield with my mother in her arms, leaving the social worker still standing on the porch. The social worker took Peggy's flight personally and would pursue Peggy as if Betty were her own child.

I heard this story of Peggy running through the cornfield so many times that it became my story, too. I was there—inside of my mother's skin as her mother ran for *our* lives. My daughter, too, somewhere inside of me. We all ran across the cornfield with my grandmother.

Peggy lived on the run. She found an apartment and a roommate and worked as a waitress to take care of my mama. She always looked over her shoulder because Richland County and the social worker would not give up. There were close calls as they kept on coming for her.

One evening, Peggy was waiting tables while her roommate was sitting with the baby. Betty-nanny was in the apartment watching the sandman floating by sprinkling baby-light magic on her blue and quiet eyes. There was a knock on the door. Peggy's roommate answered and came face-to-face with the social worker looking for Peggy and her child. "Peggy is not here. She's at work. You go on and get outta here now," and she closed the door. The social worker was employed by the devil himself and would not be deterred by words. This time she went around the back of the house and climbed in through the window, grabbed little Betty, and climbed back out and ran. The social worker kidnapped my mother.

It was a harsh time in America and Peggy had no husband at home to make her "legitimate." She never had a chance to win her children back. The courts ruled Peggy an unfit mother and all four of her children were permanently separated from their mother's care. The Glen kids, along with a million other orphans of the Great Depression, were left to fend for themselves among the religious fanatics and pedophiles and sadists that seemed to gravitate toward children's homes.

At least the Glen children had each other at the orphanage. Their bond was unusually strong, their word true. In a crucifix of rhyme and spit, each one vowed not to be adopted if it meant being separated. By swearing faith to one another they created an extraordinary sense of integrity for their family and future families, although this promise condemned each to a childhood of institutions. "Night Train" belongs to the women of my clan.

> *Here I'm going*
> *Walking with my baby . . . in my arms*
> *Cuz I am in the wrong end of the eight-ball*
> *And the devil is right behind us*
> *And the worker said*
> *She's gonna take my little baby, my little angel, back*
> *But they won't get ya, no*
> *Cuz I'm right here with you*
> *On the Night Train . . .*

My mother's stories are the heart of me, the country from which I come. Escapades of her ghastly childhood in the orphanage were the Grimm's Fairy Tales of my own. Trolls and dragons could not compete with my mother's impossibly gothic reminiscences of the 1930s and the orphanages where she grew up.

Many nights, lying there with my mother (Father was always at work) my brother and I would ask Mama to tell us one of her stories. Of course we knew them all by heart, or at least we thought we did, but we'd ask for them like you might ask someone to play a song. Play *that* one, Mother. Tell us about One-Ball!

One-Ball

Of all the people Betty Jane met—the nice cook who baked her a cake when she was twelve, or the kind, young couple who bought her new clothes and gave her a private room of her own (and then returned her to the orphanage because she refused to live there, separated from her brothers)—Mother recalled the matron, "One-Ball," with the most chortles and disdain. One-Ball alone received a name from the orphans—one worthy of her half-human heart.

One-Ball was named for the solitary ball of hair, the bun, she pinned up on her uncommonly cruel head. It was speculated among the children that the name more likely referred to the one testicle she hid up there under her skirt, thus, "One-Ball!" My mom would laugh so hard about that. Lying with us, thirty years away from that orphanage, it was finally safe for the little girl inside her to giggle out loud.

One-Ball liked to sneak up on kids, trap them, catch them as she hid in a shadow holding a belt. It was the surprise element that was the sadism. She kept children in a constant state of terror and exhaustion. After years of silent acceptance, my mother finally confronted her tormentor, redeeming a lifetime of torture. Old One-Ball almost ended up No-Ball-At-All. If you get my meaning.

Mother had her own bedroom now, being fifteen years of age; she'd earned her privacy after thirteen years in orphanages. On this particular evening, One-Ball, bored and restless, was scouting for an unguarded child to pounce on, and stealthily she entered my mother's bedroom. Betty was seated at the vanity, brushing her hair with her back to the room. One-Ball hoped to grab her by the hair—the element of surprise brought the terror that was so satisfying. Mom spotted One-Ball in the mirror and she kept her cool, waiting until the old witch was nearly upon her and then she rose suddenly, with her hairbrush raised in the air. This time it was One-Ball in the hot seat.

Mother faced her tormentor. "If you ever sneak up on me again, try to hurt me, even touch me, I'm gonna ram this hairbrush down your throat and it's gonna come out your butt."

Bold move, Mom. One-Ball staggered, her soul shrinking, and retreated like a demon caught in its own reflection. One-Ball did not catch my mother that week or any other, ever again. She was a bully and bullies can only eat the fearful.

One-Ball went into the shadows from which she came, just a page or two in a chapter about the cruel adults who abuse little children. Gentle Betty, it seemed, had been waiting for a chance to strike a blow for the little guy. Literally. Mother's years as a slave were coming to an end. She would be gone by her sixteenth birthday.

Even though her nickname was "Sarge," my mother's demeanor was unconfrontational, and something way inside—the little girl she was once—was exceptionally kind. It was there till the very end. Like an iceberg, I suspect most of my mother remained frozen under the surface. She would often demand:

"What's the use of bringing all that up?"

And she was right. All that hand-wringing and chanting of unfortunate memories, what's the point of it? Cry your tears and be done with it. My mother—and my mother's past—is always with me.

Rhubarb Pie

Mama had the most secrets and the best poker face. It was forty years before I even knew she played the piano! One evening near Christmas Mom sat down and played "O Holy Night." My mouth fell open, and my little sister and I sat silently in awe. Who knew what else she kept in that caldron of cakes and pies and blood and tears?

For Mother, the lesson of orphanage life was simple: control yourself. Mom started the rhubarb pie story with a different twist on this lesson every night: never let them know you like it or they'll take it from you. Which was another way of saying never let them see who you really are. Tom Waits used to say that, too. I never listened to either of them.

The rhubarb pie story is a testament to that one truth, and the reason behind my mother keeping so many secrets so well.

"We hardly ever got to have dessert, and rhubarb pie, they only made it for the kids once or twice a year. It was my favorite. We were lined up to go into lunch and as we entered I saw the pie on the table. I was so excited that I gasped, like this"—she sucked in air—"One-Ball heard me and pulled me out of line. They sent me to my room without any lunch."

"No pie?" I asked.

"No dinner, either."

She explained, "It is hard for little kids to stand still, especially when they're excited about dessert. Jim just couldn't seem to stand still. The male guards were much crueler than the women—they liked to flick Uncle Jim's ear, they knew it hurt him so bad. He always had ear infections. They hit his ear to make him cry. They said it was to teach him to stand still but it was really because they just liked to hurt the children."

As with the flicking of Uncle Jim's infected ear, the staff customized punishment to uniquely hurt little children and leave a mark on them into adulthood. The little girl who loved rhubarb pie was still in my mother's voice as she relived the despair of inexplicable cruelty.

For Mother's seventieth birthday, I bought her a giant rhubarb pie. It was big enough to feed all the children in the orphanage: Jim, Don, and Fritz, and all the rest of them. They are ghost orphans now. I could not reach them with my pie. I thought to shine a kindness so bright that it would shine into her past, but we can never undo what was done.

Ninety years ago, my mother's entire generation was tricked into the dust bowl of desperate poverty called the Great Depression, due to the greed and narrow interests of wealthy men. Betty's sad childhood as an orphan was so common that Little Orphan Annie, a syndicated comic strip character, became a national sensation. Child actor Shirley Temple, one of the biggest box-office stars of the time, usually played a singing, dancing orphan of some sort. In 1932, my mother's image became iconic. She got her first job as a model at three years of age, in a print ad for cake flour. She was the image of a happy child, her Dutch-boy haircut neatly framing her sweet face, her tiny fingers almost touching a yellow cake that would always remain beyond her fingertips.

My song "Juke Box Fury" opens with a little introduction, a melody my mother often hummed around the house. It was the only song I remember her singing regularly. She said it was already old when she learned it as a little girl. Dorothy herself probably sang this tune on her way home from Oz:

> *Polly and I went to the circus,*
> *Polly got hit with a rolling pin,*
> *We got even with the circus,*
> *We bought tickets but we didn't go in.*

This melody made a powerful impression on me. It told me everything I needed to know about my mother's America. "Ain't got nothin' to prove to nobody." Perhaps, then, this song is the proper title for the last and saddest of her stories—though not the most violent or most tragic. Just . . . another ticket unused.

A Bum on the Bench

My mother's father, James Glen Sr., was a "red-haired-blue-eyed-Irishman." She liked to rush through to make that collection of syllables into one word. When Jim got out of prison, he was sick with the same tuberculosis that would kill both my grandfathers and a generation of Americans. Had the media reported my grandfather's death they might have said, "A veteran of a war long forgotten died before his time in a VA hospital somewhere near a chestnut tree and a wishing well."

He was an old man by the time my mother was fourteen years old, but very, very shy Betty agreed to meet him. She was an excellent student, and so serious about her gymnastics that she wrapped her bosom to flatten her profile. She wasn't totally sure she wanted to meet the old man. What if she didn't like him? What if he didn't like her?

Betty's brother Jim Jr. arranged for them to meet in a park. "Walk through the gate and to the left, there is a statue and a fountain. Dad will be sitting on the bench by the fountain." She arrived after school with her books in her arm, something to hold onto or place between her and him. She sat down on the bench to wait.

When she bent down to tie her shoe she noticed an old man, a bum, sitting to her left. Had he been there all along? She let her eyes meet the man's. He was looking at her. Then he grinned, a mostly toothless smile. Why was he smiling at her? She shuffled, tried to look away. It was hard to breathe, she was such a shy girl. Then the old man took off his hat. It was the red hair, the famous red hair.

She realized, Oh God, it was him.

Her father rose slowly and sat down next to his daughter. "Betty Jane?" And he smiled, so big, so happy. "I'm your daddy." He had no front teeth and he looked like a poor bum in old clothes and worn-out shoes. Betty Jane stood up and ran away, crying. Her father watched her go. He put his hat on and walked back to wherever he came from. Her brothers chastised her. What was she afraid of? An old man? She would never again see her father. He died of TB shortly afterwards.

The Orphanages of Richland County

This orphanage relied on the work of children to turn a profit, but the children didn't get much of the food they harvested. The four Glen kids, my mother and her brothers, were behind the main house, shucking corn. There was a big pile of it, and six-year-old Betty pulled the sleeves off, then removed the silky golden "hair" and put each ear of corn in a tin pot. Her older brothers were nearby, gathering up old stalks of corn; the eldest, Don, standing by, pretending to help. Mother said the kids got the parsnips and turnips and only rarely (on Sundays), chicken (necks) and dumplings.

The Glen kids had decided to run away, again. The eldest boys, Don and Fritz, whispered to seven-year-old Jimmy, "We're gonna run today. Be ready."

"What, run? Now?"

"You'll know."

When old Mr. Brown or Miss Smith went into the smokehouse, the kids took their shot. Don and Fritz lit out across the cornfield.

"Come on!"

Jimmy grabbed ahold of Betty's left hand and ran after them. Don looked back to see Jimmy losing ground. Mr. Brown was already out the back door and running across the field, so Don slowed down and reached for Betty's right hand. Now Fritz picked up the slack and took his sister's hand from little Jimmy, the two bigger boys pulling her behind them. Betty was lifted off the ground and she flew between her brothers like a kite. In my child's mind I would see her up there, the wind lifting her body, floating heavenward and away as the Glen family, racing for their lives, showed my mama how to fly.

Everyone was a-runnin' as fast as they could but Don could see they were still losing ground. The old man Mr. Brown called for help ("Goddamn Glen kids") and now there were a number of adults trying to head off the Glens. Wisely, Don and Fritz dropped Betty's hands and she tumbled to the ground. The two of them ran like horse thieves. If Mr. Brown caught him this time, Don knew he was gonna regret ever having been born.

Betty raised her head, calling to her brothers, "Wait for me!" but she would soon learn to accept defeat wordlessly. Never let them see you cry. Jimmy was still running but he was only a year older than his little sister, and he couldn't get far. He cried out as the men yanked him up. One of them slapped Jimmy on his sore ear. Jimmy and Betty were taken back to the big house and sent straight to bed without supper. Jimmy was small but since he was a boy, he was whipped. Betty was not hit, not because she was too little to beat but because she really had nothing to do with what had happened. Well, maybe a swat or two just for being in the fray.

Sacrificing Jimmy and Betty to the chase allowed Fritz and Don to escape. They were hiding in a ditch making profound social calculations that no child should ever face. Don said, "Hell, they won't hurt Betty because she's just a baby. They might spank Jimmy but if they catch me they're gonna beat me to death. I ain't a-gonna be beat no more."

Years later, as I asked about the orphanage punishments, I remember my uncle Don grinning:

"The way they beat me, they like-ta killt me," and his smile hesitated as if he recalled something that was not smiling back. A flicker of pain. Then he was back to his charming, polyester-leisure-suit self.

Uncle Don, trying to jump-start a ranch of his own, once stole a semi-truck filled with cattle heading for Bob's Big Boy restaurant. He got caught and went to prison. I confess I enjoyed the dichotomy of twentieth-century-style cattle rustlers in semi-trucks. A certain family pride.

Don and Fritz finally made their way to Chicago where their mama lived. They were outside the State of Ohio's budget, and "Just let 'em go" finally echoed down a government hall. Don eventually returned to Ohio and bought a house near Wooster. He married a nice Italian lady and they offered their home to kids who needed foster placement. Fritz married a stripper and ended up in Waco, Texas.

When Mother finally left the orphanage in 1944, she headed for Chicago and was reunited with her mother at last. She moved to the North Side, went to secretarial school, got a job, and started spelling her name with an "e" at the end. Bettye. It was the first inkling of her determination to make herself into a new person. Released from the region, she would eventually free herself of that southern Ohio/Kentucky accent that might forever brand her as "un"—untrustworthy, unworthy, and unsophisticated.

Bettye was full of life and energy, the world laid out before her. She planned to stay single until she was at least twenty-eight years old. She wanted to see the world, to be somebody. She would be *anybody* except what the orphanage had confined her to.

My parents met at a lunch counter where Mother and her roommate often stopped for a quick bite before going to work. My father, the waiter, was classy. He was dark and brooding, back from the war, and handsome like a movie star. Like most World War II veterans, he drank and fought and laughed about drinking and fighting. They took a trip to Florida together before we were born. I only know this because I once asked where a photograph of Mother was taken. She was private, even secretive, so most of her pre-Rickie life went with her to the Invisible World of the Great Beyond.

Bettye was twenty years old when she got pregnant. She wasn't married. I had suspected this as a child but had been rebuffed with great condemnation—how dare I imply such a thing. One day she accidentally revealed it during a conversation when I was at least forty-five years old.

"Oh, didn't I ever tell you that?"

"No! Motheeeer! I asked you when I was a kid about that and you scolded me for asking!"

"Close your mouth, you're catching flies. It was none of your business. I guess you're old enough now to hear."

Mother's life with my father, who also bore the scars of a life without a home, was premised on a vow that they would make themselves into better people than their ancestors. They were determined to jettison their past lives and join a better stratum of society.

My parents married and lived in Chicago for the first four years of my life. My sister Janet (eight years older) was attending school in a

Catholic convent and my brother, a little soldier, attended a Catholic military school. Janet had some trouble on her vacation back home, and my father decided we had had enough of Chicago. Shortly after my fourth birthday celebration at kindergarten, we said goodbye to the Windy City and hello to the road. It was the siren call of the West.

Mom and Dad thought that together they could do anything because anything was possible with money and they had a strong work ethic. Together they worked two jobs each and double shifts as often as they could. They saved their money. Their son Danny would go to college, study law, maybe become the president of the United States. Anything was possible with hard work.

But my parents had learned as kids to avoid government, big institutions, and authority. They used cash to avoid declaring income and they avoided obligations beyond next month's rent. Their mistrust extended even to census takers, so banks and mortgages were out of the question. They pushed themselves hard but never accumulated wealth.

Once they left Chicago they never stopped moving. What were they running from? Well, they ran from cities, houses, and eventually themselves, but they never got away from their difficult childhoods or their love for each other. Long after their lives together ended, my mother would stare at the window tapping her foot as if she longed for the music Father brought to our house. My father missed Bettye's jitterbug dancing. She was a very good dancer. I oughtta know, she taught me to jitterbug one rainy afternoon in my brother's log cabin out in Lacey, Washington. We were listening to Van Morrison's "Jackie Wilson Said." Mama swung me around like a redheaded stepchild. She knew how to lead alright, because she'd grown up following.

Childhood traumas leave their dirty footprints in the fresh white snow of our happy-ever-afters. No matter what my mom did—or her brothers, for that matter—she found traces of her past obstructing her future. She built a better life but didn't escape her past. Orphanage children received clothes and schooling, but not love and affection. They had food where others in the Depression did not, but even this privilege came at great cost, for it could be withheld on the whim of an employee. In this torment, my mother learned not to hold onto the things she loved because then no one could take them away from her. Our violent past will also find our children. It echoes. Recovering takes generations.

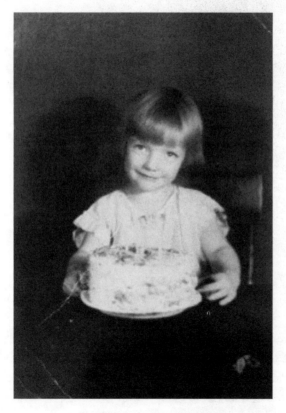

Betty Jane poses with cake

Chapter 3

On Saturday Afternoons in 1963

Rickie Lee in fifth grade

W hen my uncle Bud died of cancer in Chicago, my father flew back to help with the funeral, and my mother found us a new house. When times got tense, Mom would scour the furnished rentals in the *Phoenix Gazette*, and we knew we were about to leave our cares behind. Dad was not thrilled with the wonderful new house; it was old and rickety and he loved clean modern things. Mom and Dad were like the parents in *A Tree Grows in Brooklyn*. Their weaknesses had polarized them into being their worst selves. I adored my father when he did not drink, and hated how my mother began to hate him even when he didn't.

We moved to the house on Orangewood Avenue in the summer of 1962. It was an antebellum-style farmhouse, probably eighty years old. The last vestige of early Arizona settlers, these square wooden houses once grew like cactuses in the Southwestern desert. This one came furnished with a television set, a dining room table, three dressers and three beds, windows with venetian blinds, and an antique Victorian-type chair with velvet upholstery. I loved to lie upside down on that chair and rub my fingers through the velvet. There were five acres of dirt and a horse stall off the backyard. I was thrilled the moment I saw it. Maybe a real horse would eventually find its way into this stall.

The house sat on cement blocks and had screen doors to keep the air moving. I would lie on the cool cement porch beneath the hornet's nest, daydreaming with the drops of light splashing on my eyelashes. One day I discovered the earth moving under the house—it was a big family of garter snakes. What a discovery! Mother said to leave them alone, they weren't bothering anyone. I watched them the way children watch tattooed ladies at the circus, with a mixture of fear and delight.

Sugarfoot was more than content in the new house. There were mice and birds to hunt and saucers of milk and Purina cat food every morning. One day I watched her stalking a bird and was inspired to test her technique. Creeping slowly on my hands and knees while thinking, "You cannot see me, you cannot see me," I moved as if I was not moving. The bird was about eight feet away. It did not move as I came toward it.

I knew there was a relationship between the bird and the cat that allowed the cat to be unseen, as if nature anesthetized the prey when a predator came near. I understood this so instinctively I figured I could also have that relationship with a bird and be unseen. I was still working as God's little scientist.

I kept my unblinking eye on the bird. I *was* the cat. So smoothly and slowly I crossed the distance between me and the wren, slowly, ever so slowly. Then I moved quick—and captured my first bird!

Gently I picked it up from our front yard and brought it into the house. Nobody could be as surprised and flabbergasted as I, certainly not my mother who was more concerned about the fact of a bird in the house than my claim to have just performed magic. This was the first of four birds I would catch in my life.

In my childhood desert playground, I roamed among date trees, orange blossoms, praying mantises, and the deafening humming of cicadas singing in an enchanted dream of lost worlds. Each day was followed by a brighter sun set in a blaze of celestial colored sunsets that were erased by bigger and bigger full moons. I was slowly replacing my invisible friends with real animals.

My invisible friend, Boshla, had also moved to the new house and sometimes he still accompanied me on safaris into the desert. My mother was concerned about me talking to people that no one could see, so she asked my father to speak to me about it.

Father sat next to me on the porch and asked me if Boshla was there right now. I answered:

"Yes he is."

"You know you're getting older now Rickie Lee. It's time to tell Boshla goodbye."

I was confused.

"Your mother thinks it's time for you to stop talking to things that aren't there. So tell him goodbye now."

I could no more tell Boshla goodbye than I could tell my father goodbye. But I said,

"Okay Daddy." And then to make a show of it:

I put my finger to my lips and whispered, "Shhhhh," so that Boshla wouldn't make any noise that my daddy could hear. Dad saw me do this and smiled, then went back inside the house.

There was no more discussion about getting rid of my imaginary friend.

Years may go by . . .

Each day I would visit Wick's Market, the family-owned grocery facing the Black Canyon Highway. Mr. Wick cut the meat in back, and the cement aisles smelled like bread and milk. There were ice cream sandwiches in the deep caverns of a cold, free-standing refrigerator. Mr. and Mrs. Wick owned the market and I had a crush on Jack, their son. I was eight and he was twenty-eight, a slight man with receding hair. I proposed marriage to him one afternoon and he said most earnestly, "Rickie Lee, I think that when you grow up you are not even going to remember me. But if you do, I promise, I will go out with you." I was sure my feelings would last another . . . let's see . . . seven years would make me pretty and old enough for Jack . . .

The Wicks had a bubble gum machine filled with beautiful plastic diamond and ruby rings you could win for a penny, and I mystically conquered that machine. I could feel the bubble gum mechanism and learned how to turn it just so to get the rings. I won ring after ring. Customers marveled. "Watch me!" I called to anyone who would look. Long blonde braids, many rings on my fingers, barefoot and deeply tanned, with no front teeth, the world was mine.

I had been gathering pop bottles from the field next to the highway (they grew wild there) and was carrying them back to Wick's Market to collect the deposit, two cents a bottle. I could make about a dime, then hit the bubble gum machine. That was when I noticed the ants walking toward the desert. I had seen them many times but this morning I followed them to a newly tarred parking lot. Red fire ants with jaws like crocodiles. They burrowed into the hot asphalt, fire-walking across it to the dirt where they would attack and kill any unsuspecting bug. I found hundreds there crawling over each other as they entered and exited their ant cave. What was it like to be ant-sized? What did they see when they got inside? I was crouching down low, mesmerized. Then I felt something crawling on me—ouch—and then—ahh!—they were all over me. Red ants bite harder than black, and fire ants are the worst of all. I panicked. AHHHH!

I was running like a child on fire because I *was* a child on fire! There were ants in my underpants. There were ants in my underarms, even my hair. They were crawling on me, biting me everywhere. I was screaming as I ran, and I had quit trying to get them off me.

Mama came out the kitchen door, jumped over the little white fence into the parking lot, and started hitting me to get the ants off. So now I was getting bit and hit. She pulled me into the yard and yelled at me to stand still. Yelling saves lives! She was spraying me with the hose now, and I was naked. I didn't care.

Wait! What if Jack Wick sees me? Oh no! That would be worse than the ants and the hitting. Sure enough, he was out there too, and he heard me screaming. I looked over at him but he had quickly started back into the store, saving my modesty after making sure Mom had saved my life.

My first month in the third grade started out well enough. Mrs. Schultz passed around our new books. I loved the smell of the paper. I pressed my nose into the book imagining what the coming year would be like, all the great things I would do and the friends I would have.

Mama had bought me a six-month-old colt named Geronimo. It was a big investment, and neither of us knew how dangerous it was to raise a stallion. Buying the horse for me was the greatest thing my mother could have done in the midst of the changes that were happening to me. Even as I lost my footing at the new school, the colt meant that dreams could come true. If something as magical as a horse could land in my backyard, who knows what else might land there?

The third grade was nothing like the second grade. I could not seem to make friends, or initiate games, and my natural ability to organize was simply not appreciated. The happy and extroverted child I had been receded into a shy character. I began going to the nurse every day. Perhaps my body wasn't sick, but my heart was. I was lonely.

West Side Story

Then one weekend my big sister took me to see *West Side Story* at the Palms Theater down on Central Avenue. The movie had an immediate impact on my life. *West Side Story* became a touchstone, an initiator of friendships, a secret code between outcasts. When I finally had a chance to perform music of my own, *West Side Story* was the backdrop I brought to my stage.

I received the *West Side Story* stereophonic LP record for Christmas. Now that I had the music, Riff was alive again. I knelt with Maria in agonizing grief. I was learning the essence of theater using experimentation and improvisation. I memorized every nuance of the orchestration as the Jets and I ran through the sagebrush, snapping our fingers, and soaring over imaginary city streets.

One spring day during recess, I was singing the "Jet Song" on the playground and I noticed a little girl watching me. The next day there were two, three, and then more. I drew a crowd! For the first time at Orangewood I had an identity and a place I fit. I was the *singer*. I spent the rest of the year singing *West Side Story* at recess. Sometimes to an empty lawn, sometimes not. Music had built an accidental bridge between me and the world. Here they were at last, my peers, my audience.

The summer came and Geronimo was a yearling now, beautiful and playful. We still raced each other up and down our five-acre pasture but one day Geronimo began to charge me in our games of tag. I had to get out of his way now; the kind little colt who'd been careful not to run me over as I slowly ran in front of him now attempted to mow me down, ears back, hoofs aloft.

Fourth grade was harder than third. I was plagued by an enemy, Jo Ellen Hassle, who took every moment to browbeat me into isolation. Had it not been for Mr. Ellis, the music teacher, school simply would have been unbearable. I looked forward to seeing Mr. Ellis three times a week as I learned to play the violin. Mr. Ellis played every instrument he taught: percussion and piano, cello and bass and violin. He could take the sax out of a kid's hands and show them what to play right off their sheet music. He played all the brass, and his temperament was always gentle. I admired his patience, knowledge, and his humor. I recall my one concert recital with the orchestra, I could not quite keep up with the reading so I faked what I thought the notes might be. As he conducted, Mr. Ellis looked over at me and shook his head, nothing more. A secret between us. And perhaps the guy sitting next to me.

My dad came home from months of being away, a stranger in our house. That was when he first heard me singing harmony on "Side by Side." Father came into the kitchen and announced:

"Rickie Lee can sing harmony."

"Yes she's been doing it all year long," Mother replied (as if to say, "If you were ever around you might know something about your daughter").

Dad seemed to suddenly see me as part of his family of singers. There was a delight in his eyes, he was excited and I was the reason. Father taught me the harmony on "You Are My Sunshine," recording us together on his expensive new reel-to-reel tape recorder. I liked singing into the microphone and I loved harmony. I understood it immediately. I felt good. I had always been "different" somehow, but now singing with my father I was something special and my father *knew* it. Not only was I being included, but I was actually "number one" on the hit parade! My dad thought I was like him—a singer!

His mind was moving a hundred miles an hour. I had learned the songs easily: "On the Sunny Side of the Street," "Bye Bye Blackbird," and then Dad went for the big one—"My Funny Valentine." A challenging song, I had a difficult time with the change from minor to major (*You make me smile . . .*), and Father's expression of impatience as I tried to understand the major note for "smile" told me I was about to lose the attention I had finally won. I was disappointing him. When I finally understood the midsentence change to a new mode, I was able to sing the song pretty much as I sing it today, the way my father sang it, the way he taught it to me that day in 1963.

Dad was so impressed with my natural entertainment ability he took me on an audition for "The Lew King Show," the local television talent show. They offered to hire me but only if my parents bought an insurance policy from one of the staff there. My father was furious. Mother said they would find a way to pay for it if I really wanted to be on the show. I said no. It was a huge grown-up decision to deny myself a chance to be on television—and to have status in my lonely schoolyard hell. But this was the wrong time, the wrong place, and to accept the prize would hurt my parents. "The Lew King Show" was my first lesson in the dark corridors of the music biz, where favors are exchanged and sins offered up as collateral. Of the many exercises in integrity I have achieved or endured, or failed, this was my greatest. This performance would have served so many devils, least of all my ability to knock the song out of the ballpark. When performances are used to gain footing, or used for anything other than the purity of the performance, bad things happen. My choice to wait for a better opportunity was a turn of the dial of growing up. I went to sleep that night a little closer to my parents, for they came in a little closer to me. I knew, too, that I had something in my pocket now, made from doing the right thing. I had a compass of sorts, the one that comes to children who sacrifice their dreams for family. All around me, childhood was slipping away. But to my north I had a dream. I had one direction I could call my own.

My older sister Janet had a harder time than I in her new surroundings. She had an undeniable sexuality and it had come too soon and probably been taken advantage of. My sister had been my second mother in Chicago, but now something was broken that we could not fix.

In 1962, the higher a girl's hair was ratted the more available she was, it was simply understood. There was something immodest or worldly about ratted hair. (That was what made Bob Dylan's ratted hair so complex and interesting—it wasn't only feminine, it was nasty.) My sister ratted her hair according to her nature. At Washington High School, Janet had a rough Italian boyfriend, let's call him "Bob M." Janet was becoming a problem child, lying, sneaking out, and getting into trouble. Her reputation was being passed around like an old cigarette, and my brother got in more than one fight defending her. Bob M. was the local hoodlum, a mean teenager who would pinch me when no one was looking. He pinched really hard, intending to hurt me, and I would cry out, "He pinched me!" and he would say, "Me? I didn't do anything." No normal person would believe someone could be so cruel as to hurt a child, then lie about it, so nobody believed me. I was incredulous. This betrayal by my mom and sister? They laughed each time.

Good Shepherd

Eventually the State of Arizona placed Janet in the Good Shepherd Home for Girls. Every Sunday, we would picnic on the lawn where each family's "troubled girl" sat on a blanket eating chicken or tacos or crying to go home. Sinners on display for all the passing cars to see.

My very first public singing engagement was there in the chapel at Good Shepherd. It was Christmas Eve and I was invited to sing "Silent Night" at the big gathering. As the nun bent the microphone down to meet my voice, stage fright nearly knocked me off the chair I stood on. I sang it a cappella. Midway through my song the whole congregation started singing along. It felt incredible! I was a hit! *That*—I want to do *that* again. Sing.

Janet ascended through the privilege and trust levels of her detention. Maybe she shared my parents' wishes that she would be a good girl, but she was already a crack manipulator. Now that she was unmonitored, Janet ran away again. It was too bad, I was so proud of her when she took me to see her new "house," earned through trust. A private bedroom, she was so excited. A room of her own. A week later she disappeared from the Good Shepherd Home For Girls.

Coming home from visiting Good Shepherd, my mother sometimes whipped out a warning out of nowhere.

"Don't you ever be like your sister. Do you hear me? Don't you grow up to be like Janet."

Every time she said this to me I was devastated. I was nothing like my sister. I was me. Didn't she even know me?

It was a seed of doubt inadvertently planted by my mother. I began to wonder if I was adopted, and so began the year known as,

"Was I adopted?" Each week I'd ask a family member, "Seriously, was I adopted?" Finally Danny said, "Yes, you were adopted. Go away." Nothing they could say could make me stop doubting my place in our family.

"When the policeman come don't say nothing"

One morning I woke up to find my sister sitting at the kitchen table. I was happy to see her but she was supposed to be "bad" and this morning she seemed normal. Yes, there they were, talking like normal, my mother and Janet. Mom was smoking, as usual. I was confused. I didn't know what to do with my hands. What should I say?

"Aren't you going to say hello to your sister?"

Now that was a good question. Did I have a choice?

"Hello."

Janet smiled at me.

"What are you doing here?" I was careful not to show affection—to anyone. Janet grabbed me and hugged me.

"She's only staying for a few minutes. She can't be here."

She ran away?

"You ran away from Good Shepherd?"

"Yes. I'm not allowed to be here, so don't tell anyone. If anyone comes to the door . . . I just wanted to stay till you got up."

Janet seemed so grown-up. Mom seemed to talk to her like an adult. It was confusing.

I sat down on a chair. The doorbell rang, and as if she knew it was going to ring, Janet quickly stood up as if to run. Mother said, "Stay here," and she peeked around the kitchen door.

"I think it's the police."

My sister was scared but fierce.

"Janet don't run or they'll catch you."

Mother looked at me and Janet said, "Rickie, can you go see who's at the door without them seeing you?"

Quiet as a mouse and using my powers of invisibility, I tiptoed along the old wooden floor, over the braided rug, and without being seen I looked through the silky curtain to see one single policeman standing there. Waiting.

Janet said, "Can you answer the door? Tell the policeman that your mother is gone at work. Tell him you can't let anyone in the house because you're alone. Don't say anything else."

I was excited. I had a part in the adult's play! A part in the Jones Gang!

Mother said, "You know you don't have to do this."

Sure I didn't.

If you do something you know is wrong, is your soul discolored, your future altered? I felt excited to help my family, and ashamed to lie to the policeman. I had been taught never to lie to anyone but I didn't want Janet to be taken back to Good Shepherd. I wanted to be part of the two of them.

I opened the door. He was a policeman alright. He had a gun. I liked him. He was nice.

"Is your mother here?"

Headshake.

"So you're here alone?"

Nod.

"And what is your name?"

"Rickie."

"Janet Adele, is she your sister?"

"Uh-huh. Yes."

"Has she been here today?"

"No."

I was acting like I was there alone and I thought he believed me.

"So, she hasn't been here at all?"

"No." Wait a second, I'm practicing my Academy Award acceptance speech.

Ad-libbing then, "My mother is at work. She has to work lunch. She said I can't let strangers in the house."

He seemed to be going for it.

"When your mother comes home—when is that? Rickie Lee, can you ask her to call us? If your sister comes home . . ."

He called me Rickie Lee. I loved him.

Out of the corner of my eye, right behind the police officer, my sister was sneaking. She was just four feet behind him, tiptoeing across the lawn. A cartoon character, lifting her feet up to exaggerated heights, tempting fate when she could easily have gone another way. Implicating me because now I had to keep her secret as she escaped behind the policeman who up until this moment, I had been taught to respect and admire. Almost to the driveway and teenage freedom, she had the audacity and courage to test it.

"Uh, she . . ."

I tried to stare only at the policeman, but I saw my sister in back of him and my eyes probably betrayed my surprise.

Suddenly the officer turned and leapt in one impossible motion right off the porch and onto my sister, tackling Janet on our front lawn. It was horrifying. His body was on top of my sister, wrestling her as he pinned her arms to the ground. Janet kicked and hit and howled. She fought with all her might and she was a big girl, but he was stronger.

I cried out, "Noooo! Get OFF her!" and then I jumped off the porch, ran to the two of them, and tried to pull him off her. I punched the officer and kicked him, beating him with my little fists. I was on his back as he tried to cuff her. My mother was there then, pulling me out of this horrific scene.

"Let go of my sister! Get off of my sister! GET OFF! LET HER GO!"

The hillbilly neighbors were out of their houses. My mother yelled, "What are you looking at?" as the cop put Janet in the back of his car. Yelling at neighbors! Mom was crossing the invisible barrier to address the audience. Mother, how daring!

"Janet, I'm sorry!" I said, but she didn't seem to hear me. I was crying too hard. My PJs had grass stains on them. If I had done my part right, she'd be free now. I felt terribly guilty.

The officer, disheveled and disappointed, looked at me, just for a moment, a look that lasted a lifetime. His eyes said that I, a little girl, had lied to him. I was so ashamed. Mother seemed to be passive, neither stopping nor helping Janet—a parenting position she would always take with Janet. Now I was a liar, too. One thing for sure, cops did not shoot kids back then. Not for hitting them, not for kicking them, and not for running away. Of course, back then teenagers didn't shoot cops. Cops and kids, it was a boxing ring with rules everyone respected. Hard to imagine now.

I was crying as the cop put my handcuffed sister in the back seat. Janet looked out the window at me, tears on her face. I like to think that my sister remembered my heroic actions and turned to smile at me from the car as it drove away. She was like a movie hero on her way to the gallows. Maybe she knew she'd get away again soon. I want to write it that way, if you don't mind. Yes, she turned and smiled, as if to say, "You did good, kid."

In reality, I stood there in the yard watching the car disappear until my mama said, "Come inside now."

No one seemed to notice what had happened to me that morning. Seeing violence on my own sister on our front yard was fundamentally damaging. We did not discuss it except to laugh about how funny Janet looked just before the policeman leaped off the porch and tackled her.

My parents had fiercely protected me, but Mom considered Janet's arrest as an ordinary part of growing up because of her own childhood. I, however, had not experienced anything like this. I had an entire moral code that had just been shaken to the core.

My father would have been unhappy that Mother had involved me in this criminal scheme. He recognized that the fragile construction of self-esteem had much to do with consistency in teaching kids right and wrong (even though he was not always the exemplar of the ideals he espoused).

My sense of duty, of being a good girl, was a shield between myself and the cruel children around me. They might not like me but

I respected myself for my basic morality and kindness, and I could prove my goodness by not lying or doing hurtful things. I had dignity as my shield against childhood cruelties.

Now I was much less than a liar. I had lied and even fought with a policeman! He then confirmed my bad-girl status with his expression of disappointment. With my self-esteem shaken, I would have little to lean on when kids turned on me.

Janet was done with childhood, with Good Shepherd, with all of it. At fifteen years of age she had seen too much of a life that she did not enjoy one bit. She soon ran away again, but this time she got pregnant and moved to Minnesota with her teenage hoodlum, army-bound husband.

Janet, Bob M., their newborn daughter, and toddler son returned to our home two years later. Their firstborn, Bobby Jr., cried every night but Mother insisted his parents get up with him because Janet and Bob M. needed to be the responsible ones. Some nights no one came so I would go to him. One night I went in to check on him and found his father, holding the baby upside-down by his feet and shaking him violently. "Shut up shut up," he hissed. This was a violence far more horrible than anything I'd ever imagined. I was petrified, unable to move as I stood in the doorway.

My mother appeared behind me, then walked over to the monster and said, "Put that baby down. Get out of here." Her authority was unchallenged. Bob M. put his son down and moved past us.

As my mother held Bobby Jr., I went to comfort the baby girl. It was odd, she was not crying, not moving. I gently touched her and she woke. Why hadn't the crying and violence awakened her? It seemed the tiny baby had already lost her hearing from an ear infection that was the result of neglect and not her father's "special" attention. These children's only chance at life was to be as far away as possible from their dangerous teenage parents.

Bob M. was out of our house the very next day. One week later, both of my sister's babies were put up for adoption. Mother knew from experience the terrible realities of both adoption and child beaters, and she knew which was worse. But I did not know what to do with what I had seen.

How could I ever erase the shadow of the baby, a man shaking an infant in the dark? I could not undo it. It would color everything I saw ever after. Yes, when it comes to children, I am a ferocious mama bear.

"A Stranger's Car"

It was another Saturday afternoon and I was out playing in the field next to our house. I had my eye on a horny toad who thought I could not see him in the sagebrush. Now he jumped to the next pile of sticks, hopping from rock to rock. Gotcha!

I held him in my hands but with lots of room to breathe there in my finger cave. How wondrous you are! I thought as I carefully placed him back on the ground. What else can I catch today? I was feeling rather pleased with myself as my eyes met the horizon. Directly in front of me a brand-new car was parking on Orangewood Avenue. A man in a suit opened the door and, smiling at me, began to cross the street and walk into the field. He seemed to be speaking to me.

I had a feeling in my stomach. Men in suits didn't walk in the dirt like this, and that car didn't belong on our street. This man was the man they told us about and he was doing everything they said he would do. He was smiling and moving quickly. What was that he was saying? Something about a puppy.

"Hey there, now, do you know anything about puppies? I have a puppy in my back seat here."

As he spoke he walked toward me in the field.

"I was taking it home to my son, but it's crying. I don't know what to do. Do you think it's hungry?"

Oh, I definitely knew what to do with puppies, but I also knew there was something wrong. I wanted to feed the puppy but . . . was there really a puppy? This was almost irresistible.

Puppy ruse? Stranger's car?

Bad man! Still I did not move.

He was closer now. I could see his tie, his dusty shoes, and his smile. Taking it all in, I thought, Do not get into that car, yet I did not think, Run away. I was frozen in my tracks.

Now the stranger was only about thirty feet away. Even as I thought, I know what you are, some part of me was still looking over his shoulder to see if there really was a puppy who needed me in his back seat.

Now he was only fifteen feet away, still smiling, almost upon me when my mother called from the back door.

"Rickie Lee!"

I looked. She had come outside and was moving toward our fence.

"Rickie Lee, what are you doing there? What's going on?" and "Who is that man?"

The man hesitated, then he stopped. He looked over his right shoulder at my mother, gauging the distance between her and me and him. I was alone and exposed. I thought Mother was too far away to help but he did not agree. In one motion he turned and headed quickly to his car.

"Get over here right now," Mother commanded. As I started to run toward our house I got there in time for Mama and I to see the man drive past us.

"What did that man want?"

"He said he had a puppy. He needed someone to help him."

She was furious. "Puppy? You knew there was no puppy, right?"

"I knew, Mama. That's why I did not go over to him."

The suit was a ticket into any neighborhood. It gave him authority, it confused people. This man had done this before. He knew how to dress for the part.

Helplessness begets fury. I felt loved as Sergeant Bettye fumed her way across the neighbors' lawns telling everyone what had happened, almost happened, to Rickie Lee. I was only a second or two from being kidnapped. We both knew there was nothing Mother could have done had the stranger taken the steps toward me instead of away.

Everyone in the neighborhood was now talking about the stranger's car. The neighbors came to complain about the world we lived in. My father thought it was time to move. The attempted kidnapping was too close for comfort.

> *Come and meet the angel born today*
> *Inside another stranger's car*
> *Be still, until this wayward bird*
> *Passes over where we are . . .*
>
> ("A Stranger's Car")

The Hillbillies Across the Street

Gloria Moore was my playmate from across the street. She and I organized that song and dance performance of "Side by Side" when my dad first heard me singing harmony. All the mothers came out on the street to see our choreography. We were Vaudevillians!

Gloria invited me to go to church with her and all her cousins. They went to church all day long and I wanted to go with them. I just had to ask my mom's permission.

There was an uneasy peace between my mother and the Nazarenes across the street. Mom had lived under the oppressive rule of evangelicals in the orphanages in southern Ohio so she knew firsthand about their zeal, their sin, and their rolling around on the ground barking. She fumed when she spoke of them because Mother wanted no reminder of her roots, and she knew better than I what might be going on in those houses.

It was hard for me to understand until the first time I went into Gloria's home. Gloria's mother did her son's hair. Elton Moore was thirteen years old, the same age as my brother, and what was nearly as disturbing—it looked as if she had dyed his hair black. Mrs. Moore sat straddling Elton from behind as she watched *As the World Turns*. Oh my gosh, I couldn't breathe. They may as well have been attaching body parts, it was so horrifying. Gloria acted as if everything were normal as she led me past them and into her room. We did not speak of it except she tried to separate herself from her terrible situation with:

"My mom likes Elvis Presley."

Huh?

"She dyes my brother's hair so he'll look like Elvis."

Oh, that I could understand. If Elton looked like Elvis, then Mrs. Moore felt like she was somebody.

That year Elton and his cousin Christian went shooting pigeons with their BB guns. To get a better perch for shooting birds, they both climbed high up a power line pole. Christian lost his balance and grabbed a live power line. The current surged through his body, gluing him to the line which was humming softly as Elton watched from a few feet away. They said by the time Christian finally hit the ground, he had caught fire and shrunk, and he hit the ground as a little piece of coal. Elton was emotionally charred and never recovered.

The notoriety of Christian's horrible death brought a prestige to the Moores, and suddenly kids who never spoke to Gloria offered their condolences. Gloria's aunt was inconsolable and her faith shaken to the core. What kind of God lets a mother's only son die so brutally? Mrs. Moore would go to church alone nuld not be attending either.

My mother, the moon

To say my mother was unpredictabl⟨...⟩t the ocean is salty. It was a given, but you went in there⟨...⟩ing to float on top of the waves.

One day Mom would fight for me like a lioness, the next she would slap me across the face for spilling my milk. She was a storm of her own, reckoning with her inhumane past as she tried to create a human being to mother her children. We watched in awe as she pulled us near and softly bit us—a woman of integrity even when there was nothing left to eat.

President Kennedy was a hero in our house. Our family had an embroidered picture of JFK hanging in the living room and my brother had Kennedy's portrait in his bedroom. We were inspired by our young

Irish-Catholic King Arthur. I remember the night when my mother, brother, and I walked along the road, along acres of onion fields and orange trees, waving our "KENNEDY FOR PRESIDENT" sign at passing cars. My brother was going to run for president himself someday. This was the deciding year—1960—when youth was invited to the future. Kennedy himself extended the invitation. He was a thrilling presence, even to me at five years old. His election meant so much to our family, as if our own efforts had helped change the direction of the future.

Two weeks after my ninth birthday, President Kennedy was murdered. I got sick and couldn't go to school all week. I cried, we cried, everyone cried. There were tears in the voices of newscasters, tears in the eyes of strangers on the street. America cried for weeks and then we cried for years.

Something was lost that autumn that has never been returned to America. The land itself seemed to grieve, it rained everywhere all week long. Even when the winter sun finally came out, it seemed as if grief was now part of our collective language. My father was gone and our house seemed emptier than before.

Thanksgiving

It was Thanksgiving. I was in the same pajamas I'd worn all week. Mother took an extra shift at work because she got paid double on holidays. She told Danny and I, "I'll be back at six or seven and we'll have turkey together."

"Danny, now listen to me, after you pat on the butter and sage, and stuff the bird—I already made the stuffing—then you put the turkey in the oven at 475 degrees for an hour, and then turn it down to 425 for the next three hours. Keep it covered."

Danny felt confident he understood what needed to be done. "Don't worry, Mom, I have everything under control." He was laughing.

Mom left for work around 10:30, and an hour or two later he put the bird in the oven and set the temperature. Danny sent me out to watch television. Since Dad was a chef, it was important for Danny to do this right.

About two hours later Danny was checking on the bird but I was thinking, it doesn't really smell like turkey. Sometime around 4 p.m. we were getting hungry, but the turkey was still raw. I looked at Danny and said, "Something's wrong." Indeed, the bird was just slightly brown, still cool inside.

Mom came home at dinnertime exhausted and hungry. As she looked at our turkey she said:

"What did you do here? What temperature did you set the oven to?"

"250."

"I told you 450."

She was mad. Dan said, "Well, let's just turn it up."

"You can't turn it up now, it's covered with bacteria."

We all looked at the stove. We had waited six hours for turkey. Mother tried not to be mad when she took the bird out of the huge black iron baking pan and threw it in the garbage outside.

"I don't have money to buy another one."

That was another shock in this week of shocks. I never really knew we didn't have enough money to buy food. There was nothing else to eat in the house, maybe peanut butter and jelly, maybe tuna fish. She had spent all her waitressing money on the turkey.

I was learning that life was not safe for anyone, at any time. Presidents could be killed, food could become deadly, holidays weren't necessarily festive, and my family might not have enough to eat.

The next day I was playing out in the front yard when I told Gloria Moore from the hillbilly family across the street the news that we didn't get any Thanksgiving because Danny messed up the turkey. I guess I was looking for a little sympathy or maybe I was bragging about how tough our family was. We don't even eat turkey on Thanksgiving. Ha!

The Moore ladies overheard me and that night there was a knock at the kitchen door. Funny, I can still see them, Gloria's mother and her aunt holding big platters of food: turkey, gravy, green beans, and mincemeat pie. They backed away as my mother opened the door.

"We heard about what happened and we have so much food, we thought Rickie Lee and Danny would enjoy some turkey dinner. Please accept it, we just won't ever eat it all." I could see under the foil—a turkey leg, sweet potatoes.

"Thank you," Mama said, "but we cannot accept this." She said it so fast I didn't believe what I'd heard. She was angry again, angry they brought food.

"Oh, but . . . we have too much."

"No, I mean it, Mrs. Moore. We do not accept charity."

Mom closed the kitchen door. Danny looked at her, but I was looking out the window at that plate of mashed potatoes. The ladies were still standing there outside the door. They didn't want to go. I really did not understand. "Mother, why can't we have the food, they went to all that trouble and it's right here."

"We do not accept charity, that's why." For my mother, charity meant shame because it included pity. Pity, especially from the hillbillies, meant they placed themselves above her. Mom's dignity was hard won through sharp-edged lessons and sacrifices as she clawed her way out of an orphanage and up from the bottom of the social strata. There would be no turkey today.

Back at school some children were not as affected by the president's death as we were. One little boy in my class said, "I'm glad he's dead. We hated him. We're Republicans." I had never heard that kind of hatred before. My teacher Mrs. Halworth interrupted:

"You will not speak about the president that way. Not in this classroom."

Mrs. Halworth sat down at her desk and gave us a lesson on being American. "I am a Republican and I did not vote for President Kennedy, but he was our president and you will respect him . . . We are all Americans, and our president has been killed."

Mrs. Halworth then read to us from *Charlotte's Web* as we put our heads down on the desk for nap time. For forty minutes each afternoon, the spider, the pig, and I got ready to go to the fair. The teardrops that fell on my desk the day Charlotte died would have made a lovely pool for Charlotte's children to swim in. Indeed, my desk was my little house away from home, where I ducked and covered, ready to be saved by my magic shelter in case of nuclear war. No book ever hurt as much as that children's book hurt us all that day. It was like part of my own mother died.

There were also school fairs, the smell of tacos, and the cakewalks for the PTA. There were playgrounds of tetherball, four square, and kickball, plus the many songs that are only sung in childhood but are remembered by a few adults whose hearts keep a piece of the enchantment of their youth.

The Intruder

In the Arizona sky buzzards were always circling. Death was ever-present and always near. Someday we will circle over you too, called the buzzards, descending on the horizon.

The dust of my nightmares leaves a fuzzy coating on my daytime horizon. In the darkness of sleep, a faraway horror is always present and moving toward me. In morning, my waking molds the little clay figures of my nighttime terrors. Sometimes they come into new life in a song. Sometimes they spring back as a full recall of lost memories.

I had terrible night terrors as a child, and fear of the dark long into my adult life. This story is my long-repressed memory that only found me recently as I forced myself to recall my jumbled life in 1963. It was a childhood nightmare come to life.

I was sleeping when my mother woke me in the middle of the night. She was kneeling beside my bed shaking me to wake up. The wind rustled across the porch, and the light from the street was bright enough to almost see Mother's face. I awoke to a strange terror, the kind that only comes when your parents are frightened.

"Wake up, Rickie Lee!" Her fingers grasped my arm. "Wake up but don't make a sound. Roll out of bed. Don't lift your head up. Someone is outside trying to get in. I want you to crawl with me on the floor to the living room, do you understand? Don't stand up."

I was thrilled that something really important was happening but too groggy from sleep to understand this as a child's greatest horror.

What? Someone? Outside?

"Someone is trying to break into the house. Be quiet now."

"Mama?"

I was waking to someone trying to get into our house.

I looked at my window and saw the outline of a man. A living shadow, moving to our door to invade our safety. He was trying the doorknob! Was it locked? Even though it was locked, I was terrified. The stranger moved from the door to the windows—he was looking into our living room windows.

I was in every scary movie with rattling doorknobs and strangers' shadowy faces in the window. "Stay by me," Mom said. We began to crawl across the living room floor toward the kitchen.

Danny was in the living room, laughing like he always did. Mom was crawling on the ground, something we had never seen before. That was funny, too. Mom was laughing. Why were they laughing?

Sometimes laughter is the only way to stay sane. A child laughs at a shot in the dark, a dog beaten, a sudden raging father. It's the only way to stay inside your skin, to not be jettisoned out of it, possibly forever.

Mom was unnaturally loud now to scare away the intruder. She bravely yelled at the door, "We called the police. You better go, get out of here!"

He did not go. He pulled harder on the front door. I was making a sound of primal fear, like the one animals make before they die. A kind of uurrruuuuuuuhhh. This noise is only heard by the thing that kills them.

Hush now.

Was I crying?

The intruder was looking in more windows, looking for the voices he heard. He was looking for *us*. We were the prey and we were hiding in the shadows just like every little critter hid from me. I looked for help. The television rabbit ears. The velvet chair. I'd hit him with the chair. If I could pick it up.

Danny got on the phone to the police, and the dispatcher said, "They're on their way. Stay on the phone." Dan shouted, "Get out of here, mister!" Then, "I can't stay on the phone, he's going to the back door." Danny yelled:

"The police are coming!"

Were the back doors locked? We never locked our doors. Mom hissed, "He's going to the kitchen."

Quick! We got up and ran to the door and he was almost there. Oh my God it wasn't locked. Just in time we locked the kitchen door. The man tried to open it but quickly abandoned it for the back bedroom.

Dan went there in an instant. The man was at the door, furiously turning the handle. I was sure he would tear open the door somehow. We were separated by three feet and a very flimsy lock.

"Danny get the gun."

Now Danny was searching for the key to the gun cabinet. He finally found it and got the cabinet door open. The man was like an unstoppable monster—he kept coming no matter what we did. We were doomed, the intruder didn't care about us, or the police, or that we were going to shoot him. Danny was holding the shotgun. "I can't find the bullets." He was laughing because he was scared to death. Then the bullets fell to the ground but they were the wrong bullets. Wrong bullets!

Where in the world were the goddamn shotgun shells?

My brother turned to face the danger with an unloaded gun and a child's bluff. "I got a gun, mister. You better get out of here. I'll shoot you if you come in."

Mom was more direct and more afraid: "You son of a bitch! The police are coming!"

That just pissed him off. He responded by kicking the door. We were braced now with Danny, our empty gun, and the door that separated us from . . . from . . .

The phone was ringing.

Suddenly the man stopped and we heard the scuffle of footsteps. The police were everywhere.

We heard them yelling, "He's running!"

The police tackled the invader in the dark field next to the house. The police weren't as alarmed as we were. "He was drunk, an easy arrest." He's Mexican, he doesn't speak English. He's drunk. He thought this was his house. We were all speaking at once:

"He did not think he was at his house."

"Then why did he run away when you guys came?"

"He saw the gun from the window. He knew this was not his house."

"I think he knew exactly where he was."

The police weren't scared like we were. There were more of them, and they had plenty of guns. We were two kids and a mother. I remember the officer telling my brother, "Good thing you didn't have any bullets. We'd have to be taking you in now instead."

Outside our door were our hillbilly neighbors who gathered once again to see the Jones family show. They went back inside their homes to talk about us some more before my mom would yell at them.

That night Danny and I slept in Mama's bed. It seemed to me that sparks were flying from our fingertips. We eventually grew quiet. Before I fell asleep, I watched the lights of passing cars scrawl on the bedroom wall with the urgent movement of people going somewhere. I wondered where they were going and I wished I were going somewhere too. We fell asleep to the touch of our mother, with Danny's loaded BB gun leaning against the wall.

The next day we recast our terror as comedy as we told the story to each other over and over again. I felt that giddy exultation of the survivor and thrill seeker. It was like my body was firmer somehow, or the air was lighter inside of me. The danger had made us closer as a family. Danny, Mom, and I. Mom started locking all our doors every night, which was unheard-of in 1963. Danny started weight lifting. I simply placed the event where I would not trip over it. Somewhere back in dreamland. Deep in dreamland.

*   *   *

My dad quit his job with Bekins Moving and Storage and, at last, returned to our house. By the summer of 1964 we moved again. I would never again know the gluey feeling of family I had felt on Orangewood Avenue, the endless hours as I seemed to grow inward instead of onward, and stretched the time in every direction it would go.

Geronimo the quarter horse did not make the move with us. He had tried to kill my mother one morning while we were grooming him. He put back his ears and squeezed Mom into the wall. She yelled at me to get out of the stall, and then kept him at bay while I ran under the fence. Then she deftly ducked under him and made a run for the fence herself with the horse right behind her. No time for the gate, Mom hit the fence at full speed and flipped over the top rail. It was incredible. All that gymnastics in school really paid off.

It was terrifying but I laughed. It was the first time I laughed at something that frightened me. A giddy kind of laugh that kids do when things are too terrible. Mom was more hurt that I laughed. We sold Geronimo to a cowboy who said he would teach him to herd cattle. He said he would not geld him and that my horse would be a father to all the quarter horses of New Mexico.

Geronimo!!

Chapter 4

A Summer Song

Father, Janet, Danny, Mother (pregnant with Pamela),
and little Rickie Lee, 1963

My baby sister was born five or six weeks early. Premature Pamela went from Mother to the intensive care unit and stayed there for weeks. When she finally came home, she had an embryonic serenity but she was such a tiny creature that she seemed too small to be a human infant. A blanket of fuzzy hair covered her body but no eyelashes or fingernails and even her crying was faint. She sounded like a faraway lamb.

Those afternoons with my newborn sister, I lay with her on Mom's bed, petting the chenille bedspread with my feet. What a mystery she was. I laid my baby doll next to my sister. "Remember this," my mother said, "your doll is bigger than your baby sister. One day you won't believe it was possible."

In the languid light of the Venetian blinds, I performed improvised operas, epic melodies of my own design. I was a mommy, singing to her, rocking her, loving her so.

I was about to enter the transitory and terribly uncomfortable age of ten. This passage to adolescence is ripe for rock bands and pop stars. Young girls are suspended in time as they fall deeply in love with the larger world. I was to fall for the first and best of all of them, the Beatles, and they would remain my true love, musically at least, for the rest of my life.

Our new house on 32nd Avenue was about a mile from our old one, next door to a car wash. We had apricot trees, two rabbits, and a stereophonic console record player. When I wasn't standing by the back window trying to practice my violin, I lay in front of the record player and listened to my dad's records: Andy Williams's "Moon River," Nina Simone's "Black Is the Color," and my favorite, Harry Belafonte's *Calypso*. I was studying music theory and I did not even know it.

Just a month or so after we arrived in our new house, my six cousins and Aunt Linda arrived from Chicago. With Uncle Bud gone, Linda wasn't able to look after all six children. Uncle Richard might be a surrogate father, they hoped, but my father was the rebel artist of the family and barely involved with his own kids, much less six more. It was the summer of 1965.

I was thrilled to meet my new instant family of so many children. Cousins by the dozens! They were all Chicago attitude, thick accents smearing a "y" on the "a," so tough and mean. The girls ratted their hair and drew black eye-liner under their eyes. That summer they taught me to dirty dance.

Uncle Bud had been a prolific man, child-wise. He was the handsome oldest brother. I have only one memory of him, a memory of safety and love, the kind of memory upon which the others lean.

Uncle Bud often babysat his brother's three-year-old girl—me. Bud lived in an old wooden Chicago tenement apartment, one story up. On this day, as Mother was sneaking off to work, I just caught her leaving—the edge of her coat slipping out the room. I screamed and I ran to the screen door as it sprung back and slammed my finger. I stood there, wrecked in despair and pain, crying as the bus drove away. Don't leave me here Mother! Don't go!

My Uncle Bud bent over and picked me up. He turned and sat down in the rocking chair in front of the round black-and-white television screen. There he rocked me, back and forth, back and forth, holding me tight, until no more sobs hiccupped from my chest. This memory of being comforted by my uncle trumps all infant memories. I am sure we were cared for, but this is the only memory of love and consolation that made it out of Chicago.

"The heart is always that one summer night . . ."

My cousins' new house was on a corner where neighborhood kids came out at night to play. It was the best August I would ever know, even better than the end of summer after my debut record came out. It was the best August of all time.

After our dinners of Rice-A-Roni and fried chicken when the heat went down to ninety degrees, my cousins and I would emerge from our houses to join the other hungry desert animals in the coolness of the night. We played all-neighborhood games like kick-the-can and hide-and-go-seek. My mother was reluctant to allow me to play with "the gang." We might be related to these Joneses but they were not like us and she did not want me becoming like them. I'd already heard swear words from them I had never heard before, much less coming out of the mouth of a six-year-old.

The thing about a game like hide-and-go-seek is that if you are really good at it, then no one ever captures you. A girl has to pretend not to be very good if she wants to make friends. I was so determined to be good at everything I did that I was rarely captured. It was discouraging.

One night it was only Rodney and Debbie and Donna and I. We were ants-in-our-pants anxious to live out every summer night before school started.

"Where are you going?" Mother asked.

"Out."

"What are you doing?"

"Nothing."

"Be back here in forty-five minutes. I mean it."

Three cousins and I walked down the sidewalk. This was *our* sidewalk.

"So what are we doing?" I asked.

"We are going to ring doorbells."

"Huh?"

"We ring the doorbell and run."

"Some adult opens the door and no one is there."

"It's funny but scary because they get mad and can catch you."

It sounded so frightening that my stomach felt queasy. I was going to do something bad! Something Mother would not approve of, but I'd be part of the gang. We snuck up to a house and rang the doorbell. The interior light spilled out the front door and a man followed. Ha! He's so big and we lured him out of his house! He can't see us. We win! Ha ha hah! We conquered the adult in his own domain.

Not a nice game but we didn't realize that someone might really be afraid.

As the night wore on, it got quieter and spookier. The shadows were blending into the darkness and no cars were going by. It was my turn to ring the doorbell. We chose a house, crept up to it, and then everyone hid as I approached the door. I was alone crossing the last few feet to the doormat. I still remember the columns on the porch. Even the crickets stopped singing.

I rang the bell and bam! No porch light, no shuffling of feet—it was like he was waiting for us. There was no time to jump off the porch, no chance to run. In the microseconds of the door starting to open I had only one option. I stepped next to a column on the porch.

My cousins could see me standing on the street side of this column as the man walked out of his house. He looked aggravated. I could see his face in the streetlight.

Behind my pillar I held my breath. I willed, I prayed to be invisible. "Don't see me, don't see me, don't see me." I was standing four feet away from him when he looked right at me. He seemed to be looking right through me. It was true, he could not see me! I was invisible!

The man moved toward me now to stand on the opposite side of the pillar. I almost said, "Hi. I'm here. Fooled ya!" But no, I kept my breath in and stayed so very still. I could see my cousin Debbie's eyes were wide as saucers and she was motioning me to not move.

Then he simply turned and went back into his house. The sound of the screen door slapping its wooden frame was my cue: I jumped onto the grass and ran to my cousins who emerged from the shadows of cars, telephone poles, and shrubs. We ran halfway down the block toward Aunt Linda's, squealing with excitement.

"He looked right at you!"

"Yeah! Did you see him do that?"

"Impossible!"

"Like you were invisible."

"Oh my God!"

"I was invisible!"

Something told me that he had not been able to see me there in the shadows for two reasons. One, he didn't expect me there, and two, because I had willed myself into a different reality and it had worked. Real magic. Adult-tested invisibility. That night I became invisible using the airless spirit of night that hides what does not want to be seen.

Every school year my mother bought me and my brother Danny a whole new wardrobe. I received new blouses, skirts, dresses, shoes, the whole treatment. This year Mother decided to make our clothes and cut my hair herself. My bangs were crooked in my school picture that year and I could not tell her that all I wanted was store-bought clothes and to be like everyone else at school.

After school Mama would ask, "Did anyone say you looked pretty today?" This was her way of saying, "You are pretty if someone tells you that you're pretty." She wanted people to accept me and be kind to me, but she was also asking whether I had been accepted. Her questions never made things better. Not even when the answer was yes and she was happy for me. Her constant need for people's approval made my private moments of anguish into a family announcement of my failures.

Perhaps because school was a closed door to me, I found beautiful places inside myself. I dwelled on things most people didn't even see. I kept myself intact and part of everything around me by daydreaming.

Someday, I promised myself, I would be a beautiful lady on television accepting an award of my own. An Oscar! Miss America! I would be so beautiful, and all those kids who drew cootie lines around me would wish they could be my friend. I would create a whole wide world from my own imagination. I would teach it how to find magic. Maybe I would find others like myself.

Those long daydreams often ended up on my report card. "Rickie daydreams all day long"—as if that were a bad thing. I had a highly active imagination with nowhere to grow. This year there would be no daydreaming, not in Mr. Carter's class.

"When they know you're not watching they talk behind your back"

My fifth grade teacher was a small, square-shaped bully with a crew cut and a bad temper. He once manhandled me by my collar because I told my classmates, "Drop your pencils at four o'clock." With my stunt, I finally made it onto their social radar screen. Listen: everyone was dropping their pencils because of me! They liked me!

Uh-oh. Outside the classroom, Mr. Carter picked me up by the collar and held me against the wall. He was threatening me with a fury that almost made me pee.

"Please Mr. Carter, don't hit me," I pleaded. The door to the classroom next to mine was open so the entire fourth grade heard me reduced to begging. It was humiliating. I was a fifth grader that even the fourth graders looked down upon. Mr. Carter didn't care about a ten-year-old girl trying to get a little social footing. There is something fundamentally wrong in an adult man's physical retribution when his feeble sense of authority has been challenged by falling pencils.

I wished I would die rather than have to stay at that school. I could not figure out what was wrong with me.

There was a ray of hope when I met my very first schoolyard friend, Susan Carl. She was a sassy girl with long brown wavy hair and a sweet face. She and her mother were from Las Vegas. Her mom wore too much makeup and ratted her hair up high. Susan and I bonded over being the first girls to get brassieres, which meant we were the first young girls of our class to be recognized as little women.

The first bra ritual was a big deal. For once in my life I did not feel like the outcast new kid. My nemesis, Jo Ellen Hassle, was no longer a threat. None of them were. Womanhood trumped any playground game as far as I was concerned. A maturing body was something far more substantial than winning a tetherball game. My little bra, along with Susan's friendship, restored a modicum of dignity, just enough to get through the rest of the year.

Friends are passengers on the short flights from one place to another, and few of them manage the transition of families moving. When the sixth grade came, Susan and her mother moved back to Las Vegas. We promised to write and visit forever but we didn't.

The Beatles

I first saw the Beatles in February 1964. My cousins and I gathered around the black-and-white television in Aunt Linda's living room. The Rice-A-Roni was cooking on the stove and fried chicken was in the pan.

The Beatles were on *The Ed Sullivan Show*. With the rest of America we had waded through his usual muddy dis-entertainment of puppets and chorus girls, and now we finally got to see what this Beatles fuss was about.

What was that they were doing with their hair? Why was their hair so long?

Girls were screaming back there in New York City. A wave ran through the audience and out of our television screen. By the second bridge—"Well my heart went boom"—we were captured, defeated, and the world was remade in their image. We were not who we had been three minutes before. The entire country had the air knocked out of it. Nothing that has happened in entertainment since can compare.

The violin I was once so eager to learn suddenly seemed unnecessary. Square. Ever since Mr. Ellis put me in the second chair of the orchestra where I faked my way through performances, I knew I was never going to make it, not reading music as well as the other kids.

On the other hand, I learned every note of every Beatles song I heard. I understood this music instinctually and thoroughly. I sang harmony and matched every nuance of their recordings. I imitated, I improvised, I learned.

By summer, I had a Beatle haircut, Beatle boots, and Ringo rings. I collected Beatle trading cards that came with sheets of bubble gum, baseball cards for Beatle fans. If I could not have Paul, I would *be* Paul. In a life as unpredictable as mine, the Beatles gave me something I could depend on. In a world where my family might move any day, John and Paul gave me harmony that I could be part of.

Unlike other girls my age, I didn't want to be a girl singer or the Beatles' girlfriend. I wanted to *be* a Beatle. I was not afraid to be "the boy" if that's what it took to find a little glory. I would find a way to learn guitar. When I first had access to one a year later, in 1965, I played it left-handed like Paul. Then I understood that the strings were backwards, so I reluctantly turned the guitar right side up. That certainly helped me with the chords, oh yeah.

Now I discovered the jukebox, the one that had always been there, and grubbed a dime or a quarter to play "Louie Louie," mythic in its reputation as the most forbidden song, indecipherable in its pronunciation.

Or "Do Wah Diddy Diddy," *the* song of 1965. As my cousins and I snapped our fingers and shoved up our feet, American rock stepped close behind. We were "Dancing in the Street"... from Chicago to L.A. "Hang on Sloopy" still makes my toes curl up. Fronted by Rick Derringer, the McCoys jettisoned little girls out of the cold wet Liverpool cavern and right smack in the back seat of a '57 Chevy.

It was nasty American rock'n'roll. If you wanted to see how vulnerable our teen boys were, listen no further than "Rag Doll" on the East Coast and "Don't Worry Baby" on the West Coast. Teen emotion was exploding like acne upon the surface of American culture, and there I was, right in the epicenter. Wherever there was a jukebox, there was a connection to the larger world. The songs never got old—we were building rock'n'roll.

It would be easy to dismiss the laments of surfers and their cars except that Brian Wilson's melodies insisted, carefully, that we take notice. This was every kid's lament—"I guess I should've kept my mouth shut"—but it was incongruous with the gentle melody it was nailed to. We felt it. The Beach Boys made it alright to do a little James Dean as you hung five and then "hahahahaaaa, wipe out." Our American identity asserted and defined itself in the musical conversation taking place with the world. Or at least with Britain. Every song gave birth to another direction.

I was undergoing a social and spiritual metamorphosis. Rock music was my bible. Mine would be the first generation to make rock'n'roll both a lifestyle and a political movement.

My parents continued to strive for their American dream. That summer I had become an AAU swimmer. Mom and Dad told me that I had to take swimming seriously if I wanted to be the best. I committed, I was going to make it to the Olympics. They committed too. By August, I was fast at butterfly, I could easily glide up and over the water. I would press forward when others tired and I would win long-distance races. I loved to win and here I didn't need others in order to feel good about myself; I alone was creating approval and accomplishments.

Mother woke me up at five in the morning to practice and after school I swam laps until dinnertime. My coach, Moonie, was an old Filipino who'd been to the Olympics for his country. He was rough and inspiring, tapping me in the water with a pole if my stroke faltered and stepping on my hands if I grabbed the side of the pool instead of flipping. "Ricarda! What are you doing?"

I started school looking sharp in my Carnaby Street fashions, sporting new clothes and feeling proud of myself from the ribbons and applause of swimming and my musical summer, but Orangewood School was a kiln, an oven of sorrow, and nothing I did outside of it ever took the heat off me. I simply could not find acceptance at school. It was so ridiculous that even the brother of one of Danny's friends, who was walking near me one day said:

"I would walk with you Rickie, but the other kids don't like you. You know how the kids are."

"I know, that's okay." But it wasn't okay. It hurt.

The difference between this year and last was that I could go home and listen to the Beatles. Finally, I had something real to hold onto, something that would hug me back.

Chapter 5

The Winston Lips of September

My brother Danny

This is where we've always been
This will always come again
This hasn't even happened yet
("Infinity")

B y the time I was ten years old my skills as a horsewoman were formidable. Besides riding every month since I was six, I'd taken a Western riding course with a rodeo champion named Karen Womack. I had proven myself in gymkhana. On my first barrel race, I had come around the second barrel when my horse stopped dead and threw me. I got back up and finished the race. The audience cheered more than if I had won. My mother was proud of me even though I did not win.

My family moved just three streets away. That August, I played on the soft bridge between the child I was and the fragmented thing

I would become. In the closet of my mother's room was a herd of horses, my mom's beautiful high heels, and I often spent my mornings clip-clopping each one out, just to hear them storming down the hall. In the afternoon, as Mom got ready for work, I brought out all the medicine bottles onto the floor. This was my orphanage, where I acted out my and mother's sad childhoods. Each bottle had a personality, and here I exacted justice between children with a precise control I would never secure at school. "Put those bottles away," Mom would holler as she sprayed her hair with enough hair spray to kill an ant colony. I had to hurry out of the bathroom.

Our cat had kittens, two of them died. It was here I wrote my first poem, an ode to "Colette and Gone Wind: The Kittens in the Dark of the Ground." While Mom was at work, I would dance in the living room. "Hang on Sloopy" was on the radio every other hour. I remember these moments as if they were Hiroshima before the terrible light, and the end of what was.

About a week before school started I was asked to help a neighbor break her Shetland pony. My parents agreed, but they did not trust the neighbor nor think I should do this work for free. I was happy just to be near horses. On the second day, I had done my work with the pony and had already ridden the mare. She was not very interesting under saddle. The neighbor was out of sight, up at the other end of the pasture with her pony. When I took the saddle off the mare, I slapped her on the hind to move her out of my immediate physical space. I'd done this many times before to move the animal away.

Sometime later, I woke up in a kind of ether, in another world; half-dreaming, half-awake. Maybe I had crawled along the ground to get into a tack shed. I was terrified of something—what was it? A horse. A horse that was trying to kill me. That was why I had decided to hide in a small cupboard like a cat searching out a secluded deathbed.

In the dark cupboard I waited eons for help. No one came to get me so I crawled back out. It still felt more like a dream than the real world. I meandered over to the fence gate where I could see my neighbor. The horse was grazing. How much time had gone by? The neighbor didn't seem to notice me, or even see that something was wrong—until she came close. I saw in her face what she saw in mine.

She brought me home, pushing me through the screen door, and my dad cleaned the blood from my mouth and laid me on the couch where I fell asleep. I was so tired. I slept until Mother came home. When she walked in and looked at me, she was furious with my father. Instead of taking me to the hospital, he had waited for her to come home. At the ER, Mom still in her work uniform, we learned that I had a serious concussion. I had amnesia, and had lost a tooth.

It was many decades before I pieced the fragments of that day back together. It started slowly with the realization that the weird feeling I had of crawling on the ground had actually happened. Oh yes, now I remembered the horse had put her ears back after I slapped her rear to move out of my way. Now I remember the pain, it hurt so bad. The impact too, she was so powerful. She may have kicked me again. Or did she rear? I may never remember. I entered that weird world I cannot describe. A door. Another door. Cupboard? Sleep. Hospital. I came back to this place again. Earth.

This accident deeply affected my father, and both my parents never wanted me on a horse again. As time went by my fear of riding grew, and I was not so sure I could ever ride again. But of course I was always going to ride again. My connection with horses was too strong to be broken for good, and eventually I got my confidence back. I still own a horse.

But I was still healing when I started school. Up until this accident, my life had been improving. Lessons, races, contests, so many ways to prove my value. I knew I could win at anything if I had the chance, but the litmus test was "back to school" where no one cared how good I was at anything. I was a cootie.

My Brother's Accident

Cooties were the 1960s version of today's "cancelling," I guess, a very public way of pretending you didn't exist. Then and now, it's a kid's version of a fatal social disease. Once it was determined that someone was infected with cooties, anyone who was a friend or even seated near that person would also be cast as a cootie carrier. In kid-world, no one wants to be a cootie. The only cure is good friendships. I was incurable.

It was the end of the second week of school. A fish-stick Friday; Phoenix was largely Catholic, and we didn't eat meat on Fridays. I had sat at a table with some kids who seemed friendly enough. Then some kids at that table drew "cootie lines" around their lunch trays. Here I thought I was doing so well, a new year, new friends maybe. Maybe I wouldn't be the one they chose to pick on. To my astonishment my "friend" who had just been chatting with me drew a line around her tray. It was a chance for her to move up a peg, I guess. I don't know, maybe I took it all too seriously. I was humiliated. It was only two weeks into the school year, and I was already at the bottom of the peckers.

The lunch tables, one after another, filled with chattering children whose voices seemed to rise, talking about me. I left all my strength on that lunch tray as I rose up in shame to leave. Unfortunately there was a gauntlet of alligators I had to pass before I reached the exit door: the older, meaner kids who were waiting there to say something when I passed. Cruelty brings fear which eventually becomes paranoia. I imagined the same meanness lurking in every face in the room. This was the culmination of the year before and the year before that, losing the normal life I'd had and then being left out of friendship since the day I arrived at Orangewood. Perhaps they recognized that I was a very different child indeed, for wonderful things were coming for me.

Some of us are born to live lives on an exaggerated scale. Even as children we have a larger suitcase in which to carry all the things that will one day be on our backs. We are cumbersome, beautiful and ugly, fistfighters and bug savers. We are the living words of poems, we little kids who are abused, and we have cut-out rainbows hidden where only we can make wishes upon them. I mean to say, we have imagination, and maybe mine was always active; while others were shining their Sunday shoes, I was capturing a herd of wild horses in my backyard. I must have seemed very . . . wrong.

So I bought a little time, gathering my cool. I meandered over to the graduation pictures on the wall to summon my strength before running through the alligators. My brother Danny's graduation picture was posted there, so I stopped to intently study Danny's smiling face. As I did, the light in the room seemed to fade into a tunnel. Sound faded too. My vision super-focused on Danny's face, I felt like I was spinning into the picture. I still don't have words, exactly, but I heard a message. I heard someone say, quite clearly:

"Something is going to happen to Danny and nothing will ever be the same."

One message, clear as a bell: "Nothing will ever be the same." I ran past the gauntlet of gator-kids and out of the lunchroom, down the corridor to the safety of the chair by the classroom door. Maybe I played jacks. Onesies, twozies, eights, twelves.

After school, I told my mother about the message and she clearly understood how much it impacted me. When Danny came home from school, Mom said, half seriously:

"Rickie Lee heard a message about you, Dan."

"Oh, yeah? What? What's the message?"

I told him, "Something's going to happen to you and nothing will ever be the same."

Danny said, "What's going to happen?"

"I don't know, it didn't tell me."

Danny responded, "If something is *going to* happen, as you say, then there's nothing I can do about it. All we can do is live and what will be will be."

Mother said something about me being a witch, which was her way of acknowledging my magical preoccupations. In my depleted self-esteem I accepted this as an improvement over being a cootie.

It seemed that this message was not just a warning for Danny or our family, it was also a warning specifically to me. There was nothing we could have done with this message to escape our horrible fate, but I took on extra personal responsibility for whatever would happen to Danny and my family. The message was so pronounced and so important that it broke through my prosaic schoolyard reality and burst into my family reality. I was hearing what was coming, therefore I was responsible. Another child damaged by taking on the inappropriately adult responsibility of "saving their family."

I was still shaken up on the Monday morning of Danny's accident, so I persuaded my mother to let me stay home. She often let me stay home. She knew school was unbearable for me.

After all our plans and individual efforts, too often our fate is decided by the uncontrollable. Tragedy and loss or success and celebration comes down to the slimmest physical margin of "inches" or "seconds." Luck turns on the most innocuous of chances. The biggest things in life often do not announce themselves, and warnings seem to only be audible in retrospect. That September, what had seemed like a friendly dance with Lady Luck was actually a slow-motion explosion of our family's lifetime of hopes and dreams.

As I was dancing to "Hang on Sloopy," Danny and his friends were celebrating the end of summer at Slide Rock, the natural water-slide near Sedona, when Danny and his wallet with his driver's license took a thorough soaking. An early morning trip to the Department of Motor Vehicles for a replacement license had him waiting in the left-turn lane for the traffic signal to change. A car driven by a sixty-three-year-old retiree sideswiped my sixteen-year-old brother. I don't know what it did to the old man, but the damage destroyed Danny. It also destroyed my mother, my father, and my family. No one was ever the same.

It was about ten-thirty Monday morning when the phone rang. I was standing in the living room listening. I heard my mother's voice close up, a kind of muffled sound: "Yes, Danny Jones, yes."

I can still feel my mother listening carefully to the voice on the other end. Mom turned a pointed attention to the emerging danger. I, too, sensed it. The phone call stilled the room and triggered primitive survival skills. Mom made a very small, choked sound: "Oh no."

If Mom had been a bird, each and every one of her feathers would have fallen from her. She would have bowed her head, her mythic cigarette falling from her claws. But she could not scream. Hundreds of tiny sobs had wrapped themselves around her throat.

If she had been a bird and I was a human, I would have run over to save her. I would have caught her in my hands, then quickly cast her into the sky and said, "Fly now. Fly before you are forever destroyed by what you have just heard." But she was not a bird and I was not a god or a witch. I was a little girl. I was not responsible for Danny's fate, and I was incapable of the adult role of managing and saving my family.

Instead, I silently watched my mother and hoped the danger would end when the phone was hung up, but as soon as the call ended, Mom called Aunt Linda. I could not hear what she was saying. Then quickly, she went to the bedroom, got her coat, her hat, her purse, and the car keys. She said:

"Rickie Lee, Aunt Linda will be here to watch you. Stay inside."

"What happened?"

"Danny's been in an accident."

My "normal" ended with that phone call. The "voice" was right, nothing would ever be the same. And in so many ways my childhood became one great day that faded into a night, a moment when I knew it was over and would never return. Melancholy became my new companion. A sense of useless achievement, the understanding that at any moment all plans might be swept away by some arbitrary act. That was a ridiculous lesson, an erroneous conclusion, but understandable in the mind of a child. Considering my parents threw my sister and I out with the bathwater, it would be a miracle that I overcame lifelong depression and self-recrimination to achieve the highest star I reached for. It was always music. Music was where I found compassion and healing, a hand upon my shoulder when times were unbearable. At last I could see my guardian angel and she took the form of music.

"Yesterday"

Daddy was at work, getting the restaurant ready for the lunch crowd. My mother called him from the hospital. Aunt Linda came over, but in some ways she was worse than no one at all. Linda, born to deaf parents, had a monotone voice that offered no comfort or solace, and she had no ability to express kindness. In this spellbinding fright, she just sat there smoking.

"I'm going outside."

"No, you stay in."

Then the second phone call came, this one from my mother. Monotone Aunt Linda then cried out, "Oh my GOD!"

I turned and walked out of the house and into the driveway, where I found a stick and began to draw in the dirt. "Yesterday," I wrote, and I sang that Beatles song like I knew what it was talking about.

> *Yesterday, all my troubles seemed so far away*
> *Now it looks as though they're here to stay*
> *Oh, I believe in yesterday*
>   (The Beatles, "Yesterday")

Mother finally came home to change her clothes. She told me she would be staying all night at the hospital.

My sister and I went to Aunt Linda's for the night. And the next night, too. There was no information about "the accident." By Wednesday my father appeared and took me and my younger cousin Debbie for a walk in the park. I guess he thought Debbie would mitigate the impact of what he had to say. I had never seen my father or mother cry, but as he spoke my father began to cry. He sobbed as he said:

"Danny lost his leg . . ."

My father explained to me what had happened—the accident. But he was tearful, and I was embarrassed. No one was playing their part. His emotional state was confusing. I felt hardened, unreactive, less emotional than everyone expected me to be.

The oblivious driver made a left turn from one of the middle lanes and sideswiped the stationary Danny on his motorcycle in the turn lane. Danny was pinned between his motorcycle and the car when his foot became caught in the car's rear fender. Evidently unaware of the impact, the driver continued down the road, dragging Danny by his trapped foot. Danny's head was bouncing on the pavement as the muscles, ligaments, and bones of his leg were detaching. Pedestrians ran next to the old man's car, yelling at him: "Stop! You have a kid attached to your bumper!"

Debbie started crying with my dad but I did not cry. I felt angry that anyone thought I should cry, this was not a time for tears. This was a time to hold on tight to avoid being swept away and lost forever.

I wanted to see my brother. I needed to see him. I was also a child who had never even been in a hospital. I couldn't understand the magnitude of the events so I focused on the excitement of going to a hospital, where grown-ups went. Finally, my mother prepared me for my new reality. She instructed me on how to behave. "For Dan's sake, don't cry, and be strong." Then she added, "smile." It was all the preparation I had.

As I approached Danny's glass enclosure in the ICU, I smiled. I had that sick smiling voice of stunned nonbelievers witnessing the Lord skating across unfrozen water. My brother was awake but with wild eyes. He was wearing white virginal bandages to hide his horrific wounds. I moved inside the ICU and stood by his bed awaiting my older brother's usual protection. He could not speak. Instead, he grabbed my arm and pointed to his missing leg. I looked into the vacuum of the missing leg and said, "I know, I know."

We communicated like siblings—through our eyes and his gestures. I was still smiling that sick smile as this grotesque reunion came to a close. Oh, it was too horrible. He seemed like a wild animal in pain.

For the next week and then the one after, my little sister and I lived with my aunt. It was a desperate choice for my parents, one they and we would soon regret.

I guess they wanted us to continue living a "normal" life and they were not thinking about the fact that Aunt Linda had nothing to do with *our* normal life. I think they really hoped Linda could look after us, but that shows how deeply they had lost their way. They simply had nowhere to turn.

So we were removed from our home, school, and family to be in a temporary adoptive family with Aunt Linda.

In that short time on Dunlap Avenue, Aunt Linda ignored us as best she could, and our life deteriorated almost irretrievably. Aunt Linda did not have control over her children and the resulting chaos overwhelmed my formerly well-ordered life. Often my cousins did not even have a hot dinner, but all ate big bowls of Cheerios. They played spin-the-bottle and I made out with someone. I wore my cousin's ill-fitting clothes to school, which were not only way too sexy for an eleven-year-old but also way too big. The school saw my rapid deterioration and they called my mother.

By the time our parents took us home, the damage was done and spreading beyond control. I was not mama's little girl anymore. Mother and Father had also changed. Mom was gone. She was overcome with grief. Unlike our prior tribulations, this time we couldn't find the thread to pick up and start our lives over again. We were all different now.

It was November 8, 1965. For my eleventh birthday, my parents took me to dinner at an Italian restaurant next to the hospital. I was thrilled. They got through dinner and then they handed me two beautiful "Damn dolls"—those troll dolls that were so popular at the time. That was exactly what I wanted. Really, it seemed like a normal birthday, but they were apologizing for not getting me any presents. What they were really saying was that there was no more money to pay for my lessons in order to continue my previous ways of life. Dancing, riding, acting, swimming, new clothes. Just for a little while. I could still swim—they would manage that. I didn't mind as much as they did. It was alright with me. These were just hard times and I guess I felt old enough to endure them.

I only knew I needed to be with my family. Pamela needed her mother. It was important to stay together as a family in a time of family stress. Mother wanted to be at the hospital all the time and Dad had to keep working. From now on I would spend every day after school at the hospital. I roamed the corridors of every waiting room and ward at Good Samaritan. I sailed by the charge nurses at the front desks where other people waited for their loved ones. My passport to go anywhere in the hospital was the whispered: "That's the girl with the brother in a coma." I rode up and down the elevator to the highest floor, sneaking onto the empty new floor being constructed above the hospital. It was scary up there but at last I had privacy. I could sing as loud as I wanted. My voice echoed down the shaft and onto the floors below. And as unlikely as it might be, Bach's music was leading me out of the dark. ("A Lover's Concerto" was a lyric put to Bach's Minuet in G Major. "You'll hold me in your arms and then once again you'll love me. And if your love is true everything will be just as wonderful.")

Somehow life would wake up and when it did we would all be "just as wonderful" again.

Danny slowly woke from his coma, but two months later he still couldn't speak. Each day we tried to get him to speak. Danny always seemed angry to see me. Perhaps he did not want his little sister to see him in bed naked, broken, unable to function.

The doctors told us that Danny would not recover. He would never speak and he would never be able to do much at all. Mother did not believe them and neither did I. I kept doing as Mother asked, trying to get Dan to react to me. One night I was prodding him to say a word. He grabbed my hair and pulled it, and a guttural sound rose from him. He sounded like a monster to my child ears.

"Gooo!"

The word surprised him, the sound of his own voice at last, and a sweet smile overtook his anger. It was the extraordinary smile of a face that broke through brain damage. But he meant it, he wanted me to leave. He was still pointing at the door. "GO!" I called back to him, "You talked, Danny!" and swallowed my tears. Dan had hurt me but I would sacrifice any part of me if it meant Danny would get better. After all, I had caused all this. I had predicted the accident.

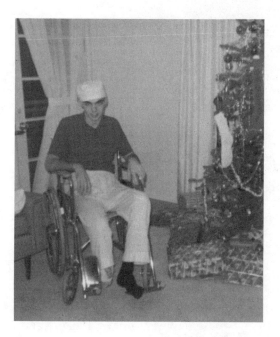

We moved just before Christmas. This time to a new school district. Finally I was out of that school. Why did my brother have to be run over for my parents to take me out of that hellhole?

Dan came home a few weeks later, speaking one new word at a time. Each word clawed back was won with great struggle.

Mom set up Danny's stuff in his new bedroom along with her impossible hopes of a normal new life for Danny. His high school football team had presented him a signed football and a letterman's jacket. It was too much, seeing all those boys there, Danny still in head bandages, smiling like a child.

Dan was determined to have his life returned to him. He thought he would go back to school, to the world he lived in just a few months ago, but the high school life he knew was over. No more football, no motorcycle, no sports. Dan had not only lost his leg; the brain injuries had done even more damage to him. He was difficult to understand: the tone of every sentence was pinched and sounded like he was on the edge of tears. He had trouble managing his emotions. His temper was short.

For a long time, he tried to regain his old life and the promise that once was his future. He kept his plans of law school and politics, but the world was now skeptical of his dreams. He could not convince it otherwise.

**"Someday many years from here where no one else can see
We'll dig up the thing they buried, and finally set it free."**

I loved my new school, things were better for me. I had a best friend, Cathy Brill from Florida. She wore deodorant. Nice. I was making lots of friends at Grandview. By Christmas, we all went caroling together. This was the way it always should have been, laughing and having fun with girlfriends. So now my guilt whispered a terrible lie: Danny had to get hurt for me to be happy. It gnawed at me and drew me away from the good feelings.

By June I had quit swimming, quit dancing, and was changing my identity from wholesome athlete. I was running around with girls who were far less capable than Cathy Brill, whose homes, like mine, kept the secrets of families in a downward spiral.

I still had music growing in me like a weed. From the safety of my room I played records all day long. I fantasized all the ways I could meet Beatle Paul. In melodramatic scenarios I abandoned my hopes and dreams for the sake of Paul who would eventually come find me as I lay dying and realize how much he loved me. This fantasy must have spoken to the lingering suffering I felt now, giving up all I had wanted in order to take care of Danny. Music was the only place I could tell a different story, feel a different feeling than this fearful darkness. A feeling something like happiness.

I memorized every detail of every Beatles song and I designed dances and one-act plays around songs like "Tomorrow Never Knows," "Anna," "Day Tripper," and the one Beatles song I eventually recorded, "For No One." I knew that I would never meet the Boys, I was just one of a million fans in a town they would never come to. I would have to be like someone they already liked and Mrs. Cynthia Lennon caught my eye. I tried to imitate her smile, to wear my hair like her, and someday when John saw me, he would be predisposed to like me. I was constructing myself out of images of lives that seemed perfect, that seemed related to the life I hoped to live. Lives as destinations. I thought, if I smile that way, maybe I will find my way to that same happy life.

In many ways, like every other insecure preteen, I was a person only half-formed, a frozen head of snow, mermaid legs underwater, formed by whims in any direction that caught my fancy.

In September I entered the seventh grade. Radio deejays were talking about a very young singer's protest against racism: thirteen-year-old Janis Ian's song "Society's Child." Ian became an inspiration because adults were listening to what she had to say. I thought, I can be like Janis Ian. She was calling me to a new social awareness. I imagined dating a boy who was not white, defying the circumstances that were already robbing me of so many possibilities.

When the Monkees came to play in Phoenix and my mother wouldn't allow me to go see them, my solution was to go directly to the source. I studied the back of their album and found two recurring names: Tommy Boyce and Bobby Hart. They were songwriters and I had a hunch they were on tour with the Monkees. I called the two best hotels and asked for Tommy Boyce.

"And you are?"

"Yes, I am ... his ... daughter."

"Hello?"

"...Uh ..."

"Hello?"

"Hi! Hello!"

"Hello, who is this?"

"Oh! You don't know me. I just called because ... I love the Monkees and I saw your name on the record."

"Oh my gosh. How did you get this room?"

"..."

"That's amazing." He was laughing now, "So hey, Bobby, this girl here, she called our room."

"She called *us*?"

Giggle.

"How old are you?"

"I am"—*say twelve, say twelve*—"twelve." That was so much older than eleven.

"What grade are you in?"

"I am in seventh grade."

"Are you coming to the show tonight?"

"I can't."

"That's too bad."

I didn't want this to end. I had connected myself to FAME!

"I have to go to work now."

"Oh, okay."

"Be good. Good luck with school."

"Bye-bye."

This was my very first brush with fame. I had succeeded in my own way, and this "initiative" would be the key to take me anywhere I wanted to go. Even at eleven I knew I had to use unusual means to be taken seriously. If I ever learned how to play guitar I'd be savvy. Growing up was taking so long, and life was almost unbearable at home.

My father had an important new job managing the Arizona Club, a private men's club downtown. He was gone all the time, but he made a lot of money and he could pay the hospital bills and save money for Dan's college tuition. Dad did the inventory, ordered food, and managed all the staff from bartenders to maids. He dealt with the members from morning to night. Dad even created a newsletter and wrote most of the articles. He published his short story there called "The Roadrunner," about a man on a road after a nuclear holocaust. It was the peak of his career, a make-or-break moment that might overcome the impact of Dan's accident and maybe even all the baggage he carried from his past. My father worked with all his soul and even so he seemed to carry the yoke of failure, as if he knew success would never belong to him.

My poor mother was unpredictable and angry all the time. I never knew who she would be each day. I don't think she knew either. One day I came home from school and she had gotten all her teeth pulled. She simply said, "They hurt."

Then Uncle Bob came to visit all the way from Pomona. He left behind the Protestants and brought his guitar instead. I had only seen the Jones brothers sing together once before, so it was very exciting, a window into a whole other lifestyle. They knew so much about music. Bob played all the jazz chords, and could translate a song into the key Father wanted. Their music revealed a language of intuition and lifelong jive; it was more meaningful than any words of love or remembrance. They played like professionals and I felt a depth, a thing between them reiterating what it meant to be a Jones. This music spirit was different than the spirit in our house or even the spirit between them when they spoke. When they sang and played, joy and comfort filled our sad little home. My uncle Bob played guitar and Richard sang: "Honeysuckle Rose," "St. Louis Blues," and "St. James Infirmary." The Jones brothers playing music again, laughing and enjoying themselves. Life would go on, wouldn't it?

I experienced the fire of the Jones family's vaudevillian ancestry. I saw us, and felt us as we truly were, not as we had become since the accident. Instead of "her and him" and "him and her and me," it was "us." Family felt so . . . safe. I wished I could hang onto it and never let it go.

"Let Uncle Bob go now," was the sendoff, but they didn't know how much Bob was taking with him as he drove away. We would retreat to our individual cabins again. That was the last time the Joneses played music together, in our house or any other.

One afternoon my sister Janet was there again from out of the blue. She was back in our lives, nineteen years old and pregnant with twins. (*Now* it was a party.) Janet was always a dubious presence. She lost her teenage years, so she coveted mine and wanted my place in the family.

She was happy enough to help Mom and have a safe place for her babies, but she took over my bedroom, then my clothes, and she took over my records. Even though Janet had been persona non grata just three years earlier, now she was replacing me as the teenage daughter. Janet came back to reclaim the childhood she had thrown away.

It seemed to me now that it wasn't only Danny who was taped together. We were all a torn and taped picture of a happy family. A family disappearing before my eyes. I stayed in my room as much as I could.

A Dinner for Strangers

My father's drinking escalated. He was becoming violent.

One incident during this time—maybe because of its unexpectedness and because of Dad's dangerousness when he was drunk—had a certain drive-by feeling that was wildly delightful. A smell woke me up. A wonderful smell but it was dark outside. The house was quiet. Was the house on fire? No, the house was not burning. Something else. I could smell my favorite smell. Outside. What was that? Someone cooking lamb in the middle of the night, right outside my window. I got up and very slowly approached the back door.

That month I had been reading the *Odyssey*, Homer's story of ancient warriors who roasted whole animals every night and had adventures, wars, and magical encounters, so when I woke to the smell of roasting meat, I was not sure where I was. Is this the reunion of Odysseus and Penelope? I heard muffled voices as I opened the back door. There was my big sister at the picnic table and my father tending to some meat cooking on the barbeque. Janet waved for me to come out, but she also gave me a look that children of alcoholic parents use to communicate: "Grave danger here. Be careful. Pay attention." I opened the door carefully and stepped into my role in tonight's dramatic episode of the Jones family movie. "Rickie Lee of Troy!"

"Hello!" Janet smiled for my dad to see. A cue. I sat down at the table. She winked as if to say, "Act happy." Dad sat down across from me. Well, anyway, I was happy but still I heeded Janet's warning and asked no questions. I was quiet as a mouse. My father looked at me: "You hungry?"

"Oh yes. Lamb chops are my favorite."

"I know," he said. "They're almost done."

He served up chunks of meat and nothing else. It was about four o'clock in the morning and we were eating a side of lamb with our hands. Oh yeah.

Dad was telling a story about work and Janet was listening to him, laughing. As the sun began to rise, my father explained that he had brought home the lamb because: "They owed me this much." I got the impression that he would not be going back to work. The lamb feast was his way of collecting severance pay from the Arizona Club.

Mama woke and looked out at our Grecian celebration and scorned, "You couldn't wake your brother up?" She was having no laughter in the house if Danny wasn't the one laughing. It would be a long time without laughter and a lot of damage before she gave up her grief.

Sugarfoot was my pet cat but also my surrogate mama and best friend. For the last five years I came to pet her quietly when life was too hard to bear. When she was thirsty she drank out of the next-door neighbor's pool. He did not like our cat drinking from his pool.

My mother found Sugarfoot dead while I was at school one day. I came home and she said, "I think your cat is sick. She may be dead Rickie. She's lying there in the garden." I did not believe her. Not Sugarfoot! Not dead! I had to see for myself. There was Sugarfoot lying in the garden where she always liked to sleep, but when I bent over to pick her up she was stiff and her fur was covered with green vomit. I picked her up gently, wiped off the vomit, and rocking her body in my arms, I cried. God, not again, don't take her from me too.

It wasn't God who had done this, it was the next-door neighbor, a man who saw us every day with our wheelchaired teenager, struggling to have some kind of normal life. A man who passed our broken-hearted house every day, *he* poisoned Sugarfoot. A monster lived next door. I still don't know how he managed it, but Danny dug the hole. He had always buried our pets and the continuity of this burial task was important to all of us. We buried Sugarfoot in the garden, right where she died. I sat there with her as long as I could, singing and crying.

Then I went inside and waited for the storm.

I spent most of my life angry, a chip on my shoulder, afraid. At some moment I simply changed my mind. I decided to be happy more or less, no matter the circumstance. Whatever I have to work with, and that's not a lot really, I tell myself: imagine you are on a ship to the outer solar system—every single experience on this earth would be welcome, good or bad. Be on that ship, for one day this will all be over. Treasure it all. Be a joyful noise.

I have met people who grew up in homes where parents did not argue and the family did not fight. They drive the same roads each day and they live in calm and predictable homes. It is hard for me to imagine this stability (conformity) in a peaceful (boring) setting.

I have no apology for my family; they were artists and I suspect we were no worse or better than anyone else. We sacrificed for each other but we were complicated. We followed an ever-changing rule book, and I intuitively understood when rules shifted. Deep down I longed for the kind of family where stability meant acceptance and consistency. I never knew if I would be rejected by my mother for some infraction, and get the silent treatment for days at a time. I understood this punishment was her way of being nonviolent. But her rejection left a scar in me I still must tend. At the same time I scorned them, I was jealous of those homes with happy, "well-adjusted" people.

Like all preteens I needed stability. My parents tried to bring stability, but nothing positive seemed to stick. My father committed to cooking Sunday dinners, but the pressure of the perfect dinner made everyone nervous, especially Mother. I'd spill my milk, my mom would slap me, Dad would yell, Danny would laugh, and it was hilarious torture. A lesson in performance under pressure.

That last year at Grandview School, with my baby sister, my broken brother, my dangerous older sister, my drowning father, my receding mother, and the dead cat buried in the garden—my family life was something like a nuclear submarine waiting for the signal to destroy all known life. Our "red phone" rang a lot. A lot. It was so bad that school had become my sanctuary from my house instead of my house being my sanctuary from school. School was the happy zone. I loved being at Grandview. Then we moved. Again. To Glendale this time, a rural area outside of town where children received free breakfasts as well as free lunches. It was here that I discovered the rock radio. I called the deejay every night, thrilled at talking to a real voice over the airwaves. "This is for Rickie," a song just for me. "City Lights" by the Box Tops . . .

All the people going places. Smiling with electric faces.

I wished I was in a city, full of people excited to be alive. There were so many other things to be besides the me I was.

The radio connected me to all the places I could not be. My one dial to the city lights I knew were shining for me somewhere. Lying in bed at night, listening to the long freight trains rumbling in the distance, I longed to be anywhere but inside my stifling life. I imagined a life running along the railroad tracks, going anywhere the wheels took me, making and losing friends, carrying my suffering heart in a guitar case.

Not much good happened to me there in Glendale, the confidence I'd gained at Grandview was squashed. The music teacher called me out in front of the entire auditorium as a prima donna and I lost my role in the school play. Then I was kicked out of class for refusing to remove my hat. The hat thing would become a habit with me, my identity. Many teachers kicked me out for my hat. But no, I was not arguing just to wear my hat, I was fighting for my right to be *different*. *I am* the girl in the red beret.

There was solace in the pink and blue walls of our house by the shivering railroad tracks. My sister had the stereo in her room. I would lie in her closet with the red light on and absorb all the music I could get my ears on. I studied Bob Dylan's "The House of the Rising Sun" and Barbra Streisand's "People." Musically, I was "Barbra Dylan," a collage of all I heard.

We moved again to a new district back in town. I enrolled in Manzanita Elementary School, on the expanding brink of Phoenix. The city was always in transition; suddenly homes sprouted up where we used to fly our kites.

The eighth grade faculty at Manzanita had devised new forms of torture for those of us entering puberty. Girls *had* to get dressed for physical education and the locker room was a gladiator's arena for shame and ridicule. Tigers roamed the concrete floors looking for weakened prey. God help the child with some kind of physical anomaly. The perfect "B-cup" girls made fun of everyone. Even the back strap of a brassiere had to be worn just so. This was the Roman Colosseum of social competition where only a few reached the top rung of the social ladder. I was spared because once they saw that I actually had breasts, they left me alone. My boobs would beat them up if they weren't careful.

I witnessed a fistfight one morning between a Navajo girl and a popular white girl. In the fray, the assailant tore at the bigger girl's blouse, and quite by accident, ripped off her bra. The crowd gasped. The Navajo girl was getting up off the ground. She was stunned, her chubby breasts exposed to the world of twelve- and-thirteen-year-old boys and girls. She tried to hug her old cotton bra and her torn plain white blouse over her breasts. She stood up, holding her shirt, her face dirty with tears and rage.

In 1967, Arizonan Natives still attended the Phoenix Indian School on Indian School Road. This young girl had chosen to attend the white school and endure the longstanding racial hatred of the children of Arizona settlers, both Mexican and white, toward American Natives. She had focused on a wider identity. Perhaps she had hoped to be part of the larger world outside the reservation. It was a fight I would never forget. I was ashamed for us all, and although we did not speak of it, I know I was not the only one horrified by what I had witnessed. The mean girls, of course, they were just a little meaner for the shame of the fight having gone too far. The glory of the kill makes monsters of us all.

*   *   *

A life that once had been gently rocking with Boshla and horses and swimming pools had come apart at the seams. My father moved out of our house soon after I started school. Home had been tense during the late afternoons when he awoke and got ready for work, so it was a relief when he quit coming home. Yet Dad being gone left a blank place in everything I saw around me. He was hard to live with, terrible sometimes, but he was my father. Life was not whole if he was not there. Somehow I was already used to my family and my life not being whole. Some part of my heart shrugged its shoulders and said, "Who cares?"

I wrote a letter to my father, and told him how groovy my life was. But toward the end of the letter I offered him my most adult advice and promise: that drinking was a bad thing, and as soon as he stopped, I looked forward to spending time with him again. I found the letter in a box of his things many years after he passed away.

RIDING SHOTGUN

Chapter 6

The Moon Is Made of Gold

My father in uniform

I was named after my father, Richard Loris Jones, a Welsh-Irishman born in Norfolk, Virginia, to Myrtle Lee and Frank Jones. Myrtle Lee was born in West Virginia, abandoned to an orphanage as an infant. Another orphan in my family.

Myrtle was adopted by the Lee family, and raised in Virginia. She died when my father was just three years old. Her death haunted him and perhaps predisposed him to finding an orphan like my mother. My mother and father shared this sad bond of being motherless children. There was no other shared connection between them that I could make out, except, perhaps, the shared dignity of work and their commitment to be better than their ancestors.

Work was their language, their tool for measuring themselves and others. The two of them both worked their fingers to the bone to make a better life for us, their children. They also hoped to have just a little bit of class. Not superficial but the kind of class that offered their kids a head start socially. Money, I think it's called. Mom was a union girl and an unaffected fighter. She did not suffer posers who put on airs. She had a natural gift for dressing well, though she rarely went out where she would be "seen." As a parent, her moral footprint might show that she walked softly, but her big stick whacked you over the head for one reason: if you lied to her. I did not lie but I suspect my father did.

Dad was self-educated, with only a sixth-grade diploma. He was proud of his knowledge and was always trying to improve it. He loved the classics; from *Don Quixote* to Shakespeare. He often read aloud, hoping someone was listening. Besides songwriting my father wrote poems and short stories. He was a singer and trumpet player, and he also played a little guitar. He was a part-time painter, mostly oils, landscapes and portraits, whatever he fancied. He would buy the canvas, nail it to the wood, draw the picture and then, so tenderly, fill it with color over and over again. He built furniture too and he did all this on his days off. I liked to watch him with his mixing knife smoothing the delicious texture on his "do not touch" wooden palette. He was rather modern. He taught me by example to be an artist and there seemed nothing I could not do, or at least try, when it came to creative studies.

In the 1950s my dad studied acting at the Pasadena Playhouse, where he was voted best in class or most likely to succeed, something like that. He was happier among strangers than he was around us. He loved being "out there" in the world—talking about theater, literature, admiring fine things. He wished to be with educated, ambitious people. He needed more to life than mere survival. Dad was about living right *now*, having some nice things, meeting interesting people.

My mother took no lessons, bought no dresses, had no manicures, no luncheons, went to no cocktail parties. She did not like being "out there" and eventually suffered from agoraphobia so debilitating she would sometimes hide in her bedroom when friends came to the house.

Instead of buying things a lady might enjoy, she spent all the money she earned and the time she could spare helping us, her children, better ourselves, nursing our interests, preparing us to be the best we could be. She was about our success, about our future. Ours, not hers.

We were her only future and we knew it. That self-sacrifice made us pity her, so we overprotected her. Our pity shackled us to her unhealthy past.

My parents are the bookends to my artistry. My connection to their past gave me my sense of momentum. I had a duty and destiny; to redeem the lost dreams of my grandfather's performance career that was aborted when vaudeville ended. Our family shared a sense of loss about it, so I would make things even, square accounts. I meant to bring my father the respect he craved. My mother and father were the perfect impetus for me to get out of the house and onto the stage at Carnegie Hall.

My father liked to say he was a Southern gentleman, but I found no evidence of this. He certainly did not grow up in the South. He did have a dignity about him, or rather an *in*dignity, and through his discontent he found his motivation and industry. He was always proving what a man he could be if he put his mind to it. How high he could climb if he kept himself alight. The indignity of loss, the chip on his shoulder, were his tools, his motivation to reach beyond his circumstances. Perhaps I have inherited the strange shape of his courage.

The Vaudevillians

My grandfather's stage name was "Peg Leg Jones." He was the original Peg Leg Jones, the vaudevillian, the one they wrote about in the newspapers way back then. He was a big star on circuits like the Pantages, where I saw his name on a bill in the scrapbooks my family kept. I was in awe of him and felt my father's tense respect for his father. He seemed to be more afraid of him than anything.

When my father brought out Peg Leg Jones's scrapbooks of notices and photographs, it was like a rabbi opening the Torah. We gazed at the book and pondered the meaning of having this famous person in our family. My father's tales of the theater life, all the hours of meticulous makeup and rehearsal, still echoed in his storytelling voice.

I also understood that "Peg" was not to be trifled with. He was a disciplinarian in a time of unkind child-rearing. He beat the boys and expected they would be as serious, and as accomplished, as Peg Leg Jones. None of them were. They had the talent, just not the luck, I guess. My father had a few notes of Frank Jones's terrible violence in him and when he drank, he could play the whole chord.

Myrtle Lee, my orphaned paternal grandmother, was a teenager in Norfolk when she met "Peg Leg" Jones, who had wowed 'em at the matinee. Frank had especially wowed Myrtle Lee and now he wanted to take her to Chicago. The Lee family disapproved and felt her rebellion was an unforgivable rejection of their parenting and adoption sacrifices.

Myrtle ran off with Frank, and her adoptive parents never spoke to her again. Too bad, since she needed them and was desperately alone without them. She had run off to be in vaudeville, but her life

Grandmother Myrtle Lee, bottom left

with Peg Leg Jones would offer little glamour and no relief. Frank too easily resorted to physical violence when easy means did not present themselves.

Myrtle did her best to adjust to vaudevillian hotels and backstages and alleyways. She raised her children in those hotels, and suffered the hard life of constantly touring. She sent them to school when they were old enough and when Frank brought in enough money that she could set up a household near the North Side of Chicago.

On the road, Myrtle had jobs dancing in the chorus lines wherever Frank went. Together they lived life vaudeville-style, outside of "normal" society. This jazz side of life, where "You're-on!" meant "You're home."

When acts were hired to play a circuit like the Pantages, they paid their own way to get there, then found their own lodgings in rooms with other vaudevillians, and shared the bill with who knows what kind of acts for two solid weeks. They played multiple shows each day, sweating out one twenty-minute performance after the other. Vaudevillians soft-shoed, flipped, joked, sang, juggled, arabesqued, and hopped. They promenaded and sashayed their risqué legs beneath the floodlights trying to make enough money to feed the kids and get a bit of glory on the side. They worked with parasol and petticoat, dog and pony, shoe and sand. Everything and anything was entertainment in these experienced performers' imaginations.

Frank's show consisted of a variety of his talents. He was a master of the ukulele, he danced, sang, and was a gymnast. My grandfather was a great soft-shoe and sanding artist. My dad showed me his routine. Gold dust. Gold dust at our feet.

The sanding dance: He would drop sand on the stage floor so the audience could hear the shuffling as he rubbed his toe and heel across the floor. It was a percussive swishing and tapping to a song's rhythm. Peg Leg Jones could flip from a standing position—impressive with two legs, but with one leg it was spectacular.

Peg had to fight harder to be taken as a serious artist instead of being seen as a pitiful cripple. He was a handsome man who had outstanding reviews on the merits of his music and dancing that distinguished him from the novelty acts of child dancers and performing animals that surrounded him.

There are no recordings of Peg Leg but there are short, perfunctory reviews that panned everybody except my grandfather. I liked that. Peg Leg was once billed above Milton Berle! We were very awed. My favorite review of Grandfather was short and to the point: "This mono-ped puts most two-legged men to shame."

I always claimed to have learned to sing from my daddy but I suspect it was really Peg Leg's oversized influence all along. His words, distilled through my father, taught me the craft of theater, from how to take a bow to how to love the stage and retain one's dignity while inviting critics and the public to judge you.

Peg

Little Frank lost his leg while playing by the railroad tracks when he was six years old. A train was passing by and he slipped. Maybe it was a dare. Anyway, Frank's father, Burrell Jones (my great-grandfather), did not suffer this loss of limb. His son would be expected to do anything any other child did. Perhaps that was how Frank developed the confidence to dance and perform. Burrell owned the general store and also worked as sheriff in their small Virginia town. I would very much like to have taken a gander at that old pirate. We have a photograph of him standing austerely in his dry goods store.

One-legged men run in our family. My grandfather, Uncle Bob, and my brother—each Jones generation lost a leg. Locusts and boils, I guess.

A curse I mean. The curse of poverty, motorcycles, and war.

Myrtle had left her family for Chicago less than ten years before, but she hadn't found a satisfactory replacement. Chicago seemed impenetrable and secondhand. Three of Myrtle's children, Bea, Frank Jr., and Richard, were playing on the sidewalk in front of their house while Myrtle and Frank were once again arguing. Perhaps this time Myrtle had had enough. She left the infant Bobby in his crib, stormed down the stairs, and stepped right in front of a bus. There remained confusion about whether or not her death was an accident. She was killed instantly in front of her son, Frank Jr.

Frank Jr.'s gasp, his breathless anguish, vacuumed his childhood out of him. When he could breathe again he could not speak. He never fully recovered and stuttered for the rest of his life. A "stoppage of speech," it was called. Frank, whom I called "Uncle Bud," died before he was fifty years old.

Richard, my father, was only two years old when his mother died. It was my mother who told us what had happened, as Father would not speak of it to us. Who knows what he experienced on that sidewalk with his mother lying on the street? What scars does a two-year-old carry from such tragedy?

My father's sister, Beatrice, or Bea, became the surrogate mother for all her brothers, Frank, Richard, and Bobby. As a teenager she started singing jazz and sitting in with the new big bands of the era. Tommy Dorsey was a friend of Bea's, staying with her and her husband when he passed through town.

Aunt Bea died suddenly while my dad was at basic training. 1941, I think. She was arguing with her husband while they were in a car and Bea fell out. Or just decided to get out while the car was moving. Or worse. My dad went AWOL to make it to her funeral but missed it because he could not hitch a ride. The army forgave him and let him come back because forgiveness included shipping him to Europe and the meat grinder of WWII for the next four years.

My dad's intrinsic sadness seemed built into his character, as if a DNA strand were woven into him by circumstance. I like to think that when we love someone we make them a part of us and our invisible skins grow together. A tragic loss of one half of a couple leaves a cavity, and the skin that grows back in recovery takes on the scarred and misshapen outline of the departed. The one who remains is half ghost. For my dad it was the loss of his mother and then his sister that ate away at his heart. I have felt my father's broken heart inside myself, an archipelago.

Vaudeville had started its long death rattle in 1922. Vaudeville theaters that had been the center of life for so many towns now installed movie projectors and hired organists. At first the live performers continued to headline with a little silent-movie showing as a novelty. Soon, the movie became the main attraction and the organist full-time. Finally, one day, even the organist disappeared and vaudeville was extinct. An entire generation of performers had no idea what to do with themselves.

Frank died of tuberculosis a decade before I was even born. Amid the crowded damp backstages and cramped hotels full of people where a single infected person with TB could spread the disease simply by breathing. The little TB bug was ready to drown the poor and the old in their own fluids, but Peg Leg Jones had died long before he quit breathing. He was a remnant of another century that was now abandoned by America. Vaudevillians adapted or found other work but my grandfather, without the stage and an audience, was reduced to what he had always fought to never become—"a one-legged cripple."

Boys Town

Richard was twelve years old when he read in *Variety* that they were making a movie about Boys Town, the Omaha, Nebraska, orphanage run by Edward J. Flanagan, a Catholic priest. The movie featured Spencer Tracy in the leading role as Father Flanagan, with a young newcomer, Mickey Rooney, as the wayward star. Guided by a dream of being in a movie, my dad left Chicago and hitchhiked 480 miles across Illinois and Iowa to the movie set in Omaha. He was exhausted, hungry, and just in time. Richard told Father Flanagan that his father didn't want him, so that Flanagan would be compelled to take him in. Father Flanagan smelled a rat and insisted on verifying Richard's tale of abandonment. However, Richard could have a bed and a hot meal until Father Flanagan could exchange letters with Peg Leg Jones.

My father didn't last a week before Frank Peg Leg Jones sent word that his son was *not* an orphan and needed to return home immediately. However, in the short week that Dad lived at Boys Town, he managed to get himself in the film—or at least, the short about making the film that still sometimes airs before the actual film. I had seen the short a couple times before my father pointed himself out. "I was working in the laundry room and as the camera panned over us I looked up and"—Dad demonstrated a kind of ta-da gesture—"smiled." A smile intended to win him a movie career. The runaway child who became my father is forever burned into celluloid.

When he returned to Peg Leg's care in Chicago, the already thin father-son bond was in tatters. Richard began misbehaving. His father sent him to a disciplinary boarding school in Georgia. There he met many old Black men who taught him the blues and gospel and how to sing low and alone for songs like "The Old Rugged Cross" and "St. James Infirmary." Those songs stayed with him for the rest of his life and he passed them on to me. I sang the latter on a record of my own, but no one could have known how much it meant to me. Omaha and the movies were the seeds of a lifelong wanderlust. Dad was gonna take the hard road of adventure. He was a rebel, his father's son. I would follow in his footsteps—or footstep. Sorry Peg.

Potato Soup

Dad's home life was over before he was fourteen years old and his new life of adventures on the road began. The Depression unraveled the ties that bind as families were unglued and unmade. Like many others, Dad caught a freight train to "anywhere but here." His train happened to be headed for Arizona.

The other men on the train taught Father how to ride. You never waited until the train stopped to get off. The railroad bulls were waiting at the stops searching for freeloaders. They were mean men.

"I saw them beat a man to death," Dad said. "No, you jump before it stops, you run, and you make sure those goddamn bulls don't see you." His stories live within me. The bulls became part of my childhood list of devils.

Dad jumped off the train just shy of some little desert town in Arizona and headed for the hobo gathering that was always nestled outside of the population center. Some of the men lived there all season long. You might be able to trade, say, cigarettes for some beef jerky or an old coat for a couple cans of beans.

"Any work in this town?"

"No work, boy."

Dad went into town anyway, and started knocking on doors, asking if he could do any work for a meal, but every door already had a hobo employed. There was no work anywhere and Daddy was hungry. Very hungry. A man walking by saw the desperate young boy and said to him:

"There is a lady who lives at the edge of town. Her yard is a rock garden. She has some work, if you hurry."

When my dad arrived he saw a line of people standing outside her back door all turning away with nothing. He got up to the door and asked if there was any work. The lady said, "No, I don't have any money or work for you." But then she said, "Hold on, wait here."

She came back with a potato. Not just any potato, the biggest of all potatoes. "Big as a cantaloupe," Dad would say. Young Richard, high-stepping now, hurried through the tiny dirt-road town back to the hobo camp. The men were trying to make dinner. Someone had made a fire and there was a big iron pot of boiling water from a stream. Dad gave his potato to the cook who smiled big, cut it up, and dropped it in. Someone else had gotten paid with an onion. They cut that up too. Somebody else had salt and pepper which went into the pot.

Now men started coming from all directions, smelling the onion and potato. As the sun was going down on the Arizona desert some eighty years ago, a big pot of potato soup was feeding all the hobo men as far as scent carried. Daddy's belly was full. Someone had tobacco,

Dad rolled himself a cigarette, and they smoked it there under the desert stars with the trains going by. It was a momentous episode for my father. He would return to this memory and this very desert with his family, just as I would return to Ojai with mine after my adventures.

Eventually though, we wander again. For every hobo there is only the road, the train tracks, and the eternal sky. The scorpions and the night-blooming cactus. The wanderlust of travel by thumb or by train, the magic of strangers without possessions sharing their meager nothings to create a community more generous than most, with bonds that outlasted the lives of those in the richest cities. Conquering an impossible survival is such a moving experience that it becomes a new reason for life. It's an unheralded accomplishment that passes so fast and then is gone, except in memory where it reshapes the definition of "the good life." It's an experience that is accidental-like. It's a glance, a smell, and a sound that leaves a memory of deep contentment. Like the night the potato soup fed the hungry masses by the side of the railroad tracks.

Dad spent four years in the army, fighting from North Africa into Sicily. He was wounded, received a Purple Heart, and was saved, more than once, by his best friend Barney Williams from Kansas City, Missouri.

Barney was a big red-necked (literally) man who raised hunting dogs and loved my father so much that he once crawled into the middle of enemy gunfire to pull my dad out of a foxhole. But Barney couldn't pull all of my dad out of that foxhole. He suffered from PTSD all of his life. Some invisible part of my dad remained buried in the earth.

The Scorpion

My father had been made sergeant but was demoted to private for insubordination to a captain. Dad was a rebel without a cause until he joined the army. The army gave him purpose. He could also wait out the terrible loneliness that surely would find him in the States where his sister no longer waited for his return.

Dad had survived the fighting in Tunisia, and when the British insisted the Americans stall their advance into the North of Italy, Dad spent time in Sicily where, I suspect, he fell in love. I guess they fought in trenches and then spent a few days in towns and Sicilian homes. Then back to the trenches, literally.

It was a long campaign of fighting and bombardment as he burrowed in his foxhole. Occasionally he checked to see who was still alive.

"Hello?"

Great relief if anyone answered, "Still here."

Father quietly hunkered down, seemingly safe in the foxhole he had dug with a little shovel supplied by the army. He set his rifle down and opened his rations for the first time. A condom. A tiny bible. He felt a bit of the self-satisfaction that comes from still being alive on the battlefield. There in the dirt, Richard filled his belly. Beans was it? Or maybe Spam? His stories were always better when food played a part in them. Dad ate his Hershey bar. He would always love Hershey bars.

He remembered he had bought a cigar back in town. "Where was I—was it yesterday? Last week?" He wasn't sure. Richard lit a match; he would smoke a cigar to celebrate his dinner and his life. As he inhaled, the glow of his cigar lit up the dark shadow inside the hole and he noticed the scorpion who had crawled in with him. Another sole survivor of the fury unleashed by World War II, the scorpion had long considered this his dry, serene world.

It was a fair-sized yellow scorpion, perhaps attracted to the cigar's light, or simply the cool earth where his kind usually congregate. Dad watched the animal walking slowly and decided to stop its advance with his cigar. He set the cigar down in front of the scorpion's path. The thing stopped. It started to go around the obstacle, but Dad moved the cigar back into its path. The scorpion wanted no part of it. One more time my dad put the red end of the cigar into the scorpion's face and this time the scorpion had had enough. It struck the cigar with its poisonous tail spike, but the cigar survived and was still lit. Now the scorpion took hold of the tobacco with its scorpion hands and pulled the burning cigar to itself, bringing it close enough to strike, and strike it did—but not at the cigar. As the scorpion brought its poisonous tail down upon its own head, it pulled the fire into its face. It killed itself.

Father was dumbfounded. Shocked. He had tormented an innocent thing, a survivor like himself. A refugee, tired and hungry, only wanting to share his safe space.

In that foxhole, surrounded by death, my father, like the scorpion, could not escape. Dad had a revelation. The scorpion was my father's spirit animal. The scorpion showed Dad his true nature of self-destruction. Dad had tormented it until it did the most inexplicable thing a living creature can do; it ended its own life. The scorpion killing itself was one picture too many for my dad. He began to cry. In a way, he cried for the rest of his life. He did not cry for his missing neighbors or his platoon. That would have broken him. It was the animal that brought him low. He saw what could happen to him.

Soon after, Dad was shot off his motorcycle by a sniper. He received a Purple Heart and headed back home to Chicago. It was the end of the war.

My father's quiet revelation with the scorpion was deeply personal to him. World War II was his generation's embrace of masculinity that showed its bloody limits in solving problems. Dad's struggle with violence as a form of masculinity came at great cost to him. He lived a tormented life as the victim, then the perpetrator of a violence that had marked his life and so many of his generation.

I like to think my father overcame the trap of masculine violence the day, years later, he went rabbit hunting in the desert outside Bisbee, Arizona, where he lived then. He shot the rabbit, and when he went to fetch it he was overcome with regret. He told a beautiful story of the rabbit's hard life out there in the desert, and how it had managed to survive coyotes and snakes only to be shot by a man with the unfair advantage of a gun, who could easily have bought his food. He cried over the rabbit just as he had cried over the scorpion. It seems some things never die.

Father did what few veterans can ever do. He brought all his proud guns out to the desert and broke them into pieces. This symbolic destruction of his masculinity marked a profound moment of growth at the end of his life—his realization that his violence, not society's lack of appreciation of him, was the real barrier to becoming the gentle man he had always hoped he was. Richard was always a lover, not a fighter. It just took him a lifetime to recognize himself. Now, riddled with cancer, revelation rendered him the gentleman he always said he was. Kind, patient—I met a new father when I saw him that day back in 1984 after five years apart. We went to a river, and a rodeo, and bought groceries so Dad could cook me a meal. A year later I had my wedding at his home, three months before his death.

Richard died young, at sixty-three, younger than I am now but older than anyone in his family had ever been. His mother and father and brothers and sister all died young. They began life in poverty, with its dead ends, but they grew into enough freedom and income to enjoy the riches of music, dancing, and looking good. They were the first generation of Americans to claim music as their youthful banner. They brought swing music and jazz singing to every home, and that was my home—full of music and a warm pool of ambitions.

Dad never gave up on creating things. His very last letter to me was about a new project we would do together. It arrived a week after his funeral, a surprise postcard from the other side.

Chapter 7

Gravity

My eighth grade graduation
with little sister, Pamela

Alone, in a world of your own
There you are, girl
Small things float to the top
Of Gravity

("Gravity")

November wind could blow a child out of her mother's arms and right across a frozen Lake Michigan. I suspect there are still babies frozen up there in the sky, and one day, thousands of thawed-out infants will fall to earth with little Chinese umbrellas carrying them safely to the ground. Perhaps that is how I see my childhood. One day it will show up here and gently fall to the ground at my feet, and at last I will grow up.

Chicago, the town I was born in, where all my relatives lived and died, was the stockyard for America. My dad once took me to the stockyards to show me the cows and the killing places. It smelled terrible, blood, feces, and the kind of smell that comes out of us all when we are about to be slaughtered. He wanted me to know Chicago history was more than Al Capone.

The lessons he felt he needed to impart were random and obscure as far as I could tell. I preferred our family stories—like the freezing November when Dad and Uncle Jim got drunk and went skinny-dipping after a night of drinking. Dad watched Jim hit the water but instead of hurrying out, he kept diving back down.

"What are you doing?" my dad called.

"I—I lost my teeth!"

My dad would laugh so hard as he told that story he'd have a hard time getting to the punchline. I liked stories better than lessons. Any time an adult wanted to teach you something it was probably something you did not want to learn.

Get your kicks on Route 66

Eighth grade was not so bad, I had "street corner" friends who stood under the streetlight just talking. I loved being allowed to join them. We listened to the transistor radio and giggled over lyrics, like "let's spend the night together now, lalalala."

It was October when I came home from school and turned on the television to *Wallace and Ladmo*, the kids' cartoon show. Mom tore into the house, she was frantic.

"Quick. Put your clothes in the car. Anything you want to bring. You have fifteen minutes."

"What's going on?" I asked.

"Just do it."

"Mother, what's happening?"

"Your father is coming. Now you have fourteen minutes. Put your stuff in the back seat, don't pack it, just throw it in the back, we don't have time to pack. I'll get Pamela's stuff. You just get yours."

My father was coming?

I grabbed my suede shoes with the buckles, my navy blue polyester coatdress with the brass buttons, my tambourine, and my guitar.

"You don't have time to get your records." Mom had Pamela's many medications. I snatched up *The Beatles vs. The Four Seasons*, I just had to bring my favorite Beatles songs. We were in the car thirty minutes later, me riding shotgun, my little sister in the middle. As Mom pulled out of the driveway I was thrilled with confusion and delight. An adventure! Where would we go?

Me: "Somebody has to feed the dog."

Mom: "I'll call Janet."

After a long while I said, "Boy, old Betsy sure has taken us back and forth a lot. Where are we going?" Betsy was our name for our car.

Mom: "Don't say anything right now."

I knew better than to ask twice. Finally, Mom lit a cigarette. All my life, Mom with a Winston in the ashtray. I rolled down the window and counted cacti. We drove halfway to Flagstaff before I dared look at her.

"What happened to Daddy?" asked Pamela Jo. Her youth made her the braver soldier.

"Why do we have to run away?" I asked.

Pamela pushed in the car lighter for Mother's next cigarette. It was now night and there were only sparkling dashboard lights as we drove, figuratively and literally, in the dark. Mom wanted us many miles away from our home.

It was well into the night before we finally stopped at a little motel. Motel living was exciting. A strange temporary bed meant *nothing* really mattered. A few hours before, I was routinely walking home from school, and now I was on an adventure without a reason or destination. We found a diner and bought two hot meals, one that Mom shared with Pamela. My mother never answered my questions about why we had to get out of there before father came home:

"Well, why do you think?"

"I don't know, that's why I'm asking, Mom."

I'll never know. I suspect her silence was meant to protect me from some knowledge of violence, but silence didn't hide the chaos. I was undergoing yet another fundamental unsettling of my world.

Mom was driving to her brother's house in Chicago. We were going east on Route 66, a road I knew well because my family had taken it to and from Chicago already. Here was no-man's-land, the Texas Panhandle, and then Oklahoma. It was late afternoon of the second day when Mother asked, "Do you want to have a picnic or stop in a coffee shop for dinner?" Ah, deftly handled, Mom. She was running out of money so she offered what no kid could resist, a picnic. With bread, bologna, and mayonnaise we pulled over to eat in a beautiful rest stop somewhere near Springfield, Missouri.

I saw so much color coming out of the earth, a rainbow of autumn leaves. I had never seen autumn colors before. I wished I could just stay there in that moment, or live in that place, or over there in that house, and never go back to Arizona.

Mom drove hard after our stop. The only radio station available out there on our trip down the dark unlit highways was talking about UFOs and extraterrestrials. I looked up at the stars, just in case. "Hey I saw that star move!" Nothing abducted us and we pulled into Chicago just after midnight.

Uncle Jim lived in a modern apartment building on Belmont Avenue, just a few blocks from the lake. We left everything in the car and took the weary elevator up to a modern, fancy apartment. Mom's brother and his family were waiting up for us.

Mom's brother bore no resemblance to her. Neither his face nor his accent was like hers, nor his unsavory spirit. He was nothing like anyone I ever thought I could be related to. He had no front teeth. He and his family all had red hair. He frightened me when he said to his wife Helen, "Well what are ya doing? Make 'em something to eat, ya idiot!" Then he smiled at me and shook his head as if I were in on the joke, as if I deserved respect and she did not. It was demeaning for my mother to have to ask for help from the one thing she had tried to leave behind—her hillbilly past.

Aunt Helen was Cherokee; her skin was white porcelain and her hair was wavy red. She looked like a doll, with a tiny waist and large motherly bosom and hips. She was gentle and had a twinkle in her eye. I liked her very much. I wondered how on earth she ever ended up with this . . . thing, Uncle Jim. He was horrible to her, spoke to her like a dog he did not like.

In the morning we woke up to find our car stolen with everything we owned gone. "Goddamn cops probably stole it," said Jim. I was devastated. On Monday, with only the clothes on our backs, Mom took me to enroll in my new school. I was still in the eighth grade.

Maybe our lives in Phoenix were chaotic but we had enough family security that I was always growing and developing. The accident had unseated us, but we were recovering. I was a good kid, I followed the rules, I studied and tried to please my parents. This trip to Chicago removed those foundations.

This mean, urban setting was so unlike the sonorous, suburban landscape of home. Our uprooting undid the tether that had kept me devoted to *good* things, upstanding things, right things. In the impoverished neighborhood I saw around me, my self-esteem was reflected in a terrible new mirror. How could I be good if we were here? Had I done something bad to cause this punishment?

A child's reasoning, but I was a child, after all. Like all children, I needed consistency. If only I had one thing I could count on, just one thing. The ugly alleyways were frightening to me and the old men were always leering. It was a jungle, and I understood in a matter of just a few days what was going to be expected of me now. I must land on my feet, I was on my own.

Walk tall, we always walk tall

Mother, sister, and I moved into a hotel on Belmont Avenue in Chicago. We lived in just one room with a Murphy bed and a kitchen that looked out on the alley. It was awful. "Temporary," Mom said as she saw my face drop. I was going to be brave. What else could I do? It was time to be tough.

Nettelhorst School on the North Side of Chicago was just a block from Lake Michigan. I pressed my 140-pound frame against the wind and risked being blown back into the water. I liked being one of the kids who knew how to walk against the wind, who wore a windbreaker against the freezing wind off the lake. *We* were tough.

As I waited for my first homeroom teacher to arrive, a large boy picked up a desk and threw it across the room! There was chaos and noise, nothing like Phoenix. I was amused, it seemed like they were showing off for the new girl. Sure, I was frightened, but also kind of thrilled.

There was a big school dance coming at the end of the week. Would it look like the dance at the gym in *West Side Story*, my only urban reference? It did. Mom bought me two or three new outfits for school with money Uncle Jim insisted she borrow. I looked pretty—I was different than the girls brought up in the neighborhood—and boys wanted to dance with me. Lots of boys were looking and paying attention to me. I loved dancing and I felt so happy. One of the tallest boys asked to walk me home after the dance. Then another boy said he'd join us, and then it was about six boys—the whole gang. Sure! The boys in Phoenix never treated me so sweetly. Yes, let's all walk home together, and there at my apartment I waved goodbye. For the weekend, I felt like I was, you know, Cinderella.

On Monday I walked into my homeroom class, and people were whispering:

"What?"

"Did I have sex with the boys?"

"With *all* the boys?"

The girls of the school were serious, it didn't stop at gossip. I ended up fighting a sad-looking girl whose boyfriend was the tall guy who danced with me and walked me home.

"Susie is going to fight you. She says you're a pig whore."

She and I met in the playground. I had never been in a fight but I could not back down. Not here. As Susie walked up to me, I thought, Why should I wait for the fight to commence? I took her by surprise, slapping her before she got a punch in. I knocked off her horn-rimmed glasses, but she was a tough girl who was about to beat the crap out of me when some teachers broke us up.

Of course, in the finest tradition of youth, she dumped the boy and we became best friends. We spent lunchtime at the diner playing "Don't You Care," by the Buckinghams and "The Mighty Quinn," by Manfred Mann. Nancy Sinatra was an idol of mine that year, primarily because my family thought we looked a bit alike. If I looked like her I must not be as homely as I thought I was. She gave me something beautiful to grow into.

Mom had paid Jim back, but we were living on very little. It felt disgraceful, poverty. We were living in a neighborhood that looked like the one in *The Man With the Golden Arm*. Was my whole life in Phoenix an illusion? Had I made us all up? Did I really belong *here*?

November came and at last, my thirteenth birthday. A real teenager. I think I went straight from child to adult that birthday. I babysat my sister that night. Mother had told me she didn't have any money to buy a gift, but I was happy to be a teenager.

When Mom came home from work that night she said, "I am so sorry, Rickie, I could not afford a cake, but I brought you home something. Somebody didn't eat their food. It's filet mignon. See, they didn't touch this part, it's good." I ate the steak. It was delicious, luxurious. I needed Mom to feel that I was alright about my birthday in our circumstances. To be honest, I felt kind of lucky, because even down here at the lowest of the low, I was having a steak for dinner.

All November my mom worked the day shift while we were at school, and then she returned at night to work the dinner shift. I watched my little sister and did my homework. I started reflecting on this filthy, sad place. I was becoming what I saw. This must be who we were. My parents made a lot of miscalculations, but something in me had always felt whole, until now.

Come PLP with Us, Rickie

I met the Puerto Rican girls the week after my big fight. They said they were a gang, "The Spanish Queens." They said, "We saw you fight and you were good. We want you to be in our gang. We like you even if you're white."

It was an offer I couldn't refuse and so these beautiful Puerto Rican girls and I became friends. I liked how it felt to be part of something bigger than myself. I was Riff, I was Tony. This was all theater until the day they told me they had murdered a girl.

"On a roof. We killed her on the roof."

"Oh?"

"We knocked on her door and asked her mother to tell her we would meet her up on the roof. And when she got up on the roof, everybody stabbed her."

Oh, I could not think. I could only feel what that girl had felt. Betrayal. Pain. Terror.

"And she died?"

"Mmhmm."

> *I try to imagine another planet, another sun*
> *Where I don't look like me*
> *And everything I do matters*
> *In the world where you are, girl*
> *In your green paint*
> *With a pin to pull at the fingertips*
> *Of Gravity*
>
> ("Gravity")

It didn't matter why. Maybe she insulted someone, maybe she danced with someone, like I had. She had been one of their gang, one of their own. In the ever-changing rule book she had been condemned to death without trial. I wondered, What might happen to me, the white girl, the outsider to Chicago, and the newest member of the Spanish Queens?

A week later, just before Christmas, Mom decided we would return to Phoenix. The leaves of the Chicago fall were long gone, the wind had shorn them all away. The sky was cloudy and the cold was unbearable. It was also an escape from my fear of being stabbed on a rooftop by the gang and my now messed-up school life. I woke up New Year's Eve in Phoenix with my dad sitting in the kitchen. How was I supposed to react to this surprise? My mother was smiling at me. From the way she and my father were smoking and drinking coffee, I knew he was going to stay. We were a family again.

Daddy moved back in as if nothing had happened. My sister moved in with her boyfriend and they relocated to Tacoma, Washington. My parents concocted a new vision of life in which Chicago would have better jobs for them. Now we'd go "back east." So in the dead of a February winter we packed our clothes and boarded an Amtrak train back to Chicago.

Small things float to the top

We settled into a one bedroom at the Donmoor Hotel on Eastwood Avenue. This was the same neighborhood where my father grew up and where my parents had lived a lifetime ago. Pamela and I slept in the bedroom, Dad and Mom on the Murphy bed. Most nights I was alone. Pamela would not sleep without her mother by her side. Or maybe it was me who couldn't sleep. The Donmoor was a residential hotel in a decaying part of the city where ruined families lived. I hated and loved the old carpet that smelled like onions and looked like decades of spilled dinners. The six blocks I traversed each morning were more dangerous than Belmont and Broadway where we'd lived just three months before. Men perched outside of bars leered at us as we walked to school.

I was now on my fourth enrollment of my eighth-grade year. This new school, Stockton Upper Grade School, was a rougher and poorer version of any school I had ever known. Still, romance was the theme of middle school, and it was no different for me. I saw a boy named Junie walking down the hall, a white stag, a magical vision in my lonely world. We smiled at each other as we passed on the stairs. He was a promise of romance—the boy in the green windbreaker.

Then, in April, Martin Luther King was murdered and the city exploded into violence. There was also an ominous battle shaping up for the 1968 Democratic National Convention, hippies were piling into the city. The police were driving four men to a car with shotguns across their shoulders, but for me the really dangerous shit was happening in school.

I'd started in the middle of the second semester, so a girl named Diane was assigned to help me adjust. She even sat behind me in homeroom. All was fine until a Black kid named Billy Raye stayed after school to do a little artwork on the walls of every bathroom on the eighth-grade floor. In twelve-inch letters was roughly scrawled:

Billy Raye
+
Rickie Lee

Unfortunately, Billy Raye's girlfriend was Diane, and now Diane hated me. *Me!* She got her girlfriends to join in hating me and now it was a Black versus white thing. It seemed that racism was in the air people breathed in Chicago. By May I had to hide during recess. The Black girls would not let me go anywhere. They roamed the halls and playground looking for Rickie. In final days of school they finally caught up to me. As I ran up the stairs to the back door, four of them were waiting. My friends fell away and the girls surrounded me:

"If you come to graduation practice tomorrow, we are going to kill you."

I walked home and took the elevator to our hotel room. I lay down on my bed and stared at the red scarf covering my lamp. "Lady Madonna" was playing on the radio as I made my announcement:

"I am not going to school tomorrow."

Mom: "Why?"

"I can't tell you."

It mattered more somehow not to snitch on my potential killers than it did to come clean to an adult about the danger I was in. I knew skipping rehearsal meant I would not graduate. No diploma. Finally, my parents extracted the reason from me, and they relented. If I did not want to go, they would not make me.

The next day my teacher, Mr. David, telephoned my house from rehearsal. "Where is Rickie?" My father listened to Mr. David, and boy was I relieved. Then it was my turn on the phone with him. "Rickie, we know what happened. We spoke to the girls and nothing will happen to you. Come now. You can still graduate if you get here in time for rehearsal. Come. Be brave."

I can still feel the eyes of every single person in the auditorium staring at me as I walked in for rehearsal. It was horrible anxiety but no one killed me. They did not even yell at me. My teacher was cool, he figured out how to save everyone and solve my teenage nightmare.

On my graduation day I spent the entire morning getting my hair done up like Jean Shrimpton's, the British supermodel. My aunt Vicki (Fritz's "go-go dancer" wife) loaned me her beautiful white lace minidress, and it was all perfect. I felt very pretty. There with my uncles and cousins, my parents, my crew, I was not afraid. I accepted the only diploma I would ever receive. I went home, took off the dress, and gave it back to Vicki.

The famous green windbreaker

I spent one more soft, sublime week in springtime Chicago, hanging out at Hull House. The day before I was to leave, the legendary boy in the green windbreaker, Junie Stamper, whom I adored but never spoke to, walked by Hull House where I was sitting. Junie saw me and without missing a step turned my way. He sat down with me on the stoop.

"I heard about you and the graduation thing."

"Diane really liked Billy Raye."

We talked a little and he asked if I wanted to do something tomorrow. I said I was leaving the next day so he said:

"Would you like to walk with me? I gotta go see my mom at work."

Would I? Walk with him and meet his mom at the same time? What a kind, well-mannered boy. We would be engaged before I got home for supper. I wanted to marry him. Do you think he will ask me?

The windbreaker was a badge of honor for Chicago kids who braved the Arctic temperatures coming off Lake Michigan. Like going barefoot across the burning pavement in Arizona or never using an umbrella in Seattle, a kid's honor was in showing they had adapted to and conquered their surroundings. Being tougher than the weather was the coolest thing of all.

Junie introduced me to his mother, which really was a very special thing for a boy to do. Just a hillbilly lady working at a store. She liked me, I think. Now we walked on toward the Donmoor Hotel. It was springtime and the neighborhood men were hanging out in their sleeveless T-shirts as the sun was setting. Between the hippies invading for the Democratic Convention and the Martin Luther King riots, the streets were a war zone now. Junie and I didn't care. We walked along Wilson Avenue careful not to touch hands.

As the sun began to set, the wind picked up and it was suddenly chilly. I shivered. Junie took off his windbreaker and put it on my shoulders.

We stood there at my door, shuffling our feet and wondering what might have been had I stayed. I still had his jacket on when we said goodbye and I wore it the next day when I took the plane to Tacoma, Washington, to spend a month with my sister Janet (until my parents found a house in Phoenix). I kept Junie's windbreaker for many years. I wore it as a flag of our possibilities.

It was probably a mistake sending me to my sister's house. Janet was violent, careless, and often cruel, but I read books in Tacoma. *The Heart is a Lonely Hunter*, by Carson McCullers and *Anthem*, by Ayn Rand. I stole Winstons from Janet's purse and went out walking in an attempt to look like Simon and Garfunkel on the back of their record. I was trying to grow up. More than that, I was trying to imitate something they had. Paul Simon had something I could almost reach. It wasn't him, it was his music. I wanted to be in his song.

By August my mom brought me home to Phoenix. It was almost time to start high school.

> *I remember walking in the rain*
> *Rain falling on my hands*
> *I don't want to live like that again.*
> *Outside it hardly gets dark now*
> *Lovers walking in the park now*
> *Children singing songs of when*
> *They'll make all their dreams come true*
> *I'm in love with you.*
>
> ("Stewart's Coat")

Chapter 8

You Never Know When You're Making a Memory

My cousin Debbie and me in the
famous green windbreaker

My First Year in High School

I was drawing on my spiral notebook. I was spelling my name but also trying to define who I was in those letters. Was I "Ric" or "Rick"? Was I "Rickie" or "Rickie Lee"? I spent a lot of time making lists of what I would do and what I would be. The more order on paper, the more order seemed to take shape in my day. Writing down what I owned was a way of holding it closer. Writing down what would come to pass was a way of holding that closer, too.

I had a whole bumper crop of music now. Jefferson Airplane was on my turntable every day. Buffalo Springfield, Jimi Hendrix, and bits of new music—Vanilla Fudge and the Mothers of Invention. New ideas were taking shape. For me, *Surrealistic Pillow* seemed to be at the eye of a storm I longed to be a part of—the hippies. Their beautiful music alluded to LSD and a grown-up life I longed to call my own. San Francisco, 1968, I was missing out on everything happening. It was out there!

My first month at school I tried to do everything perfectly. I sat in the front of class in algebra, I auditioned for the choir, I went to a football game, I went to a dance. I even took a speed-reading course. I hoped to become something greater than I was. I posed for my class picture wearing the culottes my mother had made for me.

By October I fell asleep most mornings in first period. I didn't care much about sports. I wasn't very interested in anything school had to offer. Everyone was searching for an identity which is why some people didn't even get a hello, while others were social celebrities.

"Our kind" sat at our lunch table. "Your kind" at your table. Cross the line and there'd be hell to pay. We were like jungle animals at the watering hole. What does all this matter anyway? I was oversensitive, that is clear to me now, but my sensitivity made me delve deep into my emotions. Without a constructive outlet, those feelings would have been damaging to my psyche, but I was already matching music to my emotions. I was just starting to make up my own songs.

I was turned down for the choir. It was done in such a spiteful way that I wonder now if the choir teacher was a friend of the music teacher from Glendale who had called me a prima donna. He singled me out in front of my friends, saying my voice was too "unusual" and would not fit into his chorus. I was devastated. When this dickhead rejected my voice as too unusual he also rejected me as too unusual. Being unusual was a social death sentence for a freshman.

This admonishment colored my high school experience for the next four years. I became defensive and surly. My new beginning for my high school life was ground beneath that choir teacher's penny loafers.

Did my family have a reputation in small-town Phoenix because of my sister or my cousins? Was the Jones name a brand of trouble I wore before I entered a teacher's classroom? One thing was certain: singing was the best thing I had to offer, and if that wasn't good enough for some special attention (which I needed more than I craved) then, well, fuck it.

Perhaps the choir teacher *was* just a tool—of destiny. I was made for greater things than his old vocal group and it was time for me to start down the road to find out.

Firsts

My freshman year was a year of firsts, of thrilling to the anticipation of each thing that would one day happen to me, and hopefully soon! I would spend study hall and algebra and earth science mapping out all the things I hoped to achieve that year. They were listed in order of importance, with secret indicators in case my mother should decipher my code of "not yet" or "happened already" next to each entry of a "first."

My First French Kiss

My girlfriend Raye and I were lying in front of her family's console record player listening to Frank Zappa's *Absolutely Free* and making jokes about "Plastic People." We were swooning over the intellectualness of it all. She and I bonded over being girls with boy's names. We went on a double date and I had my first French kiss. Turned out I hated having any tongue in my mouth but my own.

My First Song on Guitar

It was a weekend and I was listening to my favorite record, *Surrealistic Pillow*; the last song on side A was my favorite. The enchanted and melancholy series of images was half sung over a simple three-note guitar pattern, and then the pattern repeated over and over. I recognized my chance, and thought, I can learn this. I sat there practicing all day long, and the next day too. Sounding out each note one phrase at a time, rubbing the blisters and then the calluses, pushing so hard on the sharp steel strings. Once I figured out the guitar part of "Coming Back

To Me," the floodgates opened. Next I learned "Today," from the same Jefferson Airplane record. It was the first of many times I would learn a song by ear. Now I practiced rhythm guitar, "I've Just Seen a Face" and "Rocky Raccoon" by the Beatles. Not too hard, not like the rest of their stuff. Any melody that I could imagine untangling I did, I did not yet know "bar" chords so I was limited to the bottom three frets of the guitar neck. Still, I learned quickly in the private cocoon of my room.

My First Rock Performance

I never saw myself as the "girl" in my musical imagination. I was always the boy, the one who had the power, the one who made up the songs and stood on the stage. I would never be the "seamstress for the band"—I was *the band*.

I heard from a friend that her boyfriend, Dave, was starting a band. I auditioned and became lead singer of the California Blues Band. We thought of that name ourselves. "Blues" and "California" were kind of the two coolest words in Phoenix high schools back in 1968 thanks to Janis Joplin. "CBB," as we might have been nicknamed had we stayed together, learned Iron Butterfly's "Flowers and Beads," the B-side of their single, as well as their big hit, "In-A-Gadda-Da-Vida." We did Vanilla Fudge songs and most anything with an organ because that was what our leader played. Dave Rodriguez was a Mexican-American kid who had grown up playing accordion and now was claiming his place in American acid rock.

The accordion in ranchera and conjunto music translated well for future rock organists, although culturally the kids had to abandon tradition and head for the rock hills. "Use an accordion, go to jail," Walter Becker often quipped, and that was so true in 1968. Accordion was the most uncool instrument in the poor man's orchestra, associated with German polkas and Lawrence Welk, Republicans, short-hairs. More than one Mexican-American player struggled with the pressure of playing rock organ in a family that wanted him to stay with their tradition. I met some of the best organ players through the Hispanic musical railroad.

Our band played only one gig that year but it was a great one, possibly unlike any other first gig anyone has ever had. We got the call the day before the show. I was puffed up with excitement. Now I was a real singer in a band. Mom gave me money to buy these paisley, empire-waisted, one-piece satin lounge pajamas I'd seen at Lerner's Department Store.

I wore them out of the store. I was so proud of my first rock costume. All eyes were on me but this time *I* had invited them to look. This was different from schoolyard stares and taunts. I had found a way to turn others' dark attention into a celebration of my uniqueness. Many rock singers make this switch. It's a great moment when the underdog becomes the alpha dog for the same reason she was once the "ugly duckling."

I liked people looking at me.

I got to the venue where Dave told me we were performing at a dance for deaf people.

I was up on the stage, my first time up there, singing and dancing like crazy. There weren't many people in the audience, only a few couples on the dance floor. "Are you sure they can't hear us?"

I was thrilled to be up there. Sure kids might laugh, but I didn't really care. I just wanted to sing. Be in the band. Okay, truth was it was a bummer that no one could hear me sing but still I sang my heart out:

"Set me free, why don't ya babe?"

And then we were finished. It was over. Should we bow? I didn't know what to do.

"Thank you!" "Thank you!" The audience, all fourteen of them, clapped and headed out the door except for one couple who approached the stage. They wanted to speak to me. Oh wow, my first fans.

They smiled and said hello.

"Hello," I answered then, earnestly, going head-on with the "handicap" issue, "I saw you dancing out there. How do you dance to the music? Are you completely deaf?"

The woman signed as she spoke so her date could understand what she was saying to me:

"Yes, we cannot hear but we don't have to hear because we feel the music. Vibrations. The beat through the floor. I lost my hearing when I was little, so I can still speak."

Oh how I loved them. These deaf people felt music just like I felt music. They came to the show to be a part of the world, part of happenings, and felt their way on the dance floor. What an honor to play for them my very first time.

"Oh, so . . . can you hear my voice?

"No, but we see your expressions. You tell us what *you* feel and we feel it. We liked your singing. A lot of emotion."

I wished I could sign back to her. How did I say thank you? With hand to my lips. I bowed my head and that was the end of my first rock performance. Funny, they were teaching me the fundamentals of music, that the emotion transcends the sound.

Who can say what anyone experiences when it comes to music? Deaf people appreciate and make music for themselves and the hearing world by choosing the sounds instinctually. Who knows what the soundless would bring to music?

My First Love

Let us be lovers, we'll marry our fortunes together.
(Simon and Garfunkel, "America")

I saw Ricci Cretti in the lunch quad. He was seventeen and I was fourteen. There was something about him, his hair combed back instead of forward like most boys. He was like Jim Stark in *Rebel Without a Cause*, standing alone, leaning against a brick wall in his blue jeans and his white dress shirt. He held his left arm, palm out, in his right hand. It was an odd gesture that caught my eye. Plus, he lived only two doors down from my cousins and he was also new to this school, so maybe we could walk together. Maybe, if I played my cards right.

By February Ricci Cretti and I started sharing Winstons after school, sitting in the back seat of an old 1940s sedan that had been left in front of his house. I was thrilled, he was my kind of beautiful. I hoped he liked me the way I liked him. At last, a boy of my own. The winds of romance inside that smoky car blew away the chaos inside our teenage heads. Mine anyway.

It was maybe a week or two after we'd met. I was pressuring my mother to let me go out, it was only five o'clock but it was a school night. Mom lost her temper, took hold of my clothes, and literally threw me out of the house. I lost my balance and landed hard on my butt in the front yard. The neighbor boys laughed at me which hurt more than falling.

Listening to *Alice's Restaurant* together last August, those same boys had become my friends, but school demanded we square off and pretend not to know each other. One of the boys had a crush on me which made him especially cruel during my humiliation. *Alice's Restaurant* was closed forever.

I jumped up and flipped them off, then walked quickly in case my mom changed her mind and called me back home. It was already 8 p.m. by the time Ricci showed up at my friend's house. She had a black light in her room. I was electrified. We were all expanding our consciousness with dayglow paint.

"So your mom kicked you out?"

My girlfriend made it sound crueler than it was. I wanted to protect my mom even though I wanted to use this event to get close to Ricci. There were homes where parents never threw their children out the front door, no matter how nagging and whining they were.

Ricci asked, "Where you gonna go?"

"I don't know, California maybe." Secretly, I just wanted to be with him now, and anywhere would be alright.

Ricci obliged. "I'll walk around with you for a while."

When I was fourteen I thought happiness lay in the arms of anyone but myself. It would be a habit of self-destruction that would follow me most of my life.

It was nearly ten o'clock as Ricci and I walked. I was skipping along the sidewalk, weightless, walking on the moon.

We walked without a destination until we stopped at the Circle K and bought a fruit pie and a pack of cigarettes. At last, I was living the Simon and Garfunkel song "America":

> *Let us be lovers, we'll marry our fortunes together . . .*
> *So we bought a pack of cigarettes and Mrs. Wagner pies*
> *And walked off to look for America*
>   (Simon and Garfunkel, "America")

Ricci knew how to drive and a silent agreement emerged between us: we would steal a car and we would run away. For real. Just like that we began, tippy-toeing, sneaking onto driveways to check cars for keys.

Across from Washington High School, Ricci found a hopped-up Camaro in a dirt driveway. She was a beautiful car, sitting up high, with tuck and roll interior and loud tailpipes. There was nothing subtle about it so it was a stupid car to steal, but it was the only car with keys still left in the ignition. It was irresistible bait for teenage runaways.

My First Stolen Car

It was night-air quiet and everyone was asleep. We whispered to each other, "*Gently* pull the car door shut." The tension was so high that we were holding our breath. Then it was the point of no return, Ricci turned the key. The car roared out of its tailpipe. He threw it in reverse and burned out of the driveway. Shifted into first, then stepped on the gas and we peeled out. We figured we woke up the owner and the rest of Phoenix as we roared down Bethany Home Road to the edge of town, and onto dark, unlit roads. Our noisy machine in the sand garden.

Overcoming our fear was a giddy high much greater than the mere ringing of doorbells brought a few years ago. We were going west, following the sun. We got to the onion fields on the outskirts of the county and into the desert in no time. Uh-oh, the car was already low on gas and we only had some change between us after those fruit pies. Ricci pulled into a gas station and said, "Don't worry, I know what to do."

The tension was rising again. It was an old man who washed the windows and filled the tank. I thought Ricci was going to ask him for a favor, but Ricci asked for a map. When the guy went to get the map, we tore out of that gas station. Such a thrill! Catholic kids like us had enough guilt that we would both lie awake wishing we could go back and pay that guy the five or ten bucks, but not tonight.

I can still see the old man standing on the stage, as it were, a spotlight on his disappointed shoulders, watching us drive away. The great red flying horse of the Mobil gas station flashing until it was swallowed up by the velvet sky. I was surprised that Ricci had the guts to do all this stuff. Stealing and tearing out and the sudden violence in his determination to not get caught.

Driving all night with a full tank of gas, we hit San Diego at dawn. We found a beach with a parking lot, and we slept in the back seat of the car for maybe four hours. We awoke sweaty and tired but we emerged from the car and beheld our accomplishments; a beautiful shore and cool breeze. It felt so good, the smell of the sea, knowing we had arrived in "happening" California.

People were parking all around us. What now? I was hungry. Where shall we go? I had ruined his life and he had saved mine, or maybe it was the other way around. "Let's go to L.A.," I said, "My cousin lives near the Sunset Strip. We can ask people, someone will know her." In my mind every town and every problem was small, no bigger than Phoenix. We could find her and stay with her for a few days. I really thought that was how this story was going to play out.

The City of Industry

Except we did not have a plan. We were living a lyric. We had a map of maybes.

Somewhere near the City of Industry we were running out of gas again, and Ricci pulled off the interstate and into an unreal planet of steel pylons and concrete dioramas. "City of Industry." I wondered what that could be. A city with no people?

Yes, there were no people, no homes, nothing that looked like the world we knew. We had entered some scene of human deterioration, some place that marked the half-life of our deed, our runaway life. It was a desolation of industrial buildings, smoke, and fires. Didn't they eat? Where were the gas stations? In the stress of the moment, I beheld what appeared to me to be the gate to hell. This could not be real. Sunset Boulevard and the City of Industry could not exist on the same highway. Could they? Were there no signposts on this planet?

"Nope. This is the City of Industry, man. That's all there is here. In-dus-tree," the gas station attendant joked while eyeing Ricci suspiciously. He already knew what was coming. Nobody traveled to the City of Industry unless they wanted to be there. That, combined with a couple of teenagers asking questions—meant trouble.

Ricci asked for a map and the guy replied, "I ain't got no maps," as he looked my boy right in the eye. Ricci looked at me and I looked at him for our nonexistent Plan B. He threw the car into gear, hit the gas, and tore out. In the rear window I saw the guy run into the station and pick up the phone. He was dialing before we got out of the parking lot. Ricci and I made a crucial mistake then. We turned right—into the City of Industry. Back into the arms of the dragon and away from the freeway with our only chance to be lost in traffic. The City of Industry apparently only allowed ramps off the freeway, a one-way fish trap. Those wishing to come were welcome, but there would be no returning on-ramps into the world of the living. It was a trap for capturing the low-on-gas, the runaway teenagers, and the witless. (We were all of the above.)

Here in the mire of industrial dragons we kept searching but could not find our way back to the freeway. Perhaps we had been blinded by our guilty consciences or by angels of someone else's better nature, but our Camaro had been torn from its path to freedom and sent reeling into a bleak future.

Our world of freedom was now a world frosted with cement. Expanses of nothing at all were followed by skirmishes of factories and industrial waste while just above us, supported by a tangle of pylons, was our yellow brick road of a freeway to freedom. This was unbelievable, we were on an endless underpass below a giant centipede of bad ideas, and we just couldn't get on top of the beast. We could see and hear it above us, the rhythm and rush of sixty-mile-an-hour tires, the heartbeat of our California freedom, fading. The lonely doppler whine of truck horns above us. For all I knew Carol Jones was in one of the cars on her way home to her safe and happy life.

Ricci turned the car into a parking lot. He wasn't sure what to do, and turned off the car to save gas.

"Where are we? What should we do?"

"I don't know."

We sat there for a long time, long enough to draw the attention of the firefighters inside the firehouse whose parking lot we had violated. La-de-da, just parking our car. People always parked at fire stations, so what was the big deal?

There were railroad tracks so we thought it was a good idea to walk down them. I was carrying something. Was it my coat? His hand? Was it my broken dream dragging behind me? That must hurt, hitting your head on those railroad ties.

"These tracks have to lead somewhere."

The cops saw us at the same time we saw them. We started to run, but you can't really run on railroad tracks, and we had nowhere to go. Right there, that was the moment "Night Train" was born. Not written, born. My song was born of those three seconds of freedom lost to the realization that there was nowhere to go

The cops didn't even bother to chase us. They said, "Stop running and come back to us."

We stopped running and looked at each other. Or Ricci stopped. I think I would have run forever. It was a defining moment in our romance (he stopped) and perhaps in my life (I kept running).

Like the freeze-frame moment in the Bonnie and Clyde film just before they die. It was over. A one-act love affair in one car on one night.

Ricci said "It's over" and started toward the cops but I stood there. I thought, I could keep running.

> *Swing low, Saint Cadillac,*
> *Tearing down the alley*
> *Don't let them take me back*
> *Broken like valiums*
> *And chumps in the rain*
> *That cry and quiver*

I knew there was somewhere else down those railroad tracks I was meant to be. Surely happiness was waiting for me at "mine"—my story, my luck, my life. "Mine" would be the only way I was ever gonna find out where that was.

> *There's a blue horizon sleeping in the station*
> *With a ticket for a train*
> *Surely, mine will deliver me there*
>   ("Night Train")

Not yet.

We did what we were told and climbed into the back of the squad car. The fireman pointed to the parked car. "It's stolen," we said. APB for the gas stealers. "That was you," as much a confirmation as a question. They drove us round to the gas station guy.

He said, "Why didn't you just ask me for some gas?"

"Sure, sure."

Turned out the car hadn't even been reported yet. Late sleepers, those Arizonians. Sound sleepers too.

The cop looked over his shoulder at us, bemused.

"Where did you think you were going?"

"L.A."

"There's nothing here."

"What is this place?"

"You turned off the wrong exit, kid. This is the City of Industry."

This surreal episode was the beginning of my feeling that my travels were accompanied by the gentle pen of a divine writer. Every single event seemed cinematic. Even in my peril, my writer had my back. She stopped the story just short of prostitution, murder, and true horror. She kept it tough with a *Peter Gunn* and *Naked City* soundtrack for a night or two but then returned us safely back to *Ponderosa* and *Wagon Train*. "Raw-hiiiiiiiiiiiiiiiiiiide. Hya!"

My First Night in Juvy

My father retrieved me the next day and we flew back to Phoenix. Dad suggested I keep away from Mom for a while but there was no easy solution. Our house was not big enough to allow Mom and I to be anonymous. Dad seemed to be saying, *I am with you. She is not but give her time.*

The psychological gauntlet Mom would require me to pass through was too much. The fact was, I had changed in the past twenty-four hours. I had made a choice to be the thing she warned me of, the thing she threw out, and threw away. I had stolen a car and gasoline, I had tricked people to get what I wanted, I had imagined having to survive on my own, and I could have kept going. Of course had my mother welcomed me home with love and affection, I wouldn't need to run again, but now I had confidence in my abilities to live on the road.

My family was usually demonstrably affectionate, but not this day. I did not hug my mother when I came in and I went straight to my room. I guess we were cut from the same cloth. Mom held her ground and did nothing to repair the damage. She was so angry at me. She couldn't understand how someone could run away from a loving home, but I felt as abandoned as the orphans of her hair-raising stories. Surely my mother's devotion was not so precarious as to exchange my mistake for our family bond. Was it?

This event changed my identity. I became Rickie Lee the person on her own. You treat me like I'm the bad girl, I'm gonna be bad. Besides, I kind of liked being out there and in danger. I liked the thrill of living by my wits.

Listen:
Does this sound familiar?
You wake up every morning, go to school every day
Spend your nights on the corner just passing the time away
Your life is so lonely like a child without a toy
Then a miracle—a boy.

Now I was living those Shangri-Las lyrics I kept repeating in my head. I always felt so guilty about my mother's hurt that happened before I had even been born. I felt like I had not been there for her somehow.

Now my mom is a good mom and she loves me with all her heart
But she said I was too young to be in love
And the boy and I would have to part . . .
(The Shangri-Las, "I Can Never Go Home Anymore")

My First Time

Within this backdrop of anger and unraveling, Ricci Cretti and I made a nest of one another. I ran away a couple weeks later. This time we didn't steal a car or leave town. Instead, we slept on a mattress on the floor of a friend's converted shed. We all slept out there, the parents didn't seem to know or care what went on back there. So what if there was no velvet curtain, brocade, or balcony. Not even a bed. No matter, it was perfect.

I awoke early and walked out into my new world. In the morning dew was an old car surrounded by overgrown spring flowers. I tried to look really pretty and flower-girl childish. Even if only fairies could see our crown, I knew we were holy here in this kingdom of the Day After.

Ricci and I sat in the car. The upholstery was rotted to dust and the rusty springs poked through. The car's shattered windshield scattered the sunlight into a hundred diamonds of light that touched my body. It was a phantasmagoria of rusted ruby iron and diamond light. Steam came off our fingertips. I shared a cigarette with my beautiful storm of a boy and wondered who else had sat there smoking with their sweethearts. All trace of them was disappearing through our fingertips. Our night had ended. My first morning of my first day as a woman. I was so proud, and a little sad.

If we are lucky, childhood ends without fanfare in a moment of our own choosing. And womanhood begins.

> *What a dream I had, dressed in organdy*
> *Clothed in crinoline of smoky burgundy*
> *Softer than the rain . . .*
> *And when I awoke and felt you warm and near*
> *I kissed your honey hair with my grateful tears . . .*
> (Simon and Garfunkel,
> "For Emily, Whenever I May Find Her")

A strange, beautiful, dark forever started with that night and, though it was painful in the morning, I was starring in a Paul Simon lyric. Perfect. So much of what I did that year, the shape of who I wanted to be, was formed by Paul Simon.

I thought my "first time" was as romantic as a girl could possibly hope. I waited until our friend's parents were gone and slipped in through the back door where I took a bath and thought, This is the body of a woman now. Oh, this feeling of grace and initiation was so fantastic.

Ricci had to go home for a while and I thought, Lord, Friend, Husband, come back alive. He did not return to me any more than Romeo returned to Juliet. Our story would take a most modern turn for the worst. I mean to say, if *Romeo and Juliet* had been written in 1969, their story might have ended up just the way ours did.

That night, I was waiting for Ricci to return to our hideout when I heard a noise. Finally, he was here! The door opened and I looked up. It was Janet. My sister Janet was standing there instead.

"Time to go."

Janet was the gentle assassin, she had waited for a long time for this moment. Now she would have the teenage life she had lost. My turn to suffer as she had. I went out to get into the car and there was my boyfriend.

"YOU?"

Ricci explained, "She told me my brothers and sisters would be removed from my house." (How did she come up with that stuff?) Although I understood Janet's tricks, I could not believe *he* had given in to her. We were a mutilated version of Romeo and Juliet!

Ricci Cretti wept, then fell to his knees.

Janet drove me to the juvenile detention center (instead of home!).

Maybe she and my mother only wanted to scare me, but Mother seemed to have handed the parenting reins to her wayward daughter. It seemed suddenly that Mother related to Janet as a peer, and Father had no say at all. That was as confusing and had as much effect on me as anything else that was happening. For the next few months, Social Services conducted an investigation of our family, the direct result of Janet dropping me off at juvy, and me half-heartedly trying to cut my wrist with a safety pin while I was inside.

The social worker asked me if I was happy at home. "No!" There was a hearing, and Child Protective Services recommended that I be removed from my family.

Our family lawyer, Tom Murphy, argued that my "good Catholic family" was going through some trouble but it was absurd to consider removing me. At court my mother and father, in their very best clothes, explained that I was a good girl. I said I loved my home and did not want to leave. The social worker seemed stunned that I had changed my tune. Tom Murphy won our case, but after the hearing my parents drove away without me. Tom said he wanted to talk to me, and drove me back home in his 1969 Corvette.

"Be good" was all he had to say as he dropped me off in front of our house.

This would not be the last time Murphy kept the Joneses together. Mission accomplished, Janet would return to Washington to ruin her own family. Harsh words for a harsh reality.

My mother was still constantly angry and I no longer cared if she took me back again.

Back at school, Ricci Cretti and I were soon reunited (after my second period class). I said, "I know, my sister is a monster." I hoped we could forgive each other for what my sister had wrought. But we had no time to gain momentum. What Janet had done left more than a scar. This was the pattern. If Janet could not have it, she would make sure that I couldn't have it either.

My family moved to another school district, and we lived in a town house with a swimming pool and a big mirrored master bath. It felt like we were moving up again.

My First Bad Acid

Ricci and his friends drove to my part of town to pick me up for a Creedence Clearwater Revival concert at the Coliseum. We dropped some Orange Wedge LSD which later I understood to be STP or "bad acid." We had been told to split the tab and thank God we did. It started coming on in the parking lot of the venue and by the time the music started, I could not find Ricci. Instead I danced and danced and twirled around. The people around me appeared to have lost their dimensions, they were like flat paper people running by me but in slow, slow motion because time had slowed to crawl. It was terrifying and fascinating. Motions that normally went by quickly could now be observed in great detail.

I could not correctly estimate what I was experiencing, and the strychnine in the STP began cramping my belly. I was trying to dance it away to the song "Suzie Q" when someone grabbed my arm and warned, "Maintain, Rickie! That policeman is watching you." Injecting paranoia into my trip at exactly the right moment only set the stage for what was to come; my life with Ricci was about to go down the black hole of a drain yet again.

Whatever Ricci was seeing on his acid trip was evidently worse than the phantasmagorical world I was witnessing. He could not look at me and was hiding behind his friends. He did not want to talk to me. His friends said, "Let him go, right now he's having a bad trip," but I was devastated.

Ricci broke up with me after the concert while I was coming down. Worse, he was already with another girl. I was overwhelmed. I don't know about other teenage first loves, but Ricci dumping me that night was catastrophic.

Mother left to visit Janet up in Washington. She took my little sister with her.

I took the bus downtown to the Little Theater to inquire about acting, and though there were no classes there at the moment, I met a young teacher who told me about upcoming plays. He encouraged me to audition for "Nancy" in *Oliver*. "It's a good role for a girl like you. You have the voice, you should audition next Saturday." He accompanied me on piano on a run-through of "Where is Love?" then gave me the sheet music to bring with me for the audition pianist. I did not know how to read music but I had learned the song by ear in one sitting. No problem.

My First Beating

I was alone with my father now. He was stern and unpredictable and he was also the only family I came home to. Dad got me a job at his steak house working on the new buffet he hoped would bring in lunchtime business. He got me a social security card and opened a bank account for me. I went to work every day. He was monitoring me closely. I wasn't supposed to go anywhere without asking, so I stayed home and kept my head low.

It was my day off, a nice afternoon, and I was sitting cross-legged on the front step talking with two guys who lived in the town house a few units away. I had on a macramé sweater over my bathing suit. I remember feeling good, I had some positive attention and I was doing what I was supposed to be doing.

I heard my father rustling things inside the house. He looked out the curtain at me. Maybe he thought I was gone and was surprised to see me or maybe he was angry. The way he snapped the curtain. Couldn't be anything I was doing. Then he opened the front door: "Rickie, come here." He didn't sound right, but I had not done anything wrong so I told the boys I'd be right back. If there was something wrong with my dad, I didn't want my friends to know. Play it cool.

Before I had closed the door my father started hitting me with his open hand. He was saying terrible things: "What are you wearing? What are they doing here? You look like a *whore*." I could not breathe. My father was disgracing me in front of my friends.

He grabbed my sweater to pull it off, like it was the problem. He was so violent that my sweater ripped. This sweater was something I loved, a thing that nice people who lived in pretty places wore. The beating continued for just a minute or two but it was noisy. Him yelling at me. All I could think was, Those boys can hear this. I'll never be able to look at them again.

I held one hand in front of my face and tried to hold the sweater together with my other. I was trying to be quiet and protect my head but "Ouch!" I needed that sweater, it was how I imagined my life could be.

The sweater was ruined, he actually tore it off me. And now, to fully humiliate me, he commanded I tell the boys to go away. I opened the front door, holding my sweater together and said:

"I can't come out."

"We'll wait for you." Did they think they could stop my father from hitting me?

"Don't wait."

I closed the door, turned, and hurried up the stairs. Oh, why couldn't my life just go right for a minute? For so many years, disaster after disaster and chaos on top of chaos was my normal. Normal! NORMAL!

It's easy for anyone to make a family's life look bad. Fact is, all families struggle with terrible stuff and everyone keeps a silent bond to stay together. I cannot say why the bond broke and the ground beneath my feet fell away. I had no family to hold onto and maybe I never did. Maybe I made them up from the beginning.

Away from my dad, in the solitude of my room, I put *Electric Ladyland* on the record player and lay down on my bed. I did not own headphones, I placed the large speakers on each side of my head. Ahh, a voodoo child. Here I could escape to my paradise, listening to every single nuance of Hendrix's galaxy of sound. In the music, I had a whole universe of my own. The healing breath of "Voodoo Chile." The gentle rocking of "Dark stairs of infinity, way down by the methane sea." Musicians opened the door to imaginary places, to better realities, and Jimi's music was the place I belonged. This young man penetrated my teenage mind. He transcended. Hendrix was ethereal, and few of us ever reach that cloud. With no mother, no boyfriend, in a new school and a new house with an unpredictably violent father, I found my only solace in Hendrix music.

I remembered a poster I had seen for a rock festival. Woodstock. Hmm . . . I would have to travel all the way to New York. That was maybe too far but how about this Northridge, California, festival? I could buy a ticket with the money in my bank account. I'd go tomorrow when Dad was at work. Yes. I was going to a rock festival.

I called my mother and told her, "Dad beat me up. He's drunk all the time. I don't wanna stay here right now. Tell Dad that I went to a rock festival in California and I'll be back next month." Maybe I said the sad, magic words, "drunk" and "beat me up," or maybe it was Mom's way of repairing our relationship, but she kept my secret that I was running away to California again. I left a few days later. I wanted joy, music, and happiness, so I headed in the direction where free love was abundant.

With Jimi Hendrix evoking my voodoo child in the honey-soaked flowers of Jupiter down by the Methane Sea, I took my lipstick and wrote on the mirrors in my dad's bathroom:

"I am going to California. Back next month."

Many of the dangerous choices I would make were in fact lesser evils. Even my unseemly guide of drugs kept me from a far worse fate. I had to find my way and get back on my feet to resume my happy-ever-after song.

I packed some clothes in my purse, headed for the airport, and forgot all about my audition for *Oliver*.

If I had gotten the role of Nancy in that play, the troubles of the last year wouldn't have mattered. All my years of studying tap and ballet, learning improvisation and articulation would have borne fruit. I would have sung my way to a better future. My audition was Friday but I would not be there to give it.

Through the years I have wondered, What would have happened if I'd made that audition? What if Dad hadn't hit me and if Mom had welcomed me back from my stolen car adventure with some kind of bemused joke. I do not look back to dig up regrets. Still, sometimes I wonder.

> *Who can say where he may hide?*
> *Must I travel far and wide?*
> *'Til I am beside the someone who*
> *I can mean something to . . .*
> *Where, where is love?*
>   (Adapted from *Oliver!*)

Chapter 9

The Summer of 1969

My freshman year, wearing the culottes
my mother made for me

I caught a plane with the money I had earned working for my dad, and left a few dollars in my account for my return. I wore my favorite clothes on the plane and when I arrived in LAX I stuck out my thumb for Northridge.

What a show on and off the stage. I watched an insane performance by Jethro Tull, and the next morning I was swept up in a small riot. I was sleeping at the top of the hill when the police charged all of us sleeping hippies. I never knew what we had done, but I ran faster than the police. I got a ride with some "heads" going to San Diego and for the next few weeks they passed me among them and their friends. We smoked pot, listened to Steve Miller and for the first time, I heard the music of Crosby, Stills & Nash. Their sound was totally new and wow—those strange harmonies. There was something majestic, the

Suite: Judy Blue Eyes was like nothing we had heard before. Not a drum solo in sight, not a feedback guitar riff to run from! The blues was like an overfed baby. White kids filled it with everything they could buy and then played it to death. Where is the Man behind the lyric? Steven Stills, fresh out of Buffalo Springfield, brought his creativity to the fierce spirit of rebellion. With nothing but an acoustic guitar, he defied the current of rock à la Hendrix, Clapton, and Beck—a new plateau as simple as one guitar and three voices.

The tide that followed CSN was a decade of gentleman poets and canyon ladies who were either tough broads or whimsical fairies. They did not dance and they did not horse around, but poetic license in the hands of serious composers like Steely Dan and David Bowie brought humor, sex, and jazz to the top ten charts of AM music. Pop music was splitting and dividing. The 1970s were a prehistoric gene pool of musical possibilities. Music replicated and bore strange new cells. The virus of a new idea had taken hold and changed who we had been.

I was always a guest with no money and no home. Since I was only a child, I was used to being taken care of. In fact, I did not know how to take care of myself. I expected someone to feed me eventually. Those nights when I had to fend for myself were hard.

I crashed with three girls, then I crashed with a couple on welfare, but having no money, no driver's license, no clothes, no food, and no skills, I soon went from houseguest to house pest and tried the goodwill of my hippie hosts. They did not realize I was an immature teenage kid, because I looked so much older. It was my large breasts, they were a ticket into any psychological door. People, whether men or women, assumed so much because of their relationship with breasts. And I let them. If I got fed and people were nice to me, then let them think my age was related to my bra size.

I had no options for earning anything so when someone mentioned that a friend was looking for a girl to go to Mexico and make some good money, I was "his girl." The guy planned on buying a few kilos of marijuana, so he needed a girl to deflect attention from his being a

solitary hippie vacationing in Mexico. To me it was all just so exciting.
I did not begin to comprehend the danger.

We arrived in Tijuana and drove to a public place on the side of the
road. Four nervous Mexican men got out of the car and approached us.
Everyone was speaking Spanish and they were gesturing at me in the
passenger seat. Finally, they gave us some bags and we quickly drove
away. The gesturing and language was ominous and the driver seemed
to be more afraid of his supplier than of the cops. "They're gonna tell
the border patrol and collect a reward. We gotta drive."

Instead of going to the border, we drove south into the dark, unlit
desert across what seemed to be a roadless flatland until we came to
some rocks with people at a hot spring. How did he know where he
was going? I'll never know.

I was there in the desert far from the light pollution (and safety) of
the city, marveling at all the stars. In the morning we shared someone's
dried fruit and gave them some of our cashews. Then we drove back
across the desert to a different border crossing, where our sacrificial
carton of cigarettes and beer made the confiscating guard smile at his
good fortune while he scolded us as a naive couple bringing contraband
into the United States.

Now I had a little money from my business venture. I was crashing
with a guy named Ken who had a big handlebar mustache like David
Crosby. Ken's old lady, who was actually six, seven years older than he,
was unhappy with my staying there. Ken was cheating on her with
me. (Hippies.) So with my pay of a whole brick of pot I made enough
money to leave San Diego. I had rock festivals to go to and things to see.

A couple weeks after I left, my father somehow tracked me down
to Ken's house. Ken was surprised I was only fourteen years old and
he shared my father's worries (or perhaps feared for his legal jeopardy
in contributing to my delinquency), so he told my father *whom* I left
with and *where* we were headed. My father went north up Interstate
5, trailing his wayward daughter and hoping beyond hope to run into
me in the forest of hippies and hitchhikers that lined the highways
and byways of California in the summer of 1969.

The Road

The scenic coastal route, Highway 1, was *the* road for anyone hitch-hiking between L.A. and San Francisco in 1969. Santa Barbara was the last stop before a long haul with few rides. For a few miles along Santa Barbara the impenetrable freeway dissolved into a four-lane road. Hitchhiking hippies lined both sides of the road, waiting with signs and backpacks, guitars and dogs for a ride out. As a girl, I could get a ride much faster than the horde but being that "girl traveling alone" was very dangerous. I needed to travel with trustworthy boys for protection.

There were a couple of Canadian boys playing guitars as they waited on a ride north. We were each other's tickets to ride. I sang along with them for a song or two, then we agreed to travel together. They could get a ride faster with me, and I'd have no creepy drivers to deal with.

We made it to Santa Cruz where we were invited to dinner in a commune near the boardwalk. After brown rice (yum), we played some music together, the whole household of a dozen people sitting and listening in appreciation. Music, in hippie culture, was like payment for food or a place to crash. The audience began to thin out and while I was singing "Season of the Witch" or some such thing, a couple began having loud and vigorous sex. The Canadians and I looked at each other and just kept on singing the song. We didn't want to bring more attention to them by stopping the music. Wacka-wacka-wacka, going on three feet away (and at the wrong tempo). The show must go on.

Weird was just about to get weirder. Dylan had gone country!

The next day was Buzz Aldrin's moonwalk. We gathered in front of the television like every other American family except as we watched, we had Bob Dylan's *Nashville Skyline* playing in the background. The people in the commune were more concerned with why Dylan had gone country than with what was happening in the sky over our young cloudy heads.

The head of the commune declared his lust for me. He was (he said) a former Black Panther, which was super high status among these university-type hippies. He seemed to know how to rule the commune and he really wanted me in his ensemble. His obsession started slowly but by the third night, I could feel the thumb of a tyrant pressing upon my body and mind. He forbade me to leave. He forbade the others to let me eat dinner. He was moving toward total control over me. He wanted to own me.

I saw something bad was brewing so I literally ran out of the commune and hid under a car. Members of the house followed searching for me. I could see their shoes in the dark as I watched them from under the car. They were like *Invasion of the Body Snatchers* as they moved from house to house. There was *something in the air* alright, something evil. After an hour of waiting them out, I hightailed it to the Catalyst.

The Catalyst

Xanadu, Asgard—the Catalyst, a mythological café in Santa Cruz's St. George Hotel that was a new idea; a home to student intellectuals and hippies who gathered for music, coffee, cheap meals, beer, and pot. It was so amazing to fourteen-year-old me to see young people in charge. This was *home*. College students from UCSC, revolutionaries, psych majors, people working on the astrophysics of stars and even the moon that we just saw walked upon. And me, I was there too! And I wanted to be there from now on. Revolution and college and music and brownies. The brownies, that was the best part. I was never leaving the Catalyst!

While mankind had landed on the moon, I had landed somewhere equally amazing, at the apex of the whole California scene. I loved it, but in reality I was broke, homeless, and not old enough to hold my own. I met a couple guys who were heading to a rock festival in Seattle and just like that, I was on another trek. We stopped in Berkeley to panhandle and made enough to buy some lunch meat, then stuck out our thumbs.

Somewhere up Interstate 5 we were picked up by two men in a saucy 1962 Chevy Nova. The minute we got in the car, we knew there was something deeply wrong with these guys. They made jokes about prison and robbing banks, but they were the only ones laughing. They looked at us and then each other before asking the wrong questions.

"Are you guys together or just traveling together?" was translatable to "Will you protect the girl from us?" That meant trouble. We deflected with:

"Really, you rob banks?"

Too much hesitation before their response:

"Oh yeah."

Bank robbing might be the least of our problems. One guy had his arm stretched across the entire seat, and as he turned he took me in. When we finally reached a rest stop, Little John, Michael from the Mountains, and I had a discussion. Little John said, "We should not get back in that car. Man, they are gonna do something to Rickie." To all of us, I thought.

Michael said, "It's a long ride."

"Not if they kill us," I said.

"Listen, he just came up to me and asked about Rickie. Like, is she mine?"

"She has no chance with them if something goes wrong."

My traveling partners and I slept in our sleeping bags far away from the car where the guys slept. We woke up in the morning to face our decision but the bad guys were already gone. They took the guys' backpacks and what little money was in the backpacks. Some bank robbers. Stealing money from hippies too broke to buy a package of lunch meat.

This was the opposite of the Catalyst, the anti-Catalyst. Here men might pass as hippies but they didn't care about a better world or even the people in front of them. They were hippie imposters. My child mind had idealized people with freak flags and I automatically welcomed them all. Now I would be weary of them all. The horrible hadn't happened, but we knew we had come very close and we were humbled and quiet as we tried for another ride out of the rest stop.

"We need a ride north, some bad guys just ripped us off."

"Sure man, we can take you up the road."

The Avenue of the Giants

We rode up California 101 until we were dropped off by the entrance of the Avenue of the Giants. These gigantic redwoods glistened in fairy light, and their musky smell intoxicated me.

We walked for miles along the middle of the two-lane highway, our leafy escorts singing sweet songs of consolation. The long walk put me in a melancholy mood. Even the shade here was hundreds of years old. I was a kid, a lost girl, a moment in time surrounded by the oldest living things in the world. What was I doing out here so far away from home?

Back on the highway, I was tired, beat, and hungrier than my usual teenage famished feeling. I was starving. Between the three of us, we didn't even have the twenty cents it took to buy a McDonald's hamburger. All the people going in and out of the roadside joint took it for granted that they had money to buy food. I wanted to cry. I did cry. In fact, Michael from the Mountains had fifteen dollars but he was holding out on us and would not share. I had no dinner that night until someone on our next ride offered me an apple; a VW van heading up to Ashland. A good ride. A fox who had somewhere to go and somewhere to go back to. Suddenly I envied everyone I saw.

By the time I got to Seattle, I ditched my two mercenary friends and saw the Youngbloods at the festival by myself.

There I found someone to crash with who lived in a big house on the corner of 4th and John Street. Funny, I still remember the directions. I stayed there for a week, then somewhere else, then somewhere else. By now it was clear to me that my body was the only way anyone was going to feed me or offer that famous hippie hospitality. They might pretend they were about "free love" but once they were finished with you, it was the same old roles as in any 1950s movie. Bra-burning bitches could not protect me here, in these moments of truth when I might actually be pushed out the door—not even breakfast—which was probably the only reason I slept with the asshole. I was hungry and lonely. I thought every boy who wanted to fuck me wanted to fall in love with me. A romantic and cynical young girl like me was rudely schooled in the double standards of society—the great one or the groovy one, it was all the same in the morning.

At the yearly Seafair Torchlight Parade, a hippie "Peace" float was going to be included for the very first time. At the last minute, I was invited to participate. Somewhere there is a newspaper photograph of me in a suede fringed vest, pulling that float while singing, "All we are saying is give peace a chance."

"I've never heard this song before. What is this?" I asked.

"This song is on John Lennon's new record. You know, with his wife Yoko Ono. She's ruining him," Someone responded.

Then why are we singing this song? I wondered. Seems like everyone likes the song a lot.

Bad things came with nowhere to stay; acid, speed freaks, and each new drug brought a worse companion. I ended up in the downtown lair of Ivan Gomez, the speed freak. Somehow someone took me away from that room saying "I'm so disappointed in you" and put me up in the home of some older, thirtyish jazz aficionados. My lack of skills as an adult was glaringly obvious in these guys' company, I never washed a dish or made a bed, I was just a little girl waiting to be taken care of. Maybe I had stayed too long in Seattle. The drugs and that terrible speed bore no resemblance to the peace movement. Crime and drugs insidiously pressed their way into our ideals through the back door, disguised as mind expansion. One evening I was uninvited from my Seattle safe-harbor housing and dropped off in a no-man's-land beneath the highway. It was the skid row of concrete pylons and far more dangerous than the ambitious City of Industry.

I was scared. I missed my mother. I prayed. What would happen to me now? No cars had come for some time. Then headlights. I stuck out my thumb. I was scared and desperate. I bent down warily to look in. He looked alright so I got in. He said, "I saw you down here and was so worried that I turned around to get you. It's not safe down here." Sometimes when men say it's not safe, they are warning you that they're about to hurt you. Not this guy. He gave me a ride for a few hours, and like the angel who would show up so many times in my life, rescued me from a dangerous situation.

Every ride was a performance for me because almost every guy was sizing me up for sex. Perhaps they wanted to scare or to shame me as they drove, flicking their dicks till they quietly came, or they wanted to rape me—loud and furious. Which was it? I had to assess every ride in just a minute or two, and figure out what part to play. Am I a tough broad? Am I an innocent young girl? Am I me—which me am I? So on the occasion when a guy with long hair picked me up and did not talk sex, I filled up my empty vessel of self-respect, enough dignity that I could walk the rest of the way.

The next ride, nice looking young guy would not stop asking about sex. I had to ward off advances. I told him I had the clap. That usually worked. He kept at it, even saying, "I wonder if you can get clap of the mouth." I let him keep wondering, laughing about it as we rounded the mountain pass into the holy land—Santa Cruz. Finally I got out on the boardwalk, lay down on the sand, and fell into a deep sleep.

I woke up with slobber all over my arm and a bad sunburn. I was thirsty, still tired, and still hungry. I wandered back to the Catalyst, which I loved and wished I could make my home. The café seemed emptier now. What was missing? Was something missing from me? Something I lost in my Seattle tribulations?

I still needed a place to live.

Survival drove me forward. I figured I would go to "the real thing," the hippie kingdom, an entire city like the Catalyst—San Francisco! I put out my thumb, and in the early morning fog a student from the university gave me a ride to the edge of the kingdom. "I should take you all the way but you'll be alright," except I wasn't. I only got one ride and was stuck somewhere near Sunnyvale where a cop pulled over. Unlike everyone else, he did not believe my lost ID story. He arrested me and took me to juvenile hall.

It was late in the day when I was admitted to juvy. There happened to be a riot going on when I arrived, so they put me in solitary for my protection. Well, "solitary" except for a winsome crazy violent girl, and "protection" hardly added up. She and I were locked up for ninety hours, then surprise! My father finally caught up with me.

He had been following the rumor of me since San Diego. He got a break when the State of California called my savior of a lawyer, Tom Murphy, to tell him I was in detention. There weren't cell phones back then so I was incredibly lucky that my father happened to call Murphy during the ninety hours I was locked in a cell. Perfect timing. As I waited to be bailed out, I was put into a general population of fellow teenagers. Here they had Dr. Seuss books and jigsaw puzzles. Just what a teenage runaway needs. A child's coloring book and nothing to do all day, but it was better than being locked in with a crazy violent cellmate.

The Enigmatic Code of Jones

My family might beat you up, kick you out, but they'd also travel across the country to find you and bring you back home.

I was so glad to get out of jail and grateful for my dad's rescue, but I really wanted to run back to the hippies the moment I walked out of Sunnyvale's juvenile detention center door. I was still surrounded by the promised land of California but I got in the car with my father. As we drove north past hitchhikers who were my colleagues only four days ago, he could tell I was still wild. He took me for a meal at a Denny's restaurant and I ate a glorious banquet. An impossibility only a week ago. Dad stopped at a motel where I slept on an actual bed in complete safety. We drove now through those thousand-year-old forests, we passed the rest stop where I wondered if I would survive the night. I was safe now, here with my father.

The hillsides were covered with redwoods, a drive through Washington that remained unchanged for two decades. It is gone now. Weyerhaeuser clear-cut those hillsides.

Dad and I moved in with my mom, who was staying with my sister and her husband in Tacoma. Danny had enrolled in St Martin's

College, in nearby Olympia. I don't much like to remember those days. My sister was taking diet pills and my mother still had this habit of letting her be an equal partner in parenting—and Janet used her power to rule everyone.

I had come back home very sick from my escapades and needed medical attention as I prepared to return to high school. The prejudice of straight people toward hippies was an outrage, and my mother actually had to "rip a new one" for a doctor who brought his lifestyle judgments to the examination room. Imagine returning to high school after all I had been through.

Thankfully, at North Thurston High there was an inspiring English teacher who sparked my creativity. I wrote a poem and a haiku about Ricci Cretti and I did some acting. Unfortunately, after my first semester we moved to Elma, Washington, and then Huntington Beach back in Southern California. That was three high schools for my sophomore year. Constant moving was my parent's version of my running away, and this inclination was reinforced in me every year of my life.

I found a book at my sister's house that would become my confidant and close friend out there in the garden shack where I slept apart from the rest of the house. A little shed of my own. The book was the only one that knew what I was thinking and feeling, the one thing I could hold onto while I recuperated back there in the pretend-land of my broken family's house. That is how my family felt to me now. They had barely been pressed together after Danny's accident and now I was a stranger, a guest, but this book helped me stay home and in school.

Looks Like Up to Me

The book was *Been Down So Long It Looks Like Up To Me*, by Richard Fariña. Fariña told me I was not the first to go for this bohemian life of hitchhiking, pranksters, pot smokers, rebellion, and free love. I had lived those pages just last summer, he had lived them ten years before. I *was* Gnossos Pappadopoulis! I memorized paragraphs of my new secret friend. I read with a fervor and I laughed out loud. And by September I realized I had enjoyed an entire book; only two or three times in my life had I been able to read a book. I was sure I had a reading disorder, being so slow and unable to concentrate, but now I thought perhaps the real problem had been provincial teachers and their boring book assignments. Perhaps I read slowly because I savored the words. I *liked* to read. And so I started school optimistic, and in spite of the early morning school bus ride through rural Washington with children who regarded me as something of a freak, I felt a secret sense of superiority. I had lived, and my life was literary. I was making something special out of my life, even though right now it might look messy.

The rug was yanked from under my feet when we moved to the middle of nowhere in Elma, where hippies had not yet made land. Until Rickie Lee Jones arrived, hippies were a distant threat on a sea of news clips. Elma was a poor town west of Olympia, just off the 101 freeway. Our neighbors watched *Hee Haw*, raced stock cars, died on the road. Teenage pregnancy was a badge of honor here.

Our family shared our house with a ghost. The first night we were there, the poltergeist broke a mirror. Paintings regularly fell off the walls. There was a cold draft that ran along our bedroom walls. My little sister saw an apparition at the foot of her bed. I heard Pamela screaming in terror so I ran up and told the ghost to leave her alone. (I had some authority with the invisible world.)

Other than the ghosts, Dad making beer in the kitchen, and a lone salmon finding his way from the ocean to our tiny stream, that winter in Elma was unexceptionally boring. I first read about Laura Nyro in a magazine article where Janis Ian spoke glowingly of her. Then one day there was Laura on a PBS television show. Kismet!

Father and I sat on the couch watching Leonard Bernstein and Nyro's manager discussing "Laura Nyro" as if she were an event, or a volcano erupting just a few feet away from the camera. Laura would sing, then these men would talk about her. With their legs crossed, discussing her appeal, they were contained. Nyro was possessed. She did not utter a word. I was spellbound.

Goin' Nowhere

Laura Nyro seemed to send a message to me that day that said, "Come you young girls who are not like the others because you love Broadway as much as rock 'n' roll." There were not very many of us.

When the PBS show ended, my dad said, "Well, that girl is talented but she's not going to go anywhere with that man as her manager. Wearing sunglasses and he's so arrogant and rude. What a creep. No, if she gets rid of him, then maybe. She has talent but people aren't going to do anything with that guy. What's his name?"

"David Geffen."

Dad was right, Laura and that guy were going straight to *nowheresville*. I guess my dad mistook good manners for good business. Geffen became one of the wealthiest men in the world. Laura Nyro, not so much. But a wealth of music and influence, that she did not lack.

The Seal Motel

Finally, a miracle. Dad gave up his back-to-the-land fantasy of chopping wood and fishing for old dying salmon in the creeks around our house. We loaded up the car but left the demon upstairs in the attic. My little sister and I were in the back seat and I was overjoyed to be returning to my California. My parents were trying desperately to make room for the girl I was now, and to reel me back in from the terrible adventures that had made me grow up too fast. California, here we come.

Look! There's Sunset Boulevard! I met a guy at the diner there last year. I wonder if he's still there? We stopped for gas in Hollywood and a hand-painted Mercedes sports car pulled up. A beautiful young velvet-clad woman emerged and smiled at me. I wanted to yell, "Take me away with you. I'm one of you! I'm a freak too!" Instead, I whispered to myself, "Someday, someday I'll live here and have pretty things and friends and palm trees by the pool."

(And that is exactly what I did nine years later.)

We checked into the Seal Motel in Seal Beach, a tiny beach town just a couple miles south of Long Beach. This would be my home for the next few months. That night I hoped I could both take root in California and be part of my family again. I would go to high school and take care of Pamela Jo like I was supposed to. I was so happy that day. So many plans and great expectations. I would have a home!

For the next three months I went to Huntington Beach High. Seebu and Tina were my new friends. My dudes. We were tight right away. We were young foxes and we knew it. We loved hitchhiking up and down Highway 1, the two-lane beach route where all the surfers and hippies traveled. It was also the road that led to (and from) our high school. It was spring, and there was music everywhere.

My parents expected our California move to work out as much as I did. I knew I would not disappoint them again. They'd seen I was going stir-crazy in Elma as our ghost dropped things on our heads and scared the living daylights out of us. But we were eight weeks into our California stay and Father was still unemployed. Mom always seemed to be able to get a job. With Mom, Dad, Pammy, and I living in one large motel room with two beds in the middle, how long could we last? It cost a lot more to live in California.

I had strange urges to put myself at risk. Hitchhiking to Laurel Canyon, riding around with bikers. I wanted to but seemed unable to tame myself. Rickie Lee was a Frank Capra movie that had been overtaken by Stanley Kubrick.

Chapter 10

Walk on
Guilded Splinters

My dad walking down the railroad tracks

I f my mother was the angel of my childhood, my father was the guardian of my teenage years. Dad looked after me in those breaking years while trying to keep the peace between my mother and myself. Perhaps he recognized himself in my wanderings, perhaps he knew that if he didn't watch over me no one else would. My father could see that I was trying to keep up with my better self, but my wild side was dragging me behind it.

Walking down Electric Avenue, coming home for dinner, summer almost here, just a week or so of school left, I surprised myself by sticking out my thumb and instead of going home, I headed up to Big Sur. I had not planned it and I still do not know why I did it.

Big Sur had dramatic rising earth on one side and death by ocean cliff on the other. San Simeon to the south was a strip of motels west of Hearst Castle, the lone sentinels guarding the entrance to the mystical land of Big Sur. I was just one of five or six people hoping for a ride north. None of the comradery of the Santa Barbara roadside, and with darkness coming, rides would be scarce. People were downright unfriendly. Whatever they had they were keeping for themselves. No one offered food, water, or a shared sleeping bag. I had missed out on the whole Big Sur legend the summer before, so this time I was going to find out what was going on there. But in fact, I didn't understand what I was doing. I just wanted to be out of my house, not in the middle of a forest. Now I wanted to go home. Trouble always seemed to be the only ticket out.

As the sun set, a cold fog washed in. I was shivering, hungry, and totally sorry. Why did I do these things? I hated myself. I lay down on the ground in the shelter of a south-facing hotel wall, pulled my shirt up over my throat to flimsily protect myself from the cold ocean wind. My heart began to sink as I watched the guy who gave me the ride check into a room. I wondered if he knew how much it would mean to me to lie down out of the cold, rest my tired mind. He had no obligation to share, it was his money and his room, but he seemed so cavalier with the privilege his credit card bought him. I wanted to knock on every door of that Rodeway Inn and beg them to let me come in and get warm and take a bath—with no obligation to do anything in return. I'd sleep on the floor. Please! Not likely.

That night I cried big tears through uncontrollable shivers. I wished I could just take it all back—my mother would be so angry and disappointed in me. I stood in the phone booth and asked the operator to make a collect call.

"Collect call from Rickie Lee. Will you accept?"

"Yes."

"Oh Mama, I—I don't know why."

"Where are you?"

I didn't want to tell her . . .

"We can come and get you."

"Yes! But maybe I can come back in a few days?"

I was in the phone booth but the conversation was only in my imagination, racing ahead of my reality. The actual conversation would have gone badly. In reality, I made the call but when the phone picked up at the Seal Motel, I heard my dad's voice and I hung up. Hearing his voice was enough.

Disapproval is a powerful dissuader. Had I been sure of a loving, understanding voice saying through laughter, "What a goof you are Rickie," or "We're driving up now. Be safe, sit in the lobby, and tell them your parents are coming," I would have turned around and come home immediately. Teenagers will kill themselves rather than face disapproval. I came to think of that night (and others like it) as a spiritual payment that would earn me better things to come. I would make it through that night's cold and loneliness and I would make it through life.

As I stood there in the cold fog of San Simeon, I steeled myself. I found my strength. I knew I would survive. I had to. Even today when I run myself a bath I am grateful for the luxury. I remember that night in the cold, and I lie in the warm water for just a little longer, singing "there, there" to the frozen girl I was so long ago. "We are warm now."

I was a little kid that night, maybe for the last time in my childhood. In the morning there would be no turning back. When I woke up, I walked to the highway and caught a ride into the mountains of Big Sur.

My ride ended just south of Big Sur Village. I saw a man with golden blond locks wearing a long white robe and holding a sign that said "Free Food." He was a woman-man, a Triple Scorpio, one of the "Children of Light" from San Francisco. My ride pulled over and I went right over to ask about the sign and the Vision said, "You can either take a can or leave us a can of food."

Just what I was looking for! Ambiguity, metaphor, take some or leave some. Finally, hippies who didn't want me to clean the dishes in order to get a meal. I said, "Can I stand here with you?" My ride continued on his way, and I stood with the Triple Scorpio until we got more cans of food for all the people living in the cave. The cave? "Yes, come with me, they'll love you."

We carried the cans up the mountain to a cave with about seven people gathered. The cans of food were my ticket to join them. That night we would make a fire and feed whoever was hungry.

The "cave" was more of a half-covered alcove located above the small "Salmon Creek" sign near a bridge south of the Big Sur campground. The cave became my home for the next few weeks. At night campfires warmed us and new visitors watched our troop of singers in amazement. We slept under the stars in shared sleeping bags. Actually, we were sharing a warm body for the night. We were proud to be without possessions but welcomed anything anyone left behind. I felt like I was the *singer*. That was my place in our cave. It was as if I had always been there and would always be there. I thought maybe this was what "home" felt like. It had been a long time since I felt anything like at home.

In 1970, Big Sur was a hippie haven and hundreds of longhairs walked along the road with backpacks and hand-rolled Bugler cigarettes. Think Woodstock without the concert. In town there was one motel and a café or two where the heads were congregating. I suspect straight folks just drove on by, hoping to make it to Carmel before they ran out of gas.

Rich and poor, hippies on thumb and on choppers, we sang and shared our food. A sad trio from New York City joined us for a few nights. I recall a quiet boy who pulled out his eyelashes, a putzy guy named Mario, and a girl named Dee Dee Watts. She gave me her driver's license and I memorized her address. People in the cave were inclined to help each other.

One of the young girls who stayed in the cave was a sixteen-year-old runaway from one of the privileged homes of Newport Beach. One day she left us and went back home but returned a few days later with her parents. They had accepted her lifestyle and she in turn showed them her cave. They were so modern and well dressed and . . . understanding. I wished they were my parents.

There were some kids from Detroit, Black kids, one of them slipped on a rock and hit his head on a boulder as he fell into a twenty-foot crevice. I was the second person to reach him. I held his hand and sang to him for hours. He woke up and passed out over and over again. He could not speak. It felt exactly like it had with my brother, holding his hand that day with that sick smile on my face. Here I was, singing to another dying boy.

Eventually the forest rangers carried him out. I hoped he didn't die. Later I heard that so-and-so's cousin had been the one who fell in Big Sur. It was a small world and he didn't die. I like that version best. That's a good song.

I met a sweet-natured boy in corduroy. He was tender and good-looking. A dancer from Santa Monica. He stayed with us for two nights in the cave. I decided to go with him back to the city. It was a test, I did not know if I belonged near people anymore. I was a cave dweller.

I donwannago I donwannago I donwannago back into the city
(Adapted from Mark Almond, "The City")

The dancer had a drawerful of neatly folded corduroy pants in the wildest colors. Purples, greens, and beautiful red wide-ribbed corduroys. Let's call him Corduroy for I have long forgotten his name. I have loved corduroy ever since. I am wearing some right now. My decision to go with Corduroy had more impact on my life than I could have imagined.

We stopped to visit the Krishnamurti followers in Ojai. I was intrigued with this little mountain town so I promised myself I would someday return. I kept repeating the unusual name of Ojai as the years went by so I wouldn't forget. Twenty years later I returned to raise a family of my own with my little daughter attending the Krishnamurti school. Like I said, an important decision, but not so much because of the school and the town. A far more mystical thing was taking shape.

A marker on my journey was about to present itself in the person of Jimi Hendrix.

"After the Fair"

> *To whom does the angel sing*
> *If all below can feel his wing?*

FM radio was the new alternative to AM radio in 1970, and it filled the alternative market niche as the source of music and news for all of California hippiedom. We were simultaneously shaping ourselves through the new FM radio band and shaping the sound of radio. Bob Dylan was the pope of this new culture; his word was law. The Beatles were the source, the holy miracle that gave rise to the religion of the new hippie culture. None that came before them (or after) had the Beatles spark that could inspire an entire generation to devote themselves to music as their personal salvation. Album cuts, whole sides of records, the idea was to play music and to keep it as elusive as possible. Deejays rarely spoke, but when they did, it was as exciting as the music.

FM radio was a cultural crusade that we took to the corners of the earth to make peace and love for all. In 1970, there were even community service announcements on the radio for hippies. I recall a recorded warning from Grace Slick, queen of the San Francisco music intelligentsia, of "bad acid" circulating in California's unsuspecting hippie communities. "Stay away from the Orange Wedge." "Bad trip." Oops, too late. I was there, a witness. I was a child of those times.

Of course our message was eventually subverted and perverted, but the original impetus was so thrilling that kids today still copy the timbre, fashion, and music of that time. Today's culture bearers would return to that time if they could. Bring back some of its living spirit.

Corduroy and I heard on the radio that Jimi Hendrix was playing at the Ventura County Fairgrounds. Today? Yes! Tonight! Jimi Hendrix!

It was noon and we were only about thirty minutes away from the fairgrounds, en route to Big Sur. Jimi Hendrix—YES! Let's go!

We drove past the farms of Camarillo, the Eucalyptus Trail, and the Wagon Wheel Motel. It was early so the fairgrounds were unguarded. We scrambled to the top of the bleachers and lay down below the seats on the footrest panel. "Hurry!" We thought we had made ourselves invisible but also no one was watching. We lay there for two, three, four hours waiting for the doors to open. I had to pee the whole time so it seemed that centuries came and went as we lay there on the bleachers by the sea.

Finally they opened the doors an hour before showtime. I waited for enough people to come in that I would blend in. It was an excruciating calculation, the need to pee versus standing up too soon and getting caught at the finish line. After a dozen or so people were seated, I ran to the bathroom for a painful—but wonderful and legendary—pee. I returned to my corduroyed friend and took my seat beside him in the third row from the stage.

We had done it! Jimi Hendrix for free, best seats in the house.

Hendrix took the stage with a new band, all Black. He was more than the greatest guitar player, he was a mystic force of nature. Dressed in velvet, a headband, he did not look or move like other people. When he played music he seemed to sit in space different than we do. I knew that I was witnessing a musician unlike any other. I moved even closer to look at his hands. How did that sound come out when his hands were doing something entirely different? What *was* he anyway?

I was on my feet now checking out the whole stage and—who was that I saw? Impossible! Standing on the side of the stage was my own cousin, Donna Jones. Hey Donna! Just a few feet from Jimi Hendrix, like it was no big deal.

The last time I saw Donna was at her teenage wedding in Phoenix. What a life this was. Here I was witnessing the extraterrestrial incantations of one of the angels in one of his last concerts, Jimi Hendrix at the Ventura County Fairgrounds. I recognized again the magic of my life. I was living a life enchanted by impossible connections, narrow escapes, and the perfect timing of curiously strong coincidences.

I waved to my cousin and she brought us backstage (her husband had some connection). So you were just passing by on your way to a cave in Big Sur when you happened to hide for hours in the bleachers to see Jimi Hendrix, and lo and behold, here is your childhood cousin Donna? Of course!

There, three feet from Jimi Hendrix, I planted my body. I had the best view in the house. I marveled not only at the sounds that came out of the amplifier but at the magic of his body, for he looked to me that night the way things looked on Orange Wedge. Sounds seemed to come off his guitar even when he wasn't touching it. He was the sounds he made and neither of them were like anything else in reality. I thought he was . . . magic.

The show was shortened because a thick fog rolled in but I think he was done, anyway. I said goodbye to my cousin and I wondered when we would ever meet again. She was worried about me, so she gave me her driver's license as something I could use to survive out there. If the Man caught me I could "prove" I was legal.

She looked back at me with trepidation but I felt a stirring cloud beneath my feet as if my destiny and maybe the earth itself was changing. I was right about my destiny, but Jimi Hendrix's destiny was also tragically changing. He would die just a couple months later. And with him all the world around me was dying. All the true hippies, the tender mercies, and the adventures; all of it would end, too.

Corduroy and I began to bicker. I was not meant for the city after all. He agreed to take me back to Salmon Creek. I didn't even look back at him as I ran up the mountain. "Hey everybody, I'm back!" Nobody except for the Triple Scorpio even knew that I had left.

The Salmon Creek cave congregation was an ever-shifting event of personalities. By the time I returned, only a few of the originals remained. The cave had evolved from a home for earthy types to a bus station for transients. Many of the new kids were from the East Coast. I really wished they would take me with them but they were transients, not family. They were going on alone.

Recognizing the end, one of the long-timers said, "Let us all go away from this place but meet again because we're a family. Families have to stay in touch, so go and have adventures and then we will meet on the Fourth of July in a wonderful little town I know, Chatham, Ontario, in Canada. I'll be there. Will you?"

Everyone replied, "Yes, we will be there."

Fourth of July, 1970

> *Because there's something in the air*
> (Thunderclap Newman, "Something in the Air")

I left cave life one dusty day in late June and caught a ride with a young Texan in a pickup truck who was touring the U.S.A. before he had to serve five years in prison for possession of a couple "J's" of grass. I didn't see how he could agonize over this decision. Why would he go to prison if he could avoid it by moving to Canada? He said he did not want to lose his American citizenship, but what could citizenship matter if you were in prison? So there was a certain melancholy as we traveled across America. Me with my extreme ideas of freedom going to a rendezvous in Canada, and the cowboy in his mental shackles avoiding Canada for prison in Texas.

We were somewhere in Idaho and I hadn't helped with the driving yet. Remember, I was only fifteen years old and I had no driving experience so I avoided the wheel. Cowboy needed a break and I needed to maintain my story that I was seventeen years old, so I took my turn behind the wheel. I did okay on the highway portion because I only needed the gas pedal, but when we got into the city I was experimenting with the brake pedal for the first time in my life, and I didn't have a soft touch. When I hit the truck's brake too hard, we spun out.

Cowboy was so upset, he didn't recover. We drove a few more nights together but hardly spoke. When he dropped me off in the middle of downtown Detroit I hopped out and stuck out my thumb. As he left, his truck kind of stuttered, as if it couldn't believe that he was leaving me there that way. After such a long journey, the Texan didn't look back, he was gone.

Many years later he wrote to me and said that he had actually turned around and looked for me but I had already been picked up by my next ride. He was horrified by what he'd done, having been angry about the almost-accident. It took my exiting the vehicle for him to realize how much he cared. One of the perks of fame: old traveling companions can update you on what happened afterwards.

I was lucky, standing there, braless, hippie all the way, my long blonde hair counseling me to tie it back and be careful, but I was not having it. I got a ride soon as I put my thumb out. I looked into the car and four young men with greasy Brylcreem hair were looking back at me. I didn't feel any menace.

"Where are you going?"

"The border."

"Hop in."

It turned out they were going to the Canadian border too, they said, but later. At that point it seemed best to just agree with their plan, so what the hell, we drove around for a few hours. It's hard to say if they were weighing the idea of becoming rapists or if they were just innocent Midwestern guys thrilled to pick up a chick hitching a ride.

They were certainly enamored with having a real hippie girl in their car and I was squeezed between two sweaty boys on a tour of Detroit City. By the time they finally took me to the border it was late and they thought I should wait until morning. One of the boys offered to put me up for the night at his dad's house. I had a few days before the Fourth of July so:

"Sure, I can come to your house but I have to get back on the road tomorrow." I spent the next day with him, his pregnant sister, and his working-class father in their tenement home. I recognized this was the same poverty I had lived in in Chicago. The same hopeless one-road-in and no-road-out life.

Next day, he dropped me near the Canadian border and I stuck out my thumb to catch a Canadian truck driver. It took a few hours and two more rides but I got to Chatham.

Can you believe it? I made it from a cave in California just as we all planned! I found the rendezvous park and sat near the statue where we were to meet, but I was alone. Not a single person from California. An hour went by and it was getting dark. I began to question myself: Why am I the only one here? What have I done? I had trekked across one country and into another on a whim, supported by a belief that made this trip mean more than it did. Now I was alone in a strange country, the sun was going down, and it was getting very cold. Canada cold.

I asked a hippie-looking guy if he knew where I could crash, and as we talked I thought I noticed in the distance . . . maybe . . . did I see a familiar face there? Oh my gosh!

"HEY! Hey, man."

"Oh my God, you came! You came! You're the only one."

We hugged.

"Oh man! You're here! True blue! Welcome!"

The only one, huh? He seemed happy but I felt kind of stupid. I believed that keeping a promise for the sake of the promise was the meaning of the hippie movement. It mattered to me, but was I the only one who believed? Okay, I'm not sure what it was I believed in, but I believed in it then and I still do today. I'll still show up. You wait and see.

"Come with me, I have a place you can stay."

With the sun setting, the cold was coming on like Christmas, but knowing I would soon be safe and warm that night made everything beautiful. I'd have dinner and maybe even a bed. We knocked on the door of his friend's home and a gorgeous man opened it. Holy cow. Tall, sweet face, smile, long blond hair, friendly manner. His spirit was alive. He'd been living in Amsterdam and just got back.

"Amsterdam, I always wanted to go there."

There were four of us: Amsterdam and his roommate, me, and my cave-dweller friend. He had some great pot and he rolled us a joint which we passed around and I started getting high.

Amsterdam's roommate was an older guy, maybe in his thirties, with long dark hair and a thin body. He had a speech impediment, maybe a cleft lip or large scar. There was something sad and worn down about him, so I made it a point to be friendly to him. I smiled. That was enough, he stared at me the whole night. Stared. Everyone noticed but ignored it. We talked about Amsterdam and laws in America, revolution, smoke and let smoke, even though the guy was staring at me.

I was sitting cross-legged on the braided rug browsing through Amsterdam's record collection when I spotted an unusual record cover. "What is this?"

"Oh that's Dr. John. Very strange. Voodoo magic, Southern American music. New Orleans. You wanna hear it?"

He carefully removed the record from its jacket. As always, I studied the cover. Man-o-man-o-man, it was kind of weird: feathers, beads, face paint. "Why is he wearing that crazy stuff? He kind of looks . . . scary."

"Yes, down in New Orleans they have voodoo. It's about magic. They cast spells and stuff." Dr. John, the Night Tripper? Hmmmm.

Once the Night Tripper came on, all conversation stopped. This was the weirdest music I'd ever heard. Dr. John was singing about poison and walking through fire and I was thinking, What? Why is he saying that? A strange harmonica and guitar line that I did not recognize as two separate instruments made the whole thing seem like a spell. Then he started a chant:

Cum killy, killy cum cum.

It was scary, weird. Intriguing. Dr. John was weaving a spell while the quiet guy kept staring at me.

I was very high and the music had me. Dr. John said he walked on guilded splinters? What did that *mean*? It was like a scary movie on the turntable.

Suddenly, without a word spoken, the roommate stood up and dropped his pants. Buckle, zipper, and underwear slipped down his legs to his knees, then rattled to the floor.

I looked at him immobilized. I looked around the circle, the other two guys were dumbfounded. The exposed roommate gestured to me with his arms out like, Come to me, now, my queen, I want you. Why should we hide it?

Huh? I was still holding the Dr. John record jacket. Is this crazy priest doing some voodoo on us? Finally, Amsterdam snapped out of it and said, "Oh man, what are you doing? Oh dude, maintain, man. Please. Pull your pants up." The pantless guy slowly began to realize his invitation was a gross misestimation. I think he really believed that I was sitting on a bed of desire for him. All he had to do was make a grand gesture to break the ice and I would fall into his arms. Well, you never know.

Actually, everybody knew except him and now he had also exposed his . . . absurdity. He pulled his pants back up, then sadly turned and went back into his bedroom and closed the door, and Dr. John kept calling:

Did I murder? Did I murder? Did I murder?

Now those aren't the lyrics, but those are the words I heard that night. What he really sang was:

Till I burn up, Till I burn up, Till I burn up.

The song ended and we took the record off the turntable. Amsterdam said, "Wow, I don't know what that was. He's been having a hard time lately." Then he said:

"I'm going to the U.S. tomorrow to buy some pot . . ."

"Oh, I'd love to go with you."

"Great, we leave at 10 a.m. so you have to get up early."

"I'll be ready."

When it was time to sleep, I lay on the couch and planned how I'd get the money and move to Holland. We would be married with kids and I would ride bikes and live in peaceful coexistence with him for the rest of my life. I fell asleep to the sound of voodoo queens and bicycle tires with the ace of spades card flapping in the spokes.

The next morning we boarded a Greyhound bus for the States that stopped at the border for customs and law enforcement checks. As we approached the crossing Amsterdam took off his beret and said, "Here, wear this," and that was my first beret, its meaning forever tied to this adventure.

I'd just stepped off the bus to walk across the U.S.-Canadian border. I was in line wearing a white beret and a little dress and no bra; proudly waving my freak flag. Blending in, I thought. The guard stopped us, "Are you together?" I wasn't sure of the answer, we hadn't worked out the details of my imagined romantic life in Holland.

"Yes?"

I smiled.

He then addressed my Canadian friend: "Why are you carrying so much cash?" (We don't like hippies with money round here.) The guard disappeared for a moment, then came back and told Amsterdam, "You cannot enter the United States today." That wasn't so bad, we could come back tomorrow.

He then looked at me and said, "You, step out of line and come with me."

Amsterdam turned and left the border, knowing very well that he would never see me again. Turned out the Border Patrol also did not like braless, freak-flag-flying women entering the United States. I got a personal FBI agent who did not believe a word I said about being seventeen-year-old Donna Hawkhouse. He told me he was arresting me for "being in danger of leading a lewd and lascivious life"—a crime reserved for women and vigorously applied to braless, large-breasted ones who wore little hats and minidresses.

It was the "being in danger of" that really bewildered me. How could it be a crime to be in danger of *becoming* lewd or anything else? I simply thought these men were projecting their lust upon the woman. Me, actually. Another ambiguous message from the strange world around me that I (just as I was) *bothered* people. I bothered them a lot.

Amsterdam and I never met again. I like to imagine he went back to Holland to ride his bike. I imagine he was always pleasant and innocent and that he always wore a beret in honor of me. Perhaps he's bicycled by me as I've walked the canals near the Pulitzer Hotel where, waiting to play a concert, I often take in the beautiful city of dams. One day, perhaps, we will note each other's berets and say, "I used to know someone who wore a hat like that."

It was the Fourth of July, 1970. My cell was small with a tiny window about six feet off the ground. I heard cheering so I climbed up on the bed to try to see the fireworks. I had to imagine the beautiful colors exploding over the water. All I saw was someone else's America.

I had missed lunch and dinner and there was nothing left to eat. I was miserable. The matron that came on for the graveyard shift gave me a couple of stale white powdered donuts left over from the morning.

The inmates were screaming, literally, howling like banshees. One woman was hanging from the bars. What was going on there? I traveled across the nation to find utopia and instead I found the downtown Detroit jail. It was a terrible feeling, being in jail. I had not planned to run away, and that I got so far as Ontario, Canada, was a complete surprise. I did know I had not committed a crime, but I was an outlaw as far as Michigan was concerned, and I was treated to the same handcuffs as murderers, robbers, and rapists.

To everyone but the FBI agent, I obviously wasn't a criminal. I confessed in the interrogation that I wasn't Donna Hawkhouse, and that I was actually, get ready, a fifteen-year-old runaway from California!

"California? What on earth are you doing here?"

They had suspected I might not be Donna Hawkhouse when they asked me to spell my last name and I responded:

"Uh, H-A-W, I mean, U-K . . . H . . . O . . ."

"Okay. What's your real name?"

I smiled and told them, "Rickie Lee Jones."

With the July Fourth holiday weekend, it was a few more days in banshee jail before I was transferred to juvy.

Detroit was using mass incarceration because the deadly 1967 riots were put down with not only the National Guard but also the U.S. Army, which President Johnson had actually sent in. Years later they were still using mass arrests to avoid summer riots, which resulted in a juvenile hall so overcrowded that kids were sleeping on mattresses in the hall outside the cells. Except me. I was kept in one of three locked cells where they housed potential runners. They suspected I was a runner—and they were right. I wanted out.

The third locked cell held a fifteen-year-old murderer. She was a small, short-haired white girl who had shot and killed a policewoman escorting her from the police station for a misdemeanor. She had horn-rimmed glasses and a very unpredictable attitude. Other than the fact that she had murdered someone in cold blood, there was nothing unique about her, no fury, no joy, no soul at all. She was empty but dangerous.

I made friends with Guinevere, a tall, serene, beautiful, African-American teenage queen. At least, I thought she was a queen. She was my first Black friend. She already had a baby daughter on the outside.

Guinevere hoped for more than life dealt her and she hadn't given up yet. She was a reminder that it was a great big world out there. Talking together each day, she and I, or me mostly, began to organize a breakout. Get out there and start living. We might have made it if either of us had been real criminals instead of harmless kids.

The plan was for Guinevere to grab the matron by the hand, pull her into the cell, take her keys, and then lock her inside. Guinevere would then unlock my door and we would run to the exit, unlock that door, and run down the stairs. If we could figure out which key unlocked that last door we would be free. No one would be hurt. Two young girls finally out where they belonged on a long summer night.

At bedtime the matron came to Guinevere's cell. Guinevere pushed her down and got the keys. The tough and dangerous part of the plan was done! Easy as cake. But Guinevere was so excited that she forgot to lock the matron in. And then she forgot to let me out. And just like

Ricci Cretti when he turned the wrong way in the City of Industry, she lost her mind. She ran to the exit but instead of unlocking that door, she turned around and ran back to the cell. She had changed her mind and wanted to forget the whole thing. She was saying "I'm sorry" to the matron when she handed her the keys.

I was watching this unfold from the little window on my door like Scout in her Halloween ham costume. The matron got up and ran to the alarm. Two giant three-hundred-pound women from Mars came rushing down the hall to grab Guinevere. Then in the irony of ironies, they opened *my* door, tossed me out, and put Guinevere in. Oh, the shame.

This was beyond any Greek tragedy or Neil Simon comedy. Beyond a *Looney Tunes* cartoon. Guinevere paid the full price of my freedom from solitary. She didn't speak to me again but she didn't rat on me either. She was also good enough to not hurt me. Meanwhile the guards pressured me and everyone else for more names. I was like Jimmy Cagney.

"We know you did it."

"Then why are you asking?"

"We know you did it."

"Who, me? I'm just a hippie named California who wants to go outside like everyone else."

They had not let me off the floor for nearly two weeks. Not even for a walk. Not even for a jumping jack. I was going stir-crazy.

Finally, after crying and pleading all day long, I was escorted outside by the social worker for a five-minute walk in a tiny courtyard. I went round and round in a circle surrounded by thirty-foot-high walls and barbed wire. Yes, yes, I did wonder if I could scale that wall before getting caught. Those moments outside fed my soul so I was able to endure the next few days in my jail cell.

Armed with my real name, the State of Michigan found Tom Murphy, the attorney of record for Rickie Lee Jones. Murphy found my father living in Kansas City. It seemed my parents had separated a month ago and moved away from Seal Beach. Good thing I didn't try to return home. Dad had gone to stay with his old army buddy Barney Williams.

The social worker at the jail said my father would take me, and asked if I wanted to go to him. I said that I did.

"He doesn't have the money to send for you."

"Oh."

"We can send you to him in Kansas City and the State of Michigan will pay for your ticket. You sure you want to go to him?"

"Oh yeah, I really want to leave."

"Okay, then. We'll send you tomorrow."

Tomorrow? Suddenly jail was not so bad. Hello you funny little barred window! Hey there, you locked-down hallway, how you doing? Will you miss me?

I was lucky, there were kids who thought jail was a hundred times better than the "home" they came from. I looked at the social worker:

"You couldn't find my mother?"

"Your mother said she did not want you back."

August in Kansas City

I have fond memories of my dad and I together that hot humid August. We had no air conditioner, we'd sit by the fan all day and then toward evening Father prepared the most delicious dinners: eggs with onion and cheese, black bread and honey, all put together on a few cents. That summer in Kansas City, my father let me go to any concert I wished. I saw Eric Burdon and War and Led Zeppelin on their first American tour. Eric made a big impression on me.

Dad couldn't get a job down at the union hall so he'd come home angry and drunk. It was hard on me. By the end of August, my father and I had caught a Greyhound to Chicago. At the bus station downtown Dad put our stuff in a locker, and he found us a motel on Clark and Broadway. Watching him adeptly navigate our way down there at the bottom gave me another glimpse into his childhood of living on his own when he was only twelve years old. He was still a master of that life.

I took my dad to see the movie *Woodstock*. It meant a lot to me that Dad wanted to understand my way of life. He didn't care much about rock music, tolerating the embarrassing but earnest characters in flags and birthday suits. I glanced at him while Richie Havens was singing his frantic "Motherless Child" and saw tears streaming down my father's face. Daddy really *was* a motherless child.

One day in the future, I would send Richie Havens a message about my memories of my father watching his performance. That's a great thing about this job; the music community is a small world and sometimes I get to make sense of the random events of my life and let people know what they meant to me.

It only took until October before we runaways, my father and I, headed back to Washington State in search of my mom. I was uncomfortable now in constant close proximity with my father. I needed my whole family back together. I needed a mother. Maybe he did too. So Dad and I took a "drive-away" car to Montana, and from Miles City caught a Greyhound to Olympia, Washington, where my mom was living. Mom didn't know it yet, but Dad was going to put us all back together again.

A Bird in Miles City

Miles City, Montana, was a small village in the middle of the state. We stayed one night at an old, wooden Western hotel that seemed left over from the cowboy days of the 1890s. After dinner, Dad let me go for a walk by myself. As I approached that big highway going west I was tempted to put out my thumb and disappear again. Dad knew, he watched me from the hotel window. I looked up and waved.

I crossed the road and walked into a little dry meadow where I could be alone and consider life. As I walked, a bird ran out from the sagebrush and actually stood on my foot. I froze in midstep and gasped, "There's a bird on my foot." Then I slowly and carefully picked up the bird.

Hey, ho! Oh my! I've got a bird! A wild bird just came to me! I rushed back to the hotel and I showed my dad who said, "That bird must be sick or something. You have to let it go." I could feel him refuse to see the miracle of a wild animal running up to me to be captured. Why didn't these adults see how unprecedented this was? Wild animals didn't just walk up to people! Adults always thought something had to be *wrong* if anything out of the ordinary occurred. But maybe it was right—so *right*.

Dad didn't believe in my world of magic even though he was the one who told me about fairies and the man in the moon. He was sick of waiting on magic to lift his life. He just wanted to get back on the Greyhound.

I kept the bird there in the dark old room for an hour or two, then recrossed the road to put her back where I found her. I opened my hands expecting her to fly away immediately. She didn't move. I pushed her upward, as if to say, "Fly," but she held on. I wanted to stay there with this magical thing and never go home and never grow up. I threw her up, up, and said, "I'm sorry!" She flew low and into the brush. I stood there pondering the magic. Was I the only one who recognized this miracle? Did others simply throw magic back into the brush?

I returned to the hotel and went to sleep in the bed next to my father's. Next morning, Dad and I caught our Greyhound to Olympia. We were out of money by the time we arrived. I mean, maybe we had seventy-five cents; two bucks, tops.

It was early in the morning when Dad and I lugged our old-fashioned suitcases up the hilly two-mile route to the Rib Eye Coffee Shop. We ordered glasses of water and he called my mother. It was do or die, the end of the road, now or never, etc., but we were saved again. Mama came and got us with my little sister Pamela in the car. It was good, really good to see them again. My mom, my sister, my dad, and me.

We drove to Mom's house, a small trailer in King Arthur's Court trailer park. Ah, a special nod to Father's love of the classics. There, lying in the back bedroom, was my guitar. My mom had brought my guitar with her all the way from California. She hadn't thrown it away! While Mom and Dad were inside making up, I stood outside and played the guitar with all my might.

Chapter 11

Olympia

Rickie Lee at fourteen

The Adventures of Rickie and Julie

Julie lit a match and the dark exploded into strings and paisley
Patterns, comets of gooey, viscous light.
I hollered to the Lord, "I seen light!"
Julie guffawed, "And it's burning my fingers!"
Which is very funny stuff on LSD.
All night long we laughed
Our minds peeled open for any passing revelation,
Playing on words and lying on the cool sheets
In the dark that was lit up by the lights in our dilated eyes
A couple teenage girls safe at home
Higher than kites fly on a windy day.

I slipped through school with a B average in spite of not being able
to read very well. I could read but I could not concentrate. My mind

drifted beyond the page. My imagination was far more interesting. The beginning of every school year I always had high hopes. By November the idea of reading an entire chapter in any subject was simply overwhelming and I abandoned it. I don't know how I passed tests but, curiously, I did much better than most of the class.

In hidden places around our little trailer in the Court of King Arthur, I would make out with my boyfriend Eddie. Eddie was the first boy in Olympia to challenge the school board and win the right to wear long hair at school. His hair was to his waist and he was a good kisser. But Julie had a spirit that teenagers were drawn to. I preferred her company to his any old day.

When I started at Timberline High in Lacey, it was already four weeks into the sophomore school year. Timberline was a nontraditional school, inspiring young people instead of teaching them by rote. The success of an early alternative school in England called "Summerhill" rippled into my local school system, which was trying to be current and to integrate the new ideas of this social revolution. Problem was our faculty was not totally committed to the idea, and without absolute confidence and guidance, this free-for-all was never going to work. I brought my guitar to play during free periods and introduced myself to people. They told me about another guitar-slinging girl. Really?

We arranged to meet at a free period. Julie walked right up to me, like Wyatt Earp in the showdown at the O.K. Corral.

She pulled out her fingerpicks as if they were bullets and carefully applied each one. I handed her my guitar. When she played "Sugar Babe" by the Youngbloods, she slapped those fingerpicks against the strings with authority. I would never be able to play like that. I was humbled.

Could I try? She handed my guitar to me. I played the opening notes to "Suite: Judy Blue Eyes"—an ambitious reply. I did my rendition in regular tuning, not easy. I had taken aim and hit my mark: respect. We respected each other right away and were destined to become the best of friends. Julie would teach me the jazz chords that

ended up in "Chuck E's in Love." We were on the frontier of the
teenage wasteland of high school, sharing our food, the music that
kept us both alive. We understood each other as only musicians can.

> *If you smile at me I will understand*
> *That is something everybody everywhere*
> *does in the same language*
> (Crosby, Stills and Nash, "Wooden Ships")

My brother now owned a pool hall, and Julie and I learned how to play
pool there, listening to Yes's "Roundabout" over and over on Danny's
jukebox. Julie became protective of Danny and I, making sure no one
treated him badly and no one bad-mouthed me. She was a sister to
us both.

High school was smoking pot out in the woods, then pacing back
and forth in our cars as we drove to one end of town and back, endlessly.
We would sometimes park at the tiny airport to watch the moving
lights in the sky grow into massive airplanes landing over our heads,
or sometimes we'd stand on the brewery bridge and look down into
the water. We also meandered through cemeteries or met up with our
friends to crowd into the Red Eye photo booth, smoking, laughing,
and having fun.

We were at the end of the hippie movement, when it went into its
slow death spiral, and at the beginning of the 1970s. We lost friends
to the Vietnam War; it seemed like every boy who went came back
in a casket.

Noble Elements

Vice Principal Bozak was the real life version of Dean Wormer of
Animal House. He eventually dismantled the "alternative school" in
favor of a traditional school with a regimented curriculum. There was
an ideological battle being fought in high schools across the country
about the orthodoxy of education. We hippies were the foot soldiers

sacrificed on the front lines of this battle. That included kicking me and eleven other "heads" out of school before the end of our junior year. Even long-haired students who didn't touch drugs and carried straight A's were ejected from school. We would have been part of the first graduating class but Bozak was determined to strike a blow against longhairs. No hippies would make it to his school's graduation podium.

I was fundamentally against the requirement that girls learn the skills to become housewives—a role I would never accept. I'd tried but wasn't allowed to enroll in the boy's woodshop class. I showed up in Home Ec one morning ready to learn how to hem my skirt and the teacher told me to remove my hat. Thus, once again, I was suspended from school for refusing to remove my hat.

I returned to class four days later and the teacher expelled me again. She evidently didn't know I had been gone. Daffy dame. I explained this to Mr. Bozak but his issue was never women's hats. He cut me off with, "I don't care. You are an undesirable element here."

Later, joined by my parents, we met in his office and he offered this as the reason he was uninviting me from continuing my education at Timberline: "Rickie is an undesirable element." He was kicking me out of school. It was too much for my dad. My parents had been fighting to keep me in school but now the fight was over. Father recognized the situation for what it was as he stood up from his chair and hissed:

"I wouldn't let my dog go to your school."

I thought he was going to punch Mr. Bozak right in the jaw. I was so proud of my parents.

As we walked through the Timberline High School parking lot for the last time, I felt part of a family of rebels. My parents understood what I had gone through and they righteously defended me. We were hoping we could reason with Bozak, but his small-town authority was all he had. Though it was horrible to be kicked out of school, I had my family fully behind me that day. I was hopeful we would become whole again and for longer than just that one day. It was us against the world! We had lost a fight with Bozak but won an encouraging battle for our family. Unfortunately, it would be our last battle fought together in a foxhole, the last scorpion of our tired history.

Father and the Piggybank

My family had moved from the trailer court to a cottage on Offut Lake about ten miles from Tumwater. Dad's bad luck with jobs continued. He couldn't get hired anywhere and he wasn't doing well. He was always looking through us at some other life he was missing. When we came home from school, my little sister would bring Dad a beer and they would sit together on the dock and look at the lake. She loved the father-daughter time and he loved his little girl's adoration and acceptance. It would be hard for her to lose him.

It was early October, Mom had gone to work. I was home with Pamela when my dad started packing a duffel bag. I knew right away he was leaving us. "You're leaving while Mom is gone?" I was so angry I could spit. How could he do this? I went into my room and sat on the bed. I wished I was anywhere but here. Pamela was crying.

In his final act of diminished fatherhood, Dad came into my room and said, "I don't have any money. I need to borrow some. You said you had three hundred dollars you saved for a vacation. I will pay you back soon as I get somewhere. I'll send you the money."

"No. I don't want you to go."

I swallowed. How could I say no to my father?

"I'm not giving you my money. I have been saving it all year. I worked hard for it . . . You . . . why are you . . ." And finally, "I want to keep my money Daddy. Just don't go."

"Daddy don't go," Pamela sobbed.

Dad told Pammy to wait in the living room, that everything was alright, but I could see her behind him, she'd thrown herself on the floor crying.

He argued with me that I owed him, blah blah, then he walked out into the living room. I braced for his next barrage but he snapped out of it and said:

"No, you keep your money. It's yours."

My father had given up. He picked up his duffel bag and went out the door. Then I heard my eight-year-old sister:

"Wait! Daddy."

I stood there glaring out the window when Pamela did the most remarkable thing. She caught up with my father on the path and said:

"Here Daddy, you can have *my* money," and handed him her piggy bank.

Oh my heart! I went out on the path and stood there by my baby sister. Not to challenge my father or protect Pamela's piggy bank, but I thought that if he saw us together he would turn around. See us, your children?

Daddy did not take Pamela's piggy bank. We watched him walk around the corner of the blue-and-white guest cottage with the roses growing by the door. He was gone again. I held my sister and rocked her. We rocked and rocked and rocked. When Mother came home from work I had to tell her that her husband had gone. She was furious about what he did to us kids. She did not mention that perhaps her own heart had been broken too.

The week after my father left was my mother's forty-third birthday, so I decided to surprise her. Mom could smell secrets a mile away so I had to buy the ingredients and hide them next door. After she left for work, I baked a homemade layer cake, frosted with sugar and butter, as well as scalloped potatoes and halibut. I got it all from a magazine.

Mom was exhausted when she arrived home for the last two hours of her birthday, but she took in the scene: the cake, the place setting, the dinner. She set down her purse and kind of smiled. A very small and quiet smile.

This was the first time I put my mother or father before myself. I offered something to my mother made with my own two hands. I was leaving something behind and stepping up. Where I had been my only center just a year before, I was taking care of my family now. They needed me.

One month later it was my seventeenth birthday—finally, the real seventeen! Julie took me to dinner at the Falls Terrace. We shared cheesecake for dessert. My mother was our waitress. Even though Julie brought money to pay, my mom picked up our dinner. It seemed like Julie and I were suddenly adults, women who took care of our parents, and each other, and ourselves. Women who did whatever needed to be done in order to become what we must be, in order to turn the page to the next chapter.

Postscript to a Friendship

Julie and I had a life-or-death trip together before our friendship drifted away. We drove to Eastern Washington, and on our way back, Julie's brand-new used car broke down. We unleashed our thumbs to hitchhike home over the mountains. Our first ride dropped us right on top of the mountain, but we couldn't catch another ride because the steady stream of cars had petered out. Worse, the weather was changing, the sun had set, and it was getting dark fast, so we began to walk with our thumbs out. Hours later we were walking in the total dark, singing, talking, and laughing, but still no cars were coming. We were in trouble, out there in the thin mountain air with the temperature dropping and now snow falling, too, and if we didn't get to warm shelter soon, we might not survive.

We were scared. What would happen to us? They were gonna find us frozen there with a Neil Young song on our lips. "Old man, take a look at my life." I liked singing that but not as an epitaph. I was only wearing a light jacket against the cold.

Finally the only headlights we had seen in hours appeared. It was a snowplow, able to go where cars couldn't. The driver slowed down, "What are you guys doing out here? They closed this road an hour ago." We climbed in and warmed our hands. "You're lucky," he said, "I'm the last thing coming through."

We looked at each other's faces and it was as if this was the last time for us, too. Our last night on earth, coming through. It was a long ride over the pass to civilization. We never told our parents how close we had come to death in the wilderness. After that night we slowly drifted apart. Without school and without living close together, Julie and I had to work to stay in touch.

Julie could turn on the Eddie Haskell charm with our parents. Yes, she could converse with them, but the main reason our friendship faded was because my boyfriend Eddie's father and Julie were having a "romantic" relationship. I couldn't wrap my mind around it. As far as I was concerned, he was a lecherous pedophile, but to her he was just a "romantic, older man." Since all the grown-ups thought Julie was the level-headed one in our crowd, they never suspected that she might be more reckless. The courtship of Julie and Eddie's father harmed both of them and everyone else who was even tangentially involved.

Although we seldom saw each other, our friendship was deep. Many years later, Julie saved my life with a golf cart and helped me begin my second album, *Pirates*.

Peg Leg Jones

Rickie Lee Jones, Australian platinum record cover bears some
resemblance to my grandfather's publicity shot   (*Norman Sheef*)

At the "Makin' Whoopee!" video shoot with Dr. John and baby Charlotte

Walter Becker producing *Flying Cowboys*, 1989

Lenny Waronker and Robin Williams backstage at the Roxy, 1979

Recording "The Moon Is Made of Gold" and Grammy-nominated "Autumn Leaves" in London with Rob Wasserman, 1986

With Tom Waits on the pier in Santa Monica

With Chuck Weiss on New Year's Eve in L.A., 1986

My grandmother and grandfather with the vaudevillians.
Grandma in the first row, third from right, grandpa directly in the middle.

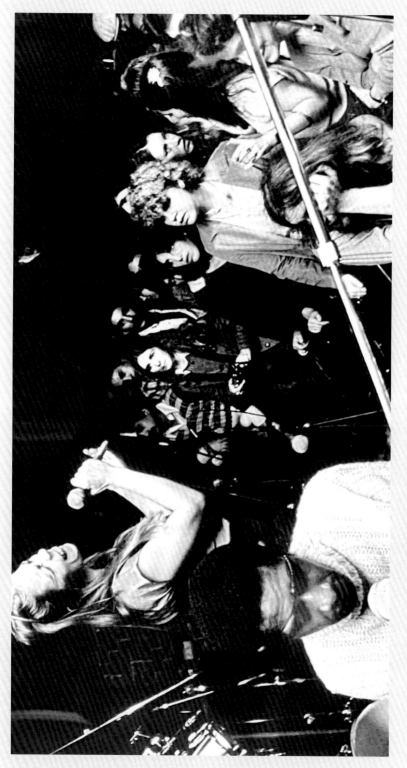

Performing with James Booker in New Orleans   (*Michael Smith*)

My maternal grandmother, Rhelda

Grandmother, mother, myself, and
my daughter, Charlotte, Ohio, circa 1993

Mother in Florida, just married

Mother and father and their first child,
my sister, Janet

Jones kids: Richard, Bea, and Frank, circa 1924

Daddy in the alleyway, Chicago, 1940s

"Sometimes I feel like a motherless child."
My father and his mother, Chicago, 1923

My father in his new Cadillac

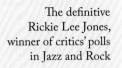

Glamorous photo from my first
photo session with Bonnie Schiffman

My great-grandfather, Burrell Jones, on the left, in his dry goods store, circa 1922

Grandfather holding an Airedale puppy
in front of the theater

An artist practicing his
nom de plume

On tour with Ray Charles in Israel, 1987
(Included are Michael Lang and Rob Wasserman)

On tour with Lyle Lovett (middle) in 1991. That's Sal Bernardi on the right end.

Stills from my first video

Playing with RatDog at President Clinton's
second inauguration in Washington, D.C., 1997

RLJ on tour in America, 1990s

Meeting Alfred Johnson for the first time
on the boardwalk in Venice, CA, 1977

Letters home

Reunited 30+ years later,
Santa Monica pier concert, 2012

Thursdays in September at
The Ala Carte, 1977

With Bob Dylan at the Grammy after-party at Chasen's in Beverly Hills, 1980

Performing with Bruce Springsteen at Jazz Fest in New Orleans, 2014

Danny's portrait of me in
the second grade

Me entering the fourth grade

1968, I've been posing with cars for a long, long time

Putting makeup on with Charlotte at the "Makin' Whoopee!" video shoot, 1989

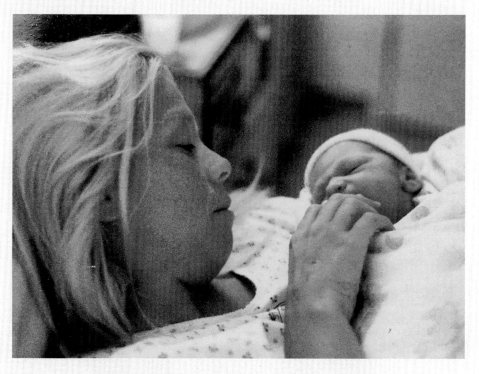

Just born, Charlotte Rose and me, Santa Barbara, 1988

Aunt Bea with umbrella

Rickie Lee with umbrella   (*Annie Leibovitz*)

Chapter 12

Surfer Girl
on the Waterbed

Julie and Bruce

I enrolled in Olympia Vocational Technical Institute where kids who were kicked out of school got their GED or learned a trade. Once I passed my GED, I enrolled in Tacoma Community College, making me the first of my entire high school class to go to college. My brother bought himself a cabin, so we Jones women moved in with him. All of us girls in one bedroom, Dan in the other. I had a horse, there were chickens and a rooster (until we ate him), and I was thinking of myself as a kind of "back to the land" mama. The reins were looser. It was summer.

My high school buddy Bruce and his girlfriend invited me to join them on a trip to Los Angeles. Mother wisely relented, understanding my summertime wanderlust wasn't anything she could successfully stop. At least this time I wouldn't be hitchhiking. We started the two-day trip from Olympia to L.A. with a bag of cashews, forty-one dollars for gas, and a couple tabs of LSD. We drove twelve hours, then spent the first night in a cornfield outside of Sacramento. We woke up hungry and hot, but drove on through to San Francisco where I got a speeding ticket. On Highway 1 through Big Sur I showed them the Salmon Creek cave where I had lived. It seemed smaller now somehow.

We stopped near San Simeon (just past that hotel I had shivered outside during the summer of 1970). The sun was going down. Each of us dropped a tab of acid and I got behind the wheel to drive. Soon I was flying over the two-lane Ventura Highway. *Hey, were we actually flying?* The roads seemed like ocean waves. I can still see the face of the driver in the oncoming lane, frozen in terror. Was I driving wrong? Sixty miles per hour, that was normal, wasn't it? Bruce said, "Pull over."

Well, shoot. I had my driver's license but I didn't recall anything in the test preparation about LSD. Once again, everyone was pissed off about my driving, and again I was unceremoniously dropped off, but this time I was at good old Seal Beach. I'd find Seebu and Tina and we would be the Rickie-Tina-Seebu combo once again. Here I was with nowhere to go, no money, and an LSD-warped reality. Rickie's home!

I knocked on Seebu's motel door and said, "Surprise!" She had not seen me since the day I disappeared from Seal Beach on my way home from her house. I wondered what she knew about my travels. I told her that I'd gone up to Big Sur but I didn't tell her everything, not yet. Seebu was happy to see me. She took me to Jay's house, he was one of three sailors who lived by the beach. One of the guys was deployed on a submarine, so I could take his place for awhile. Jay looked after me like a brother for most of the summer. He took me to the naval base, taught me things about life in New York City, and most importantly, shared his humanity. He did not load any sexual expectations onto his kindness toward me.

Jay and I smoked a little pot and then we listened to music and lounged around on his king-sized waterbed. Jay said he was Puerto

Rican by birth, and his Jewish adoptive parents had "a little money." Jay was making his own way in the world, as far away from Brooklyn as he could be without a submarine, here in Seal Beach, California. He was an everyday working Navy man. When Jay was away on maneuvers, I would lie on his bed and in the soft light of his aquarium, watch the fish and wonder if I would marry Jay. I wasn't attracted to him, really, but I was still considering every boy I met for possible marriage.

There on Jay's waterbed, I sketched out my life to come. Writing it down made it real, gave it substance and direction. I could check things off the list as they came—how satisfying that would be.

I wanted to go so many places. List: Ireland, France . . .

1. I want to be a singer.
2. Or an actress.
3. I want to have things (list on next page).

I'd have two of everything. Two guitars. Two *Buffalo Springfield* albums. Two shampoo bottles—why not! Two antique satin dresses and two pairs of suede boots. I excitedly bounced on Jay's waterbed as suddenly everything belonged to me. Oops. I shouldn't bounce on the waterbed. I was so happy being by myself in someone else's house. Being part of something that was not me, part of a life already seized, already whole.

I rolled off the bed into Jay's forbidden zone—his albums. "Do not *touch* my albums." Oh, all the beautiful covers. Four bucks a pop, lots of money spent here. I knew he was rich! Just looking, sir. New Riders of the Purple Sage. Sons of Champlin. What was this nameless cover, Neil Young? Hmm. Oh I like this Little Feat cover—woman as shoe? Ho, what was that?

I discovered important new music that summer, names that I carry with me today, records that influenced what I recorded. These artists were Rod Stewart, Neil Young, Van Morrison, and of course, Laura Nyro.

Laura Nyro, that name sounded so familiar. Oh yeah, back in Elma—Janis Ian . . . I remember *New York Tendaberry*. What's a "tendaberry"? I took the record out and placed it carefully on the turntable. I was instantly captured. Stark and lonely, the chords unlike anything I had heard before. She sang:

"To mainstream die."

Is that what she said? What was she saying?

"You don't love me . . . when I cry."

Before I discovered Laura Nyro I was imitating other women to relate to them. Janis Joplin called women to suffer on behalf of their men in a very loud way that meant socially, we are fighting—but on the Man's same old battleground. Dignity attached to our ball and chain. I was intrigued by Janis's rough persona and her unbeautiful voice. But there was nothing about me that was like Janis, I had to work to be like her.

Laura Nyro made up her own Gershwin-esque operas. This record —*New York Tendaberry*—made me not only want to be a part of her world, but to think I could make a world of my own. I *recognized* her, I recognized myself in her. I confess I didn't know exactly what she was trying to say, but I understood the feeling. She was a woman ready to lead the world, defending Black Panthers and Native Americans with the bold strokes of unflinching intimacy. There was no masculine bravado here.

Laura Nyro was not like anything else evolving out of the 1960s, as if the singer of the Shangri-Las had been raised by Leonard Bernstein.

Somehow, the moment I fell in love with Laura I loved myself just a little more. I believe an invisible cord came out of me and attached itself to Laura Nyro that summer. Or vice versa.

Laura Nyro was a teacher for me at a time when I was starving for musical direction, when I needed emotional enunciation. Her dignity didn't transcend circumstances, it celebrated them.

There, that was the direction I wanted to grow in. A sun formed and brought an orderly orbit to my randomly scattered planets.

Neil Young's music was the other side of my teenage identity, the boy side, the continuation of my Beatles-inspired technique of owning what men seemed to be entitled to and take for granted. By imitation first, I wore his flannel shirts and patched blue jeans. He seemed to know how I felt as I walked through the fair when I was only ten, and how I thought about being so old while still so young. His voice was odd and I liked it. Mine was odd, too. As I whined out my vocals in such obvious (though not to me) imitation, Julie would say:

"That must be a Neil Young song."

His album *Young Man's Fancy* was a live performance sold as a bootleg, just him by himself, stunning. I bought mine in Long Beach that very week I heard it at Jay's. I still own it today. But there was something very un-California ("back to the land, peace and love") about Neil. Why did he write about heroin? Heroin was city-ugly, and I had not seen it here in hippie land. "A little part of it in everyone . . . every junkie's like a setting sun." I sang along and sang along.

The gentle San Francisco idealism of my idols that seemed within reach during my first time out into the world of 1969 had now become commercialized. The once-threatening images of long-haired flower girls and their long-haired boyfriends were now co-opted by the media; shag haircuts for men and women. My hippie clothes that got me arrested at the Canadian border were now accepted on American television sets as wholesome Brady Bunch costumes. Yesterday's unique hippie identities were now the couture for all. As mandolins banged away on *Every Picture Tells a Story*, Rod Stewart carried the banner of a new unisex decade.

These were the records I listened to day after day from the vantage point of Jay's California King–sized waterbed.

The social upheaval that had given birth to musicians fighting for a greater good would give way to the personality-driven decade of the 1970s. Yesterday's hopeful revolution was today's impotent storm on an empty beach of cynicism. We were back to who we had been before, a nation broken by violence, with feckless leadership, and now something terrible was creeping through the cracks. Heroin had come in the back door with the hippie pot smokers—just like "they" always said it would!

A Slow Easy Mark

Mark Vaughan was a tall slender Oklahoman with a mustache, a Gibson guitar, and a VW. He lived with Debbie and her little brother Zachary a few houses up from Jay's place. He was our neighborhood pot dealer in Seal Beach, and his house was a constant revolving door of hitchhikers and friends of friends. He was only twenty-three, but he seemed much older than everyone else. It would always be that way with him.

Pot dealers know everybody, so when Kenny, a reputed leader of the Berkeley chapter of the Students for a Democratic Society, came to stay at Mark's house, we were duly impressed. While Debbie and Mark had loud sex, Kenny and his wife had even louder fights. We could hear them at end of the block.

Kenny was a short, dark guy who hid his eyes behind dark-tinted glasses. We pondered his appearance, he was here but he was also not here. He was slippery to even look at and he felt dangerous. What we heard was that he regularly beat his wife. Violence was his manifesto and he was not fucking around.

The SDS activities of that year in the "People's Republic of Berkeley" were legendary. Kenny had been a part of shutting down an entire school, so he had a notoriety and respected status among the hippies and radicals.

The killings of white students at Kent State University in Ohio and Black students at Jackson State College in Mississippi gave additional weight to his spiritual manifesto. Kenny and other protesters were seen as the vanguard of progress and the protectors of us. Kenny was living the guns and violence version of my high school battles with Bozak. That was the long and short hair of it. Us versus them.

So Kenny was esteemed, if not feared. He had come to our Seal Beach neighborhood to buy some dope and take a rest from his revolutionary activities. He was another friend of a friend. His wife was a tiny, bespectacled mosquito of a woman whose atmosphere was as unpleasant as his.

Mark and Debbie's hippie house on Seventeenth Street was full now, with Debbie's brother, Zachary, Kenny and his wife, plus two hitchhiker girls from Europe who brought with them more than their knowledge of Germany. (Only Zachary and I escaped the need for the free clinic's penicillin shots.)

I was standing inside Jay's tiny yard talking to Seebu and Sailor John, one of the guys living in Jay's house. Kenny walked out of Mark's house and up to my yard. Seebu immediately said goodbye and Kenny immediately invaded:

"You have been watching me. Tell the truth."

"Huh?"

"You're interested in me. Admit it."

He scared me so much my tummy tickled. Jay had come out from his bedroom to rescue me. To Kenny, he pointedly said, "We heard you were here. Are you gonna be here long?" Kenny turned and walked away.

Then Jay turned to me and said, "Stay away from that guy, he's bad news." Mark also warned me, "Stay away from Kenny. He's got his eye on you. He's my friend, but you don't want to get involved with him. Big hassle."

Later, Kenny saw me and again it was:

"I want to spend some time with you."

"But, well, why are you here? You're married."

"That's not your business."

Back in the house, Sailor John shook his head. I admitted I was intrigued by Kenny's forcefulness. "What did he say? Is he coming back? You should go somewhere, anywhere but here. That guy is gonna be trouble." Right on cue, there was another knock at the door. This time it was Kenny's wife, the little woman with glasses. A still life in black and blue. I opened the door.

"Hello," she started, nodding, sweet. Her words touching my body somehow. She had a blackened eye.

"I am Kenny's *wife*, are you Rickie?"

"Yes."

"Was Kenny just here to see you?"

Hard to breathe.

"So listen to me"—total change in her voice—"I want you to keep away from my HUSBAND. We are *married*. Stay away from him or I will come back here and kick your ass. And do not tell him I spoke to you."

John and I were still looking at each other incredulously when there was yet another knock at the door. John peeked, I hid. This time it was Kenny.

"She's not here," John yelled.

"Yes, she is," he replied. "Rickie come out here. Now."

He was yelling at me. What did *I* do? I came out. It was exciting.

"Rickie! Was she here? Was my wife here? I saw her leave here. What did she want?"

"She said I had to stay away from you."

Behind the dark glasses I could see his eyes bouncing around. It was like he had red eyes. If this cartoonish sequence was actually a cartoon, smoke would come out of the top of his head. It was funny and frightening. Could my world end on how I answered Kenny's questions?

I watched Kenny and his invisible revolutionary guard march back to Mark's house. Even invisible snipers could do nothing to stop him from beating his wife, and now he was loaded for bear. His she-bear wife was standing on the porch watching him walk up. She seemed to know what was coming, yet she turned and stepped into the house. Why did she do that? I was still learning about the horrific psychology of abusive relationships. Was she trying to win back his attention by threatening his will?

He beat her badly. Loudly. The sound of a bony hand hitting a bony face and ribcage. It is a gruesome sound. If you are close enough to hear it, you are close enough to intervene. The sound is as unforgettable as the lesson: domestic violence is a ritual of abuse. No one interferes with the ritual except to his or her peril.

Mark Vaughan had had enough. He defied the "do not interfere" directive of domestic violence by opening the front door and entering the fray. Between Kenny's mortar shells, Mark screamed:

"Stop it! What's the matter with you? Both of you—stop."

Kenny said, "This is not your business, you're stepping over the line."

"It *is* my business—you're gonna bring the Man down on my house and the entire neighborhood is listening to you. Stop fucking beating your wife, man."

Turning to her, softer, he said: "And you, you better leave him now while you can."

Mark had intervened and no one was sure what to do next, but the beating stopped so he went one further: "This is too much hassle. You two have to leave now or *I'll* call the cops."

No one ever threatened to call the police in hippie land. It just wasn't done. It was an even crazier idea for a pot dealer to call the cops, but Mark was not fucking around. Kenny and his wife left the next day. Kenny's "I'm sorry man, she just makes me crazy" didn't cut it anymore. Mark and the rest of us recognized there was a strain, not of revolution but of pure evil, in Kenny from Berkeley.

I heard a few years later, Kenny beat his wife to death. I guess she went back inside the house with him one too many times.

First Time is Free

As kids in Phoenix, watching television movies and stirring our ice cream to the perfect consistency, Danny and I watched *The Man with the Golden Arm* so many times I knew passages of dialogue. The movie was an adaptation of Nelson Algren's novel about an uncanny drummer, Frankie Machine, deftly played by Frank Sinatra. Frankie returns from prison (for heroin addiction) to start his life again, but he is back in the same house surrounded by the same people. Chances are slim.

It was the Elmer Bernstein music that moved me into the story. As Sinatra walked back into the dealer's house and succumbed to relapse, what captured me was Bernstein's music. It was the music that made my heart pound. It was the music that showed me what Frankie Machine was *feeling*. I wanted to know that feeling too.

As a kid watching that movie, I wondered what siren could call my name so loud that I would walk across the street into a demented basement and work like a slave just to have some more. What could own someone's soul? What could ever feel so overwhelmingly fantastic that I, Rickie Lee, would do those things?

I wanted some of *that*—that music, that feeling. Some thrill, some fear was subtly lodged in my head the first time I saw that movie, an invitation to the lowdown.

Damage Done

One late afternoon in July when the sailors were gone and Mark and Debbie weren't around, Zachary asked if I wanted to go to Long Beach to get high. Sure, get high on what? He just raised his eyebrows. We were going to take heroin. I thought I could just watch.

We drove to a little wooden house under a radio tower. Next to it was a field full of oil rigs that grew wild there, like baby dinosaurs. We were escorted into a spartan room with just a kitchen table and a bed where a skinny nefarious old creep with green skin nodded. He was like a needle-less cactus. Sucked up dry. "That's my uncle," said a younger man, a lifelong prisoner to his drug-addict relative. The uncle had cursed his nephew to the same fate by introducing him to heroin, and now Zachary held my hand as we stood at the gate of hell.

First, the uncle sat in a chair. The dealer tied off his arm just like in the movie. They cooked the drug in a spoon.

"Has to be silver or you can get poisoned."

Then—the music, the *Golden Arm* music. He closed his eyes and smiled.

Then it was Zachary's turn, and then:

"You want to try this?"

Me: "Yes."

"I won't give you too much, you're gonna fly."

The feeling was so overwhelming, I could not stand. Someone laid me on a bed and all the music faded into shapes and time stood still, or maybe it went running back to Seal Beach, looking for the shade of the girl I would never be again. For the price of a shot I had bought a lifetime in the shadows.

After a while—I don't know how long—they got me up and we all drove back to Seal Beach. I threw up on the sidewalk. I went back into the sailors' house, but things were different. The devil had come. The light of magic was not as bright. The thrill of the ordinary was gone. Easy for it to be restored, just never go back there again.

But of course I wanted to try it again. Some days later the Long Beach guy was back on our street. "This stuff is not free, little girl. You get some money and you come back." He sized me up:

"If you want to make some money . . ."

I did not shoot up a second time. I had seen *that* movie before. I was embarrassed at how cliché it all was. Really? Just like they said it would be?

The repercussions of that day were not over. Jay heard from one of the sailors that I had used heroin. Heroin was not allowed in hippie land and he was furious that I broke this unspoken code. He kicked me out of his house. I had nowhere to go.

I crashed here and there and then a few days later I heard Jay wanted to talk to me. He apologized and let me come back. Jay, always wise and decent, said, "That was the wrong thing to do, to kick you out. I'm sorry. Please come back."

Jay offering an apology was more kindness than any man had ever offered me. I nearly pouted my way through it. I stayed for a few days and recovered, but I knew my California month was over.

I had hardly seen my friend Seebu. She had not gone to Long Beach and changed her destiny. She was still a teenager, carrying her baby sister wherever she went. I was growing like a heat-seeking missile

on my way somewhere I did not belong. I wondered, Where was I going
so fast? I said goodbye to my friend, never expecting to see her again.

I filled up my thumb with a tank of gas and got a couple of long
rides. Near Sacramento, I was picked up by a farmer with a truckful
of honeydew melons. "I never had a honeydew melon," I said, so when
the farmer dropped me off, he got out of his truck and gave me one. I
carried it like a trophy all the way back home to Olympia. My mother,
sister, and I ate it the day I arrived. We took pictures that day, me with
my little sister and my spotted horse. I was glad to be home.

I did not think about heroin. In fact, I quit taking all drugs. No
more pot, no more LSD. I was not made for drugs, but heroin was
not done with me. We would meet again, waltzing in the ballroom of
Hell until the sun rose and set again, leaving my grandest dreams laid
to waste. For a while, but not forever.

Chapter 13

Turn Her Over
and Go . . .

FEATURING ME,

MY BANDS NAME.

I DID the ART WORK.

My early artwork ca. 1976

Mom thought I would stay with her in Olympia and work at Weyerhaeuser. We could do what she had always wanted to do, tour Europe.

I heard that Zachary was locked up at a California youth facility so I wrote him a letter. He seemed so lonely and needed someone to plan his life around. A few letters later, we planned to move in together. I was never sure why he ended up there but he was released on his eighteenth birthday and was waiting for me in Los Angeles.

Mom was extremely disappointed the day I left for California, but on my eighteenth birthday I caught a jet out of town. I wound up in a three-bedroom Newport Beach house with Zachary, Zachary's father, and his father's business partner.

Zachary's father did not like me. Two months later, the long unraveling of our relationship began.

It was a very cold New Year's Eve. We were in a coffee shop near Seal Beach to celebrate the new year. Zachary poured a pitcher of water over my head sometime around midnight. I caught bronchial pneumonia and had a dangerously high fever of 104 degrees. The sickness and malaise overcame me as I lay in bed:

"Zachary, you have to take me to the hospital. *Now.*"

His father protested: "Let him finish changing the oil."

When Zachary finally took me to the emergency room, the doctor looked at him: "Why did you wait so long to bring her?" He was referring to the week before the oil change. I was done with this situation. I told Zachary he could stay or return but I was going back to Olympia. Unfortunately, it was a week before I was well enough to travel home. More unfortunately, Zachary came back with me.

My mother disliked Zachary one degree more than his father disliked me. Mom was tough.

Zachary had no experience with animals. He was touched by my easy way with them. He tried to lie with them in the middle of the afternoon.

"Why is he out there lying by the horses? He looks like an idiot," Mom said. "I hope one of them steps on him."

"Mom! He just wants to feel a part of us. Feel like someone likes him."

Then I laughed. "The horse is about as good as it's gonna get around here." Mom was funny, yes, but she left me no choice but to defend him. That was both our mistake. Maybe he *was* an idiot, but I felt sorry for him.

This was the pattern that would plague me throughout my life, the inability to hurt a lover's feelings by saying, "This is not working" or more precisely, "I don't want to be involved in your trouble" or simply,

"This thing is over." If I did not value the other person's feelings before my own, I was not a good Catholic and this religion was the basis of my morality. I sacrificed my own plans for whomever I was with long after the affection had ended.

Many men of 1972 used the new "women's freedom" as an excuse for brutish behavior. Traditional gender-based rituals such as a man opening a door for a woman were discounted by the women's movement because they implied women couldn't open their own doors. Men used this as an excuse to not offer even the simplest of courtesies. Many of the guys I knew used the movement to do as little as possible for women.

Zachary and I found a tiny bungalow on Martin Way. We were trying to be a family but with nothing to do and nowhere to do it. We sat in coffee shops or drove up and down Interstate 5 while Zachary serviced the gas stations with bootleg cassettes filed in the back of his panel truck. I thought it amazing that truckers listened to the Mahavishnu Orchestra bootleg. It really sold quite a lot.

I probably was already pregnant in Orange County but by the time I found out I was sick. Mom was not talking to me (she was boycotting Zachary) so I could not ask her for anything. I had no help, friends, or money and I badly needed advice. By March I was vomiting all the time so I didn't care much when Zachary brought home a couple of hitchhiking girls. Let them stay the night, take them to a better on-ramp in the morning.

I lay down for a nap and when I woke up later and walked into the living room, the father of my unborn child was on top of one of the girls while the other girl sat on the couch watching television. That did it. Ten minutes later they were back on the freeway. I told Zachary that I was getting an abortion. There would be no family for us.

The trip to the newly legalized abortion clinic by Sea-Tac Airport in Seattle was silent. Not even Crosby, Stills and Nash would sing today. It was hard on me but not nearly as hard as it would have been if I had not gone at all, or had to go to some horrible house in Shelton for an illegal abortion. Abortion had just been legalized but it had the air of illegality on top of the overwhelming shame. There were many patients in the waiting room, all of them trying to be invisible. So many accidental pregnancies. So many hitchhikers, so many Zacharies and Rickies.

In the doctor's exam room the nurses were friendly and animated. They turned on a vacuum cleaner, then the doctor began the procedure. I felt tissue rip away. Too much. They tore me. Blood. Something went wrong.

Back home I cried and I cried and then I cried again, but I was also relieved. Thank God. A few days later I was still bleeding, which was normal, but when I did not stop bleeding three weeks later, then four, then six weeks later, I returned to the emergency room again and again at Evergreen Hospital on Black Lake Road.

It was the third time I'd come back for the bleeding and this time they were ignoring me. Finally, after two hours in the waiting room, a doctor came marching down the hall, blustering and furious. He examined me once again but this time he said, "You keep coming here wasting my time. I can't help you. Go home and don't come back."

I was stunned. The female nurse who was watching attempted to cover for him by saying, "He's only slept a couple hours." I went home and continued to bleed. We had nowhere to turn, and staying put was to watch my life trickle out of me.

Zachary decided to try his luck in Chicago where his dad had moved and said Zachary could have a job. We climbed into the panel truck and drove across the floodplains of Washington State, the grasslands of Montana, and the Badlands of the Dakotas. We drove past the hotels to stay in campgrounds. The desolation fit the mood. I was sorry I came. I was still bleeding and my cervix, my belly, hurt all the time. Isn't it sad what poverty makes of us?

I was living like a refugee. It was all I knew, this bleeding and disrespect, helplessness and shame. Had life always been this way?

As we pulled into the Chicago suburb where Zachary grew up, we finally got a motel and slept. In the morning Zachary called his father, at least he might give us some money to pay for the motel and maybe even to get our lives together.

> *How does it feel?*
> *To be on your own*
> *With no direction home*
> *A complete unknown*
> *Like a rolling stone?*
> (Bob Dylan, "Like a Rolling Stone")

I was such a long way from the barkers and the colored balloons.

> *You can't be twenty on Sugar Mountain*
> *Though you're thinking that you're leaving there too soon*
> *You're leaving there too soon.*
> (Neil Young, "Sugar Mountain")

But innocence is just a dandelion, and it blows its beauty away at the slightest breeze. Still, tiny seeds find their way to other parts of your life. Perhaps you will find that you can never really erase your innocent self from the story.

The Ballad of Officer Larry Miller

Whatever Zachary and I thought we had in common, it dissipated there in the ugly suburban landscape. His father's poisonous voice summoned him to lunch on the condition that he not bring me. Zachary said, "I'll bring you back something."

Walking around the neighborhood, I was trying to keep the motel in view so I could scurry down there when Zachary came back. I climbed up a small embankment to get a perspective on my future life as it would unfold on Zachary's return. He pulled up with his father. They were arguing. This would be my future.

Zachary went into our room, then came out with his arms folded. He went back in the room and put our bags in his father's trunk. He walked to the sidewalk and he looked up and down the street. He stood now, his hands on his hips, his father gesturing for him to go. Hey, look up! Here I am! Why was I playing this game? Because I wasn't going to scurry after him. This time he'd just have to wait for me. He didn't. He left me there and drove away with his father.

The decision was made for me. Good riddance. Then a terrible realization came over me. I had no money, no clothes, nothing. I waited an hour, maybe more, but he did not come back. I was still hemorrhaging. Sad, scared, and yet somehow I felt incredibly liberated. I felt a little saucy. Here I was again: me. All by myself. If I had nothing, what had I got to lose? Heartache and pain was the satisfying answer.

A policeman drove by and I waved my arms at him. He pulled over for the hippie girl.

"My boyfriend left me here and I'm stranded."

I explained to him what had happened. How Zachary's father was Jewish and I wasn't good enough for his boy. That story. They left me, and no, I had no phone numbers, no address, and no money.

His partner was mute. Officer Miller said some numbers to his police radio thingy. "Let's go into the motel and look around the room." Nothing there and no sign of a crime. At the desk: "The older man paid cash for the room but only for one night and it's past checkout time."

In the car I decided to tell him that I was unwell. The words tumbled out: "I'm bleeding, I can't stop bleeding." Sigh. "I had an abortion months ago and I'm still bleeding." When privacy and self-esteem become unaffordable commodities, a person will say anything and everything in the first minutes of meeting someone who grants them any courtesy.

Officer Miller actually said to his partner, "I'm going to help this girl," and to me he said, "Let's get you somewhere." First, we went to the station house where his partner got out of the car. The station was like a clubhouse where all of the officers seemed to stop what they were doing and kind of wink at Officer Miller and the young hippie girl. He was unflustered, I was serious police business. He had the decency to see my situation not as another unsolvable human tragedy but as a problem he was qualified to address. He did not see "hippie" or any other word that might separate and quantify and allow folks to withdraw when they should offer a hand. He let his humanity speak for itself.

Officer Miller called his wife and then a doctor he knew. He let me call my mom. She moaned sympathetically and said she would buy me an airline ticket home. That would not be easy, as she'd have to drive to Seattle's airport.

Still in uniform, Officer Miller took me to a hospital where a doctor listened to my story. Shaking his head he said, "Since you've had everything else, I'm going to prescribe something usually used for allergies, but maybe it will help you." Then Officer Miller took me to a pharmacy and purchased my medication out of his own pocket.

Next, he called a woman he knew at a Salvation Army shelter for young runaway girls. I was a year older than the cutoff age for the shelter but she had a space, and she would allow me to stay for one night. One was all we needed. Back at the police station, Officer Miller said, "Call your mother back now." Mom had purchased a flight for me to Seattle the next day. Officer Miller had fixed it all. His day complete, he put on his street clothes and we headed for downtown Chicago.

Right in the middle of downtown was the small Salvation Army shelter for runaway kids. Officer Miller handed my medication to the young woman who greeted us there and said to me, "I'll come back tomorrow and take you to the airport."

My room looked out over a dire city of dark lives. No bright lights here, no sweet home Chicago, just vacant parking lots abandoned even by the cars. I was trapped in the Salvation Army demilitarized zone, surrounded by crocodile men with hand grenades and mouths of spittle. They passed by my sanctuary in their filthy, stiff, stained coats, hoping to prey on some idiot child. Well, I mean, I thought it looked that way at the time.

I was safe there in the Salvation Army, really safe. Safer than I had been in a long time. I had a bed and quiet where I could now think about the sadness of being alone. Zachary was an imaginary boy anyway, nothing like the boy I thought I had met two years ago when we were sixteen and life was new and Seal Beach was heaven.

In the morning I woke up and there was no more blood. The medicine had worked. My old life was no longer draining from me and now I could start building a new life. Officer Miller wasn't working that day but he came in plainclothes for the one-hour drive to the airport. He jumped out of the car and actually opened my door for me. We walked together to the ticket counter, and then he walked me to my gate and said:

"You take care of yourself."

"Thank you."

"I would like to write to you and see how you're doing from time to time. Would that be alright?"

"Yes, that would be great. Yes."

I gave him my mother's address and I also promised to write as soon as I got somewhere.

"Okay, you're all set. Get on that plane and go home. Be happy and have a happy life." He left O'Hare probably feeling like I did, that I was going to be safe.

The offer of friendship is always precious, but the offer of kindness where others might have said "Serves you right" is a testament to the best qualities of human beings—qualities that few people actually ever achieve. I was privileged to meet one who did.

I was in line with my ticket, about to board the plane home, when the gate agent stopped me:

"You don't have any shoes."

Was there something she wanted from me?

"My boyfriend took all my stuff, long story."

"Well, you can't get on this plane without shoes."

The blood drained from my skull. Panic. I was so close. I protested, I cried, but that plane flew away without me. All the good efforts and sacrifices of extraordinary people came crashing down through the arbitrary action of a woman who did not know or care. I made it through the hell of compromised people only to get stopped by a pretty blue suit. I sat in a chair and cried. What would I do? I sat in another chair. The hours went by, the flights stopped, and the passengers disappeared. I walked up and down the empty airport for most of the night. I slept a little, then morning came. I had been there for twenty-four hours and had zero options, zero plans. I was going nowhere.

I kept going through the ticket line pleading for relief. They eventually told me not to come back. "We'll let you know if anything changes." It was heart-wrenching and it left a mark on me. I cannot fly now without great anxiety, without some part of me wondering, What will happen to me at the airport?

I panhandled enough money to buy a Snickers. Defeated, I called home collect. My mother heard my shoeless story and said, "Ohhh, that's ridiculous." She would buy another ticket and bring me home. It would take a day or so. Her consolation instantly restored my confidence and I regained my ability to think on my feet. I got another idea. Back then there was no internet or cell phone, just a mom and directory assistance to find the number of an old friend who was a reliable helping hand.

I had no money to make a long-distance call, so I called Mark Vaughan's number in Tulsa, Oklahoma, "person-to-person collect." It was the hippie's method of signaling to Mark that he could call me directly at the pay phone's number. This was way cheaper than accepting the person-to-person collect call. He recognized the game and we were happy to hear each other's voices.

He said, "Come to Tulsa. I'll buy your ticket. Come here now, we're having fun. It's summertime, girl. Go-karts and BBQ." I called my mother back collect and said, "I'm going to Tulsa! Mark is buying the ticket for me. Don't worry, I'll be home soon."

"What about your shoes?"

"Oh, I'm getting on that plane, even if I have to punch someone."

"That's my girl. Sons of bitches. I wish I was there."

An American Airlines agent walking by me, responding to my question about the chance of getting on a plane today with: "My God, what are you still doing here? I've been watching you walking up and down the airport since yesterday." I told her my story. She looked astounded. "What flight was that? Who was that agent? Ridiculous. For Christsakes. We have a lost and found, I'm sure you can get shoes there. I don't know why no one took you there and found you a pair of shoes."

I was on my thirty-second hour of trying to get out of O'Hare airport when that same agent who had barred me from boarding the plane saw me again. This time in shoes. She knew those shoes belonged to someone else but she had nothing to deny the hippie girl from boarding this time.

On the plane, I sat between a nun and an Oklahoman in a ten-gallon hat. They were both praying over their cream cheese canapés so I thought, Why not? and bowed my head. Thank you for letting me get on this plane. Please don't crash it now.

"I love all the clouds," I said to the nun, "but I'm also afraid of crashing."

"I am never afraid," interrupted the cowboy. "We are always in God's hands."

The nun and I exchanged looks, we were not so sure about the cowboy's command of aeronautics or math (faith plus jet equals safety), but ninety minutes later I landed in Tulsa.

Twenty-Four Hours from Tulsa

Mark met me at the airport in Tulsa with his Southern-Baptist, nineteen-year-old Oklahoma gal. She was jealous of me the moment she saw me. I don't know why, maybe it was my new shoes. I, on the other hand, thought she was beautiful, all hair, like Bobbie Gentry.

We spent that summer racing those summertime go-karts, eating BBQ short ribs and BBQ long ribs and anything else we could sink our teeth into. We drove up and down the highways of Oklahoma, long drives with oil rigs pumping in a relentless visual monotone. Little towns came and went, nameless grey ground beneath the cowboy moon of blue over blue. There was droning noise between horizons. If I wasn't careful I could slip on the Oklahoma shade and not be seen again.

Merle Haggard was very popular there "cuz he didn't smoke marijuana," but we sure wished we did. Today, it might be fine to say the song was a joke, but Merle sure didn't act like it was a joke back then. The war between the "Okie from Muskogee" and the hippie raged on that summer. Even as it was happening, my month in Tulsa felt like a long-ago dream, the sleepy cadence of pages turning as the bedtime story faded into unconsciousness. Nothing happening at all. I saw a building on fire. I saw a red 1956 Lincoln convertible coupe. It was that certain stillness before the real performance begins. California.

As August wore on, Mark prepared to move back to Los Angeles. His girlfriend didn't seem on board with the plan anymore. She was now jealous *and* angry, or maybe she was just afraid to leave Oklahoma. She relinquished her seat as girlfriend, and I sat right down next to Mark on the passenger side of a VW Bug.

Mark's plan was to drive the distance in twenty-four hours straight. No sleep, no rest, barely time for bathroom breaks. We changed the VW's oil, cleaned the windshield, and topped off the gas tank. Mark packed up the car with his stuff and half-filled the glove compartment with all my worldly possessions. We yee-hawed it out of Merle Haggard's land of "living right and bein' free." Like so many Okies for so many generations before us, we hit Route 66 and headed west to the promised land of California.

Driving through the Oklahoma Panhandle into New Mexico, we hit Albuquerque at dawn. A "five-minutes-only" gas and restroom stop there, a Dr. Pepper and a cup of coffee to go, hurry hurry, then back into the passenger seat. Mark had refilled the tank. He was waiting. Five minutes? Six. Okay, okay.

Woowoo! As the morning sun rose behind us, it warmed every rock and dune and cactus and lizard skin while illuminating our path. I will always remember that two-lane highway on the western slope of that flat little town. Which, obviously, had no slope at all.

We were on the western side of Arizona by midafternoon. This time I managed to keep the car on the road. I drove a short while through the desert where I had once been a wild thorn. Mark and I smoked cigarettes, drank cold drinks, and played games to pass the miles. The alphabet game was fantastic. We started looking for "A's" in Arizona and ended following a "Q" outside Palm Springs.

Date palms and a giant plaster T. rex once ruled the great deserts of Palm Springs. It was so fabulous seeing that T. rex rise out of the sand, the only thing motorists saw for many miles. It is still there today but now chain food stores hide it from view. Hard to imagine that someone built life-size dinosaurs in the middle of the desert, just for fun—and this wonderful sight has thrilled kids stuck in back seats for decades. I thought of how many times before I had marveled at that creature as the Joneses sped by in our 1959 Pontiac.

We found some "Z's" somewhere outside Riverside. Finally Mark pulled off Interstate 10 and took us into Venice Beach, late in the afternoon. It was as Mark planned it, twenty-four hours since we left Oklahoma, twenty-four hours of memories stuffed into a VW Bug. We had come West, like pioneers, and we had left our past behind. Mark took the alleyway to Horizon Avenue and parked right by the boardwalk. We had arrived.

Exhausted and thrilled, we climbed out of that Volkswagen wet with sweat, and slowly trudged up a flight of stairs to Debbie's apartment. She opened the door and smiled, kind of. "Don't leave your stuff down there, it's not safe." Debbie helped Mark with the bags and we all sat down on the couch. So, there we were in Venice Beach, California.

Chapter 14

Doyt-Doyt–
Venice Beach

Mark Vaughan and me

V enice Beach wasn't always the overcrowded marketplace of
humanity it is today. This was the "before" picture. Venice
was once a paradise of canals and gondolas, modeled after
the original city of Venice. By 1970, the neighborhood was an abandoned story, left by somebody who ran out in the middle of a sentence.
Everything about the boardwalk was "left over." The only place open
for food, or anything else, was the hot dog stand next door, run by a
couple female entrepreneurs. Debbie bought us chili dogs which were
the best, absolutely the best chili dogs I ever had (or ever would have).
I was four-states hungry and still completely broke.

Debbie's apartment was full of books and skis and strangely, in the middle of the living room, was a Volkswagen engine. With a VW manual as her guide, Debbie had disassembled and then reassembled it, to teach herself how to take care of her own car's engine so that men couldn't run her around anymore. Pistons and nuts and screws were labeled and numbered.

I was intrigued. Here was a woman who had decided to understand and capture the world around her. She was making a life of her own. She came from the same place as Zachary but she had escaped her family. She did not need a man to tell her what an engine did and she was not beholden to any past. She bought skis! She was going skiing as soon as she rebuilt that engine!

"She wants to go skiing down a mountain laughing like an idiot," wrote Woody Allen in *Play it Again, Sam*, and that image played in my head as I thought of Debbie Herman skiing.

Debbie brought a pillow and a blanket for me to sleep on the couch. I slept so well that night. Mark joined Debbie in her bedroom, so I was the third wheel. As usual.

The next night as I crouched among her books, Debbie peered at me from the hallway and said, "Have you read that?" I was holding James Joyce's *Ulysses* and said, "No. I can't really read very well. My mind wanders. I can't concentrate."

"Try this," as she handed me something called *Slaughterhouse-Five*.

I opened it up. Billy Pilgrim had come unstuck in time, Hmm. What was this? I read on, curious about the beginning. I knew how it felt to be unstuck in time.

I couldn't sleep that night because I was engrossed in reading the book. Sometime after midnight I dozed off, eager to start again in the morning. Kurt Vonnegut had reached me there in Venice. Billy Pilgrim was powerful enough to overcome the wandering mind that had kept me from reading continuous pages. In Debbie's living room, my life began to change—*I* began to change. I was a plant that had finally found the sun. Green was glowing all around.

Next I met Captain Yossarian of Joseph Heller's World War II novel, *Catch-22*. Oh, I loved Yossarian. *Catch-22* was a complex story, funny and thick with characters. I like characters, they're in my lyrics. The type was small but still my eyes navigated the pages. I liked reading! I could read books at last! I would be able to talk with people about them. I had read *Slaughterhouse-Five* in three or four days and now I was on my second book.

The third book Debbie handed me was *On the Road*, by Jack Kerouac. That one didn't move me so much. While Kerouac was declaring the virtue of the guy parking the cars, I was watching a twenty-one-year-old girl disassemble a car engine in her living room. Besides, I'd traveled by thumb for years and my family were on the road for as long as I could remember. I understood Jack Kerouac because I lived, and then surpassed, Jack Kerouac. And I didn't really like his literary style. Three books and already I was a critic.

Outside Debbie's apartment and library was an equally exotic adventure in the unique space and time that was Venice in 1973. The local theater, the Fox Venice, was our Mount of Olives, the holy land and community meeting place where legends were born. Divine (from *Pink Flamingos*) and Goldie, two famous transvestites, regularly appeared there. The now-legendary Mystic Knights of the Oingo Boingo called the Fox Venice home. The best of cinema could be found behind that big velvet curtain. While the rest of L.A. was watching *The Waltons*, we had *Cousin Cousine*, *Mean Streets*, *Performance*, *Children of Paradise*, and *Night of the Living Dead*.

The urban legend of a topless beach stems from 1974, when a few of us girls lay topless in the sand. It was convenient, right at the end of my street. Not convenient for anyone else (the traffic was jammed for a mile) trying to get a peek at some Beach Boob.

Bluesman "Uncle Bill" and I busked together. Oh, it was a great time to be young in Venice. We had *our* breakfast diner and *our* best bar. It was *our* town.

And just like that, I belonged.

The beachfront was a bleak landscape, a mile-long strip of board-ed-up oceanfront. A few small groceries at the north end served a very select clientele of synagogues and tenements. Ancient people with numbers tattooed on their arms sat on benches and passed the time speaking Yiddish to each other. They were Nazi concentration camp survivors. Black men pounded congas every afternoon in drum circles by the sand. How did so many survivors end up here on the Venice Boardwalk? Same way as me, I supposed. We were a band of refugees. Old and young, Black and white, à la carte and prix fixe.

It's hard for me to remember just how Mark and I became a couple. Was it back in Tulsa? I don't think so. Was it after Debbie or before Debbie? It doesn't matter, we moved in together and lived in Venice for the next three years. Mark and I lived in the east corner apartment at 21 Westminster, an elegant, redbrick beauty with an ivy-covered garden door. It is still there today much as it was. Our building had memorable characters on every floor, but the teenage lovers down the hall, Cici Brown and Nick Mathe, would figure into my life for many years. Britt Leach the actor was there and next door, Dennis Dean, Canadian hockey fan and divorcé, was my new best friend. Next to him, the bisexual bartender who kept both a girlish-looking boyfriend and a boyish-looking girlfriend in his bedroom. Couldn't make up his mind, I guess. It was a fun building.

Sexuality was being redefined right there at 21 Westminster and every apartment in Venice was sticking to that new premise. "Nothing is true, everything is permitted." *Performance* with Mick Jagger was playing at the Fox in Venice, and this notorious line became my personal maxim. Meanwhile, a mile inland, the Crips were just beginning to take form. They had very real interpretations of what was permitted. Soon the living brotherhood that was Venice would come to an end. The uneasy peace and brotherhood between Black and white dissolving into a disco ball of cocaine and addiction.

I became a fixture in Venice, skipping barefoot along the board-walk with my long blonde hair and still no bra. I played music on the boardwalk, bluegrass, soul, piano, anything. We felt a great life was coming and we waited at the imaginary train station every day. Me and Venice. Waiting.

Mark was now a graduate student at UCLA, working after school for his department head, pushing for his doctorate in economics. I'd help him grade papers. On weekends, we would get dressed up in our best hippie clothes and go to the movies or to our favorite Lebanese place in Westwood with pictures of Danny Thomas over the bar. We lived on food stamps and school grants.

I got a job at Mr. T's Rental in Culver City, a business that advertised on soul radio stations, renting televisions to the Black community. Mr. T had two gun-toting repo men on minimum wage. It was tough, dangerous work, pushing their way into houses to take back those televisions. Try wrestling a four-hundred-pound console out of Grandma's house while an angry grandson tries to physically "dissuade you," and babies are crying, sisters are hollering. I think the repo guys liked the adrenaline.

I had been bonded to get the job so I was surprised when they fired me after six weeks. I never knew why people fired me but I got fired from nearly every job. I never understood my effect on people. But the first step to the top of my budding superstardom was out Mr. T's back door.

Me and Mr. Jones

My next job was at Mr. Jones' pub on the boardwalk. I'd gone to check out this new bar and heard, "Come on in" over Marvin Gaye blasting from the jukebox. The owner was a handsome bearded Black man who looked very much like Marvin Gaye on the cover of *Let's Get It On.* I was hired on the spot as a bartender. Problem was, I was only twenty years old. I would not be twenty-one for months.

Mr. Jones was hitting on me daily. I could see his mounting frustration and I was concerned. Mr. Jones's wife came in more than once with a black eye and bruises. I quit my job after a month because I was afraid of what he would do if he got busted because his lady bartender was underage.

The radio had taken a turn for the worst pap: "Seasons in the Sun," "I Honestly Love You," "(You're) Having My Baby." I could not understand how this crap was all the radio offered when great music was right down the road in the form of Marvin Gaye, voice of morality and reason in this last-ditch epoch of white-man hedonism. He brought a social message when no one else was bothering. Marvin Gaye was musical salvation, creating invisible bridges across society's boundaries with pure soul music and joy. I was also crossing those bridges every time I sang along with him, "Who are they to judge us, simply because our hair is long?" Marvin Gaye, the gentleman revolutionary.

It was just before my twenty-first birthday, Mark threw me a surprise party. Mark, Nick, Cici, and I were playing pool at Mr. Jones' pub. Marvin Gaye was singing "Make me wanna holler," as I was dancing by the pool table drinking burgundy wine, lining up my shot. "Father, father, we don't need to escalate, you see, war is not the answer for only love can conquer hate . . ."

I noticed a long-haired bearded guy in an army jacket looking through the window. Ten minutes later, the police had stormed the place, arresting Cici and me for being underage in a bar. It was a birthday I would never forget, for its exaggeration of struggle between hippie kids and the establishment. There was no good reason for the police to raid Mr. Jones' other than the fact that it was owned by a Black man. Plenty of bars had far more sinister goings-on than a couple of twenty-year-old girls playing pool for a buck a table.

My mother sent me a letter from Officer Larry Miller asking how I was doing. I told him I was going to school and thanked him again for his kindness to me that day in Chicago. There's truth in the common saying, "no good deed goes unpunished," because when we are down and out and we accept help, we feel grateful for the hand up. However, when we get back on our feet, we are embarrassed that *anyone* saw us down there, and we treat our former savior as an unwelcome guest.

When we meet again introduced as friends
Please don't let on that you knew me when
I was hungry and it was your world.
                    (Bob Dylan, "Just Like a Woman")

Officer Miller's kindness to me was the tiniest weight that tipped the scales of my destiny. He not only helped me but he offered me dignity in a year of my life when I had none at all. Officer Miller was a stand-up guy, a gentleman in a world of bums.

Mexico, 1976

I took a train to Mazatlán, Mexico, with an iron sculptor named Norman. When we arrived he went off alone and I stayed in town where I met Jose Pena, a tall and terribly handsome Ricardo Montalbán kind of guy. "You look like a native in those sandals," he called to me as he walked behind me along the seawall. I turned and smiled. We continued walking along the seawall together to watch the cliff divers. Before long Jose and I were laughing and flirting as he walked me back to my hotel. I was startled when he told me that natives were not allowed to enter. "This is Mexico," he explained. "I'll wait for you out here."

I moved into his little house next to the dump a few days later. His living room was filled with large, stretched canvases and oil paints and brushes. His bathroom was full of tarantulas, bigger than your hand, hairy, slender, and grey. The tarantula family claimed the shower area, living dangerously near the hot and cold handles. I would turn on the cold water, then they would charge me if I tried to add some hot water. The novelty of the whole thing was thrilling.

When we went out to eat, Jose knew most of the locals. I recall so well the mariachis singing the plaintive "Cucurrucucú Paloma," a song I still adore. Jose would go free diving and bring lobsters up from the bottom of the sea, carry them home, and there by the garbage dump we ate lobster and drank fresh smoothies made of milk, banana, and an egg right out of a local chicken. It was a weird paradise. I thought maybe I would stay there and have babies, never return to the hard choices that awaited me back in the U.S.A.

Jose's family owned a shoe store in Mazatlán so they had a little money. Jose had spent many years living in Texas with a gringa wife so he understood American customs and his English was great. It was obvious that his family didn't like me, or maybe they didn't like Jose's preoccupation with American girls. Another gringa. Why does our Jose keep bringing home these American women? The answer was simple: Mexico was his birthplace, but it was not his home. He had successfully migrated to the United States but was kicked out after his divorce. He had been trying to get back home to Texas ever since and to him, "gringa" translated to "green card." I didn't mind. It was hard to believe that he was imprisoned in this godforsaken place when all he wanted to do was live in America.

I got a serious ear infection from swimming in the ocean so I decided it was time to go home. I'd planned to return, but then there was the abduction. That may have tilted the scales against a life in Mexico.

I was almost raped and killed when a cab driver drove me to the jungle and demanded I take off my clothes. As I started to remove my shirt, a miracle happened. A bus full of Federales appeared and parked next to us—out there in the middle of the jungle! An angel sent them, obviously. The would-be rapist and I looked at each other and knew we were in some divine plot far larger than the one he had in mind. Yes, he drove me back to where he picked me up. I did not tell the Federales because I was not sure if they were more dangerous than the rapist. And just like that, I took the train back to America.

Mark Vaughan and I ended a few months after I returned from Mexico. Just . . . ended. The hours of our time were over. I had grown out of him at last. It was a sad goodbye. Yet Mark was always there for me. I could always count on him to fetch me when I ran out of gas, loan me a ten-spot when I was low. I often visited our cats and sometimes I'd stay the night in a platonic sort of way.

Perhaps we grow out of people like we grow out of shoes. They become uncomfortable, too loose or too tight. We remember how much we liked them at first, but now they just don't fit. There is no use saying hello backstage. We would not remember why it had ever mattered so much. A sad glance, just enough to break the heart. No, best leave it lie where it fell. It was good, our journey together, but then we crossed a bridge, and it was over.

I Meet Sal Bernardi at the Comeback Inn

By 1976, just after my twenty-first birthday, I started hanging out at the Comeback Inn. I was alone, Mark was not interested in jazz. I on the other hand was both interested in jazz and in developing my own little corner of life separate from Mark. I knew I could sing jazz standards because it was the music I grew up with. I started sitting in with the jazz bands that played there, singing "My Funny Valentine," "Since I Fell for You," "I Loves You Porgy." My generation was ignoring traditional jazz so there were no young singers in the house. Maybe the house musicians were skeptical about a young girl's jazz chops when I first stepped onstage but once they heard me sing "My Funny Valentine," they were knocked out. I could feel my father with me as I sang. I had something in jazz I would never have anywhere else: the voice of my grandfather, tradition.

I met many new and fascinating people at the Comeback Inn; Pamela, the African Queen, and Mary Simon, who came up to me and said she wanted to go to bed with me (interesting), and most important Sal Bernardi, who was playing piano for a couple mimes. They weren't very good but he was. In what would become a kind of initiation ritual into my closest friendships, Sal, Queen Pamela, and I sang "Jet Song" from *West Side Story* to each other in the courtyard of the Comeback Inn. We exchanged songs and adventures, and I thought

Sal was one of the most interesting people I'd ever met. He made me laugh out loud. Still does.

Sal was working at Nero's Nook pornographic bookstore in downtown L.A. The State of California brokered the job and by their calculation, Sal working the retail jail of a pornography store was better than Sal collecting any more welfare checks. Hilarious. So there was Sal behind the counter surrounded by dildos and inflatable dolls and such articles of sexual congress. I had never seen such exaggerated sexual fantasy on display. It was truly awful, the men lurking in the fluorescent lights. That was when I first realized that Steely Dan was more than just a very big band, it was also a very big dildo.

Sal had to yell at people to get out of the film room down the hall. Always the artist, he offered the film critic observation, "They sit in there and jerk off." Cleaning up cum and selling dildos, Sal's cost of living the California dream.

"A job's a job."

I didn't visit him there again but loved hearing his descriptive assessment of his life each time we spoke. His ordinary was exotic. He lived in a hotel paid for by the State of California. ("It's an old men's hotel with winos and accountants, and the halls smell like curry.") When I visited, the lobby was full of greasy men. I wondered what a young man like Sal was doing there among those old perverts anyway? How did he find these places?

Slipping through the cracks was Sal's speciality. He knew that by not being challenging, he would not be challenged. It made him a kind and gentle ladies' man. He always had a beautiful girl on his arm. Sal was so gifted in music but he preferred a second chair in life.

I lost track of him. Rumors of a commune in San Francisco, then points beyond. I had enrolled at Santa Monica College and was in a work-study job at school where I had access to a trunk line so I could call anywhere in the U.S. for free. One boring afternoon I tried a phone number for Sal that I had saved for over a year. A voice told me Sal had returned to New Jersey and gave me a new number. I called the number and he answered:

"Oh my GOD, I can't believe it! I was just talking about you and how you sing. I was telling my friend Joey here about how you sang, 'My Funny Valentine.'

"Hey Joey! That girl I was just talking about, she's on the phone.

"The best version I ever heard. Better than Ella. Maybe even better than Frank Sinatra. And here you are, calling me!"

A faint background shout, "Hello Rickie Lee Jones!" as Joey yelled in New Jersey-ese. "Hello New Jersey!" I shouted. I knew I would see Sal again.

DRIVER'S SEAT

Chapter 15

Easy Money

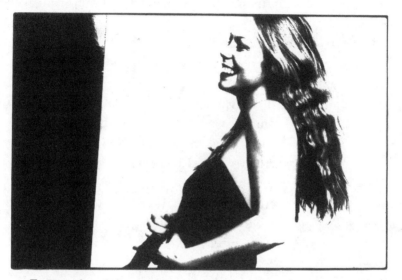

From my first photo session with Bonnie Schiffman at A&M Records

I n 1976 I got a job singing with a band in Venice that played their own music, à la the Grateful Dead. We had one gig playing for our locals on the boardwalk and we did a great job. I wore my best colored Levi's and a sleeveless vest. I guess this was my first live rock performance.

Then I became the "chick singer" in a country rock band called Easy Money. There were eleven of us and it was impossible for us to make any money.

Easy Money had only one gig in Bakersfield, and each of us had to work audience members for a floor to sleep on for the night. Walking around the next day with four of the musicians, I was treated to a pawnshop owner saying "nice tits," so I slapped him across the face. He slapped me back but none of the men I was with said anything or stepped up to my defense. This was the hippie version of equal rights that translated the gender-based courtesies into an absurdity, and said, "a woman has to stick up for herself without a man." I did get one thing out of it, though. I was inspired to write a song. I liked that phrase, "Easy Money."

The 1970s was the apex of the country rock scene, and Emmylou Harris was the Goddess. Linda Ronstadt topped the charts. I didn't sing country very well, always coming in late like a jazz singer.

I got a job with a disco band. We also had only one job, this time in Big Bear where I sang KC and the Sunshine Band covers for the weekend skiers who came to drink at the bar. There was better money in disco than in shitheel country bars. The musicians were accomplished, professional, and serious about getting paid. I was never going to be normal enough to keep a Top-40 gig. There was nothing *un*-special about me. I was glad when I got hired and got some experience, but I was happier when I got fired. This penny-ante circuit was going nowhere.

If I was going to break into the music business, I was going to have to learn something about the industry. I knew the only way in was through the unguarded back door because everybody was banging at the front door—sending demos, doing 8x7 black-and-whites. No, there was a way in already waiting for me if I could find it. But where was—and what was—the back door? I found mine soon as I started to look for it. A matter of timing, luck. If you wait for the right moment you will see what you are looking for.

I was at a friend's house browsing his albums when I came upon Randy Newman, *Good Old Boys*. This music was stunning. I read a name on the back cover and got a funny feeling: "Produced by Lenny Waronker." That sounded important. Lenny was where I needed to go.

The vision that came to me at that moment propelled me to find Lenny Waronker. It was as if the future had already taken place. I saw Lenny and I, we knew each other, worked together. In this premonition, I was in his office, standing on the other side of a large desk, talking to him.

I was supposed to find this man. He was the way *in*. I just knew it. Lenny Waronker was the back door to my future in music.

And so the vision came true. For Lenny kept a photograph of me on his desk until the day he left Warner Brothers. Indeed, I stood in a picture frame on the other side of his desk for many years.

I was broke and going to Suzanne's Kitchen on the boardwalk once or twice a week. I had maybe seventy-five cents to spare on coffee this week. Suzanne's was a small room with a couch and a piano, a kind of private house that Suzanne sometimes opened up to customers. I would stare at the piano, dying to play it, to touch it, but not having the nerve because Suzanne was kind of grouchy. Finally, one day I got up the nerve and started playing chords and then singing "Up on the Roof."

With my pencil and notebook, I would work and work, trying to develop interesting lyrics, or an idea that was uniquely mine. How to write a song using my love and feelings, my humor, my life, that wasn't just another love song about me me me? One afternoon in Suzanne's Kitchen, I began a story about other people's lives that touched the edges of adventures I had almost had. Imaginary people. I had found what I was looking for:

> *There was a Joe*
> *Leaning on the back door*
> *A couple of Jills*
> *With their eyes on a couple bills*
> *Their eyes were stating*
> *They were waiting*
> *To get their hands on some*
> *Easy Money.*

And what did he say when she asked him if he wanted to make a little easy money?

> *He say, "Yes! Oh Yes!*
> *Just tell me what you want me to do."*

With this lyric, I broke the ropes that had tethered me to other musicians' styles and the conventions of first-person love songs and replaced them with the strings of my own kite. At last I was writing from my imagination and it was flying. I changed the common "Jane" to "Jill," establishing an idiosyncrasy of my style to make a personal statement out of the common vernacular.

> *Saturday night there was a terrible, terrible fight*
> *Between two dames losing the same game*
> *It wasn't clear but I hear*
> *Somebody was looking for some*
> *Easy Money.*

Next I wrote "Weasel and the White Boys Cool," inspired by my time with Sal Bernardi.

> *Sal was working at Nero's nook in downtown*
> *Selling articles of congress to these people downtown*

Yeah, two gritty songs. I was a sexy girl and my sexuality was infused into everything I wrote. That's part of the magic. More goes into the words than what you intend.

I got a coveted job at the Great American Food and Beverage Company where I could wait on tables and *sing*. Every singer in town wanted to work there. Who wouldn't want to sing while they work? Important people chowed down in there (as if they would hire anyone off the floor). I met my longtime friend Katey Sagal there, she was then a blues singer and eventually became a very successful actress.

I started seeing Guy, a guitar player, and my first boyfriend since Mark. Guy was a "Clear" Scientologist. After I was fired from the Great American, we got an apartment together on one of the worst blocks of Hollywood; the XXX Western Avenue where the porno theaters operated.

This part of town was further from Venice than I had ever lived. The sidewalk was sticky with semen from porno marts, porno theaters, the porno billboards surrounding the once elegant apartment buildings. I would drive my orange Chevy Vega the one block to the laundromat just to avoid the jizz-coated intersections of Western and Hollywood. I mean it was lowdown.

Guy started treating me badly. He spoke condescendingly to me in private and public. He even questioned whether or not I had *really* written "Weasel." He was always auditing me.

I decided to do something about feeling beholden to him. I recognized that I could not sing very loud and that my voice did not have the power of my always-strong feelings. My voice was locked up too low in my throat. I read a book on singing.

At that laundromat of hell, right there on Hollywood Boulevard and away from the demon Guy, I studied the book. While my clothes were drying, I practiced in my portable rehearsal studio, my orange Chevy Vega. With my hand on my chest, "Lalalalala." Alone in my car I could make the huffs, growls, and sounds the lesson required. I had plenty of reasons to roll the windows up tight—I would have been embarrassed for Guy or anyone else to hear me making the growling, gurgling sounds I needed to conquer.

I rapidly improved. Now that I could push sound through my body, I could feel the difference when I sang. Mastering this one ability gave me confidence in my natural gift. As I got louder, my confidence rose. I had always been a good singer, now I could be a professional.

Little Caesar and the Romans

I got a call about an oldies band looking for a female backup singer. The band had a couple of hits in the early sixties. I was graduating from cover bands; it would be my first real professional gig. These were Black musicians who had experienced success and expected professionalism from me.

I didn't recognize their hit songs because they were before my time, but Little Caesar and the Romans had a 1961 hit called "Hully Gully Again" that piggybacked on the success of "Hully Gully," by the Olympics. They also had a hit with "Those Oldies but Goodies (Remind Me of You)," which was the perfect song for their gig at Art Laboe's oldies club down on the strip where all the greasers and old folks went to hear fifties songs. Old folks, you know, forty-year-olds.

Little Caesar and the Romans' success ended when their singer, David Johnson, went to prison for about fifteen years. It sounded serious enough to be murder but I wasn't going to ask. I got dressed in my best green Levi's and drove the Vega over to La Brea and Wilshire. I was going to audition for the part of a "Roman."

I heard, "Those oldies but goodies" coming from the door. "Reminds me of you," I answered before I knocked. "Hello!" as I entered. It was a roomful of Black men, and ahhhh, one young Black girl. Oh thank goodness, another singer. She was a plump girl with straightened hair who was already in the band.

"I've come for the audition, I'm Rickie Lee Jones."

The audition was being run by a compact man with a giant Afro. "Rickie Lee, I'm Jesse Lee Floyd. This is David, the leader of the group. Caesar, if you will. I do the choreography and costumes." Jesse Lee Floyd had rhinestones on his stone-washed, dry-cleaned, immaculately creased blue jeans. His Afro was as large as the state of Maryland. He commanded the room and he, only he, proceeded to get things going. He was the boss.

"Are you ready? Let's try some steps!"

He showed me a couple turns, a clap, a turn, a step, and then handed me my music. "Here's your part, Rickie Lee." I was always a quick learner of dance steps and harmonies although I could not read music.

"Can you just sing me the part? I'll hear the harmony." Even if I couldn't read music, I picked up music faster by ear than anyone could ever teach and I learned in one listen.

Jesse Lee said, "Can you sing this at the same time as you dance?"

They hired me on the spot, and gave me a small advance so that I could buy an outfit for the performance. I still have that black velvet pantsuit I bought from a tiny shop on the corner of Kingsley and Sunset. Jesse Lee told me not to worry, it was going to be great, and I felt like I fit in as a fellow professional. We had three more rehearsals, and that was that. We knew our steps and parts for our twenty-minute segment of the show. Oh, it was going to be fun.

On Saturday night we showed up at Art Laboe's club on the Sunset Strip for the big oldies extravaganza. There was a line of 1950s and 1960s acts doing their one big hit, but Little Caesar and the Romans commanded the stage with a half-dozen songs. Slow and mellow for "Oldies but Goodies," then we blasted out the finale, "Rollin', rollin', rolling on the river." Twirling around like Ike and Tina Turner's version of "Proud Mary." It was a good performance. Everyone felt happy and on a music high. I got paid, I really got paid!

I felt good that I got my steps right and I sang loud with vibrato, but what I remember most was Jesse Lee's decency, kindness, and consideration for me. Unlike most men in charge who prey on young ambitious female musicians, he respected me as a person and as a professional. He didn't hit on me, he didn't use me to affirm his status, and he put professionalism on display in areas I never expected. For instance, before the show all the musicians from all the acts were in one large room getting dressed. As happens backstage, there was zero privacy for anyone. Jesse always kept his eye on me, the newcomer: "Let's give Rickie some privacy, she's not used to this type of thing." He taped up a blanket he had fetched from another band so that I could dress in privacy. Jesse Lee was a stand-up guy.

Getting this gig on my own and writing "Weasel" and "Easy Money" had me feeling like there was some part of me that Guy could not run down. I had gained a secret power that only I possessed. I could take control of my life without Guy, Mark, or anyone else. After the show, I put on my street clothes and quietly walked out to my car, but I was a different girl than the Rickie Lee of before I got this job. I heard a voice from the theater:

"Rickie Lee, Miss Rickie Lee, wait a minute." It was Jesse Lee calling me back. "Are you leaving without saying goodbye? I know you're shy, but people might think you're snubbing them." And then he paused and carefully rethought the situation.

"I'm gonna give you my home number. If you ever need anything, if you're ever in trouble with anything, you call me. I'll be there." He handed me his card and handwrote his home number on the back. Also this: "Jesse Lee. If you are ever in trouble, call me."

His words stuck in my mind:

"If you ever need anything . . . If you are ever in trouble."

What did he see in my future that changed his tune from "Come celebrate with us" to "Call me when you get in trouble"? Who says stuff like that to a stranger? It meant as much as the gig to me. His card would mean the difference between a lifetime of success and a lifetime of . . . who knows what. Jesse Lee's words were in shiny gold leaf across the air, right there in my book of destiny.

After my Little Caesar gig I got a job waitressing at a pizza joint on Sunset called "Two Guys from Italy." The cook looked very familiar. "That's Salvatore Po, he doesn't speak English." The busboy smiled. "Just like he couldn't speak English in the *Godfather* movie. He played Frank Pentangeli's brother who comes from Italy to sit at the trial." Wow. Yes, that was him alright. I was getting closer to show business.

Things were not so good back at home. Guy seemed to be losing his mind. Too much pot, too much anxiety. His sexual appetites had become bizarre. He started putting on my dresses and makeup, then wanting to have sex. With me? You want to have sex with me in a dress? It was, well, it was interesting. No, to be honest it was humiliating. Maybe that was his point because one morning, in a jealous rage he beat me up.

He was sure I'd been with someone else the night before (because he had been with someone else the night before):

"Where were you all night?"

"Here."

"No you weren't. You weren't."

"I was."

"You weren't."

"What do you care where I was anyway? You were gone all night."

In the background I heard, "Get along, get along Kid Charlemagne." I had Steely Dan's album *The Royal Scam* on the record player while we argued. Maybe it was during Larry Carlton's guitar solo that I picked up Guy's guitar. Guy said:

"Put that guitar down. Put it down or I'll kill you."

I sat the guitar down. "Okay, okay."

He then picked it up and hit me in the kneecap with the little knob on the end of the guitar that holds the guitar strap. I immediately understood the verb "kneecapped." I couldn't walk so I couldn't get away from him. He started pounding on me. Beating me. It was the same sickening sound of big male fist against small female flesh and bone. I struggled to get out of the house but my knee failed at the top of the steps and I fell down a flight of stairs. I was battered and bruised, but it is hard to say which hurts more when someone you love hurts you: the physical pain or the humiliation. Or the shame when no one does anything to help you.

I hobbled down to a friend's house a couple blocks away and asked if I could stay the night. I had nowhere to go and it wasn't safe for me on Jizz Avenue:

"Guy hurt me, I need a place to come inside for a while. Please."

My so-called friend said, "I have troubles of my own" as he closed the door.

Remarkable. I waited around a while, who knows where. I had no options, I had nowhere to go. Just like Kenny-from-Berkeley's wife, I went back to Guy and my apartment. I knocked. He opened the door and let me back inside. That's what domestic violence does to its victims.

I tried makeup and clothes to hide my injuries but I went to work the next day with big black bruises on my neck and arm and multicolored bruises on my shoulder and breast. Orange, brown, and almost black. To bring even more attention to my bruises, I was limping. The Italians felt they had to fire me because it looked so bad for business—the blonde waitress beat up at the Italian place.

However, the brothers didn't abandon me, they had another job for me waitressing at the legendary Sarno's, which was just a few more bus stops away (Vermont Avenue, east of Hollywood near Griffith Park). Opera fans liked to come there and sing light opera, drink cappuccinos and espressos with lemon rinds. The place was a Los Angeles mafia café, with real Goodfellas snuggling into the booths and bossing the waitresses around. Maybe a bruised waitress worked to enhance their image. Alberto Sarno himself ended up murdered not too many years later. In another weird "L.A. is a small town" coincidence, one of his relatives was my seamstress during the *Flying Cowboys* tour. And that's entertainment! Finally one night when there weren't too many customers, I too sang a song. "I Left My Heart in San Francisco." Just keeping my hat in the ring.

I came home from work expecting an awkward conversation but instead Guy's friends came over and took Guy and his packed suitcase away from the apartment for a red-eye flight back to New York. Guy had secretly planned to return there without me and bought his plane ticket weeks before. He manufactured his entire accusation of my cheating on him and dealt me my subsequent beating to impart maximum physical and emotional hurt. It was his dysfunctional way of breaking up with me. He even enlisted his friends (formerly *our* friends) in his charade. I was silent as I watched them all drive away.

It was a hard, hard night for me but I finally fell asleep. In the morning I was startled by loud knocking on the door. The landlady. Angry. Holding the rent check, she said:

"Your check bounced."

"But I gave Guy all my money to pay the rent. He took all my money."

"You must leave. You cannot stay here now."

"Could I just stay one day? Give me some time to get myself together. I'll call my mom, get money sent."

"No. I'm sorry. When can you be out of here?" She wasn't sorry. She wasn't sorry at all. Nor was Guy—the beating was over, but the blows kept landing for days after.

I called my mother. I didn't want to. I wanted to be a grown-up, like she was, like Dad. People made it on their own, they didn't go back home. I was looking to find my dream in Los Angeles, or at least a decent life. I didn't wanna call home again, like I had in Chicago.

"Oh, Mama."

"I will find a way to get you a ticket. If you have to go somewhere and wait, call me collect."

Mom restored something in me just as she had done in that Chicago airport a few years before. I hung up the phone and collected myself.

I went through the papers and notebooks of my lyrics and lists and big ideas. I was looking for something but I didn't know what. Then I got more focused. Where was that phone number of Jesse who said if I ever needed anything . . . Where was his card? Piece of paper after piece of paper, I searched through my life. Finally, there it was. The way out. The way back. I was in a story. On the way to happy-ever-after. The phone number of Jesse, the Good Pimp.

The Good Pimp

"If you ever need anything . . . you call me. I'll be there."

I called the number. The phone rang. No answer. I went into the apartment to put my clothes in a bag and brush my teeth. I was long past the landlady's deadline. It was almost dark outside where I would have to survive the night. I called again. This time he answered.

"Yes, oh yes . . . Of course I'll help. What do you want me to do?"

He listened and then said, "Hang on, I'm coming to carry you outta there. Be there in forty minutes." Carry me out of here. Wow. Jesse was coming. I'd have a place to sleep. Would he want me to sleep with him? I'd never slept with a Black man. Would my mother get mad?

I was looking out my room's window at the landlady, who was looking out her window at me when a *golden limousine* pulled up on the curb. Right there, in front of my lowdown apartment building and lowdown landlady, came my savior. Out jumped Jesse Lee Floyd with his Afro and his platform shoes polished to reflect the sunset. He waited at the limo while his assistant rang my doorbell and carried my bag and banjo to the trunk of the limo. We drove off literally into the sunset, leaving my life with Guy, his monster friends, and the landlady with a heart of mud. Just like that it was over. The worst day of a terrible season until Jesse Lee came to deliver me somewhere better. My prince, in a gold Cadillac limousine.

Yes, someday my pimp will come!

Jesse had been a pimp long enough to know that all young ladies need a hand eventually. His game was to be there in time to catch the ones who couldn't be helped.

I stayed at Jesse's house for almost a month. Jesse never abused me or tried to turn me out. Well, not until the very end. He told me he was a pimp. I nodded my head as if he had told me he made macramé shoes and said, "Oh, that's . . . interesting. How does that work?"

Jesse showed me his route, taking me with him on drives to visit or collect money from his girls. Getting his clothes ironed and melting gold into necklaces. It was appealing, a life outside of a nine-to-five. I asked him all the questions that nobody would dare ask.

"Jesse, why do they give you their money?"

He said, "Say they wanna go home, see their family, I buy them some nice luggage, get them a plane ticket."

"Well Jesse, why can't they buy their own luggage?" He was getting irritated that I did not seem to be with the program. Jesse and I remembered that we had a professional music relationship, and so my time with the Good Pimp was over. The Western Avenue Cinderella story of 1976 ended and a new, much grander fairy tale was about to begin for me.

On my last day with Jesse, his assistant gave me a ride in one of Jesse's more inconspicuous cars, maybe a '74 Buick, back to the west side of town. As we turned down Rose Avenue and onto Sixth Avenue, the cops came up behind us with flashing lights. We pulled over and Jesse's assistant calmly said:

"Put your hands on the dashboard."

I said, "What?"

He said, "Please, put your hands on the dashboard where they can see them. They will shoot me if they wanna. Maybe you too. Show 'em your hands. Like this."

I put my hands on the dashboard and waited. He said, "Hello, officer, sir." The policeman was a young white man, flanked by a second who stood at my window. They both had their eyes on the Black man in the wig behind the steering wheel. They wanted to know who I was, where I was going, and why I was with this man. They asked him why we were in Venice and what he was doing.

I picked up on the danger here and realized it was not the time or place for my angry confrontational hippie-girl approach. I could not challenge their attitudes. I had no more rights than the Black man next to me. That was the lesson to be gleaned, everyone ends up with the lowest common denominator when racism replaces good police work.

I did not get my privilege, I got his exclusion. I realized we were both completely at the mercy of these cops. This was a much more dangerous version of the "white slavery" accusation that tripped up Amsterdam and I when we traveled across the Canadian border. I learned my civics lesson there, so I was a nice girl who politely said, "He's just giving me a lift, officer. I'm going to Horizon just a few blocks away."

Everyone involved knew the game we were playing, and there was nothing honest or truthful about pretending this wasn't about a white girl in a nice car with a Black man. It was hard for me to bite my tongue as I felt the wave of racial hatred from the cops. It left a coating on my skin, but the Black man at my side had worn that skin all his life. He wanted nothing more than to get as far away from me and my situation as he could.

"I'll get out here," I said. "Thank you for the ride."

I got out of the car and stood on Horizon Avenue with my banjo and my little duffel bag as that old Buick disappeared into the morning fog. He did not look back but I was home in Venice.

Chapter 16

Young Blood

Tom Waits and Chuck Weiss back in the day.
(Tom wears that shirt I bought him.)

They say this city will make you dirty but you look alright!
("Young Blood")

From September to November 1977 I crashed on the couches of people I met on Horizon Avenue. Yusef Rahman was one, for the next few months he employed me singing backup on demos he was creating. He introduced me to Jackson, another great singer on the demo circuit. We dreamed of becoming Steely Dan's new background singers as we waited to perfect our harmonies for Yusef's soul and disco productions.

Rita Carlyle was the wife of a singer in a well-known San Francisco band and she had a lot of connections locally. Rita said she would let me sleep on her couch for the week if I would give her singing lessons. In the lower echelons, little favors mean everything. Respect is currency. Even though homeless, I had a skill someone valued, and this was enough dignity to lift me, almost magically, up from the very bottom of my life. She soon kicked me out when our lessons bore no magic fruit. Had she not, I may have become another local hero, and never had the rocket fuel needed to jettison my life from the tiny capsule of circumstance.

Rita lived next door to the man who was to help me become a musician by trade, Ivan Ulz. Ivan was connected to famous musicians like Jackson Browne and Lowell George, he had been a neighbor to them ten years before, selling pot out of his ice cream truck. We met one morning as I was walking out of Rita's house. He was a fantastic, animated older guy, late thirties, personable and intelligent, thinning blond hair and electric blue eyes. He invited me in for coffee and I stayed for the next month.

Ivan and his roommate Christina became my escorts out of home-lessness and everything just happening to me, and into life as lifestyle. Culture. They were part of the mechanism of my future, everything fit-ting—pop! pop!—and right on time. This culture was not based on the pretense of wealth but on a shared literary, musical, bohemian way of life. History beyond my history. A world bigger than me. Christina turned me onto Edith Piaf and Colette, the Frenchwomen of the 1920s and '30s who knew no shame in their liberated sexuality. I could feel a new life turning, a thrill in every hour of the day, and a pressure, as if every move I made mattered. I needed to learn about Piaf even though she seemingly had nothing to do with Venice, 1977. I needed to fly to San Francisco just to drink a cappuccino, especially because I did not have a dime to my name. Fate was watching me. Christina hipped me to the "European style" hotel, a place poor people could live and feel like they were as worthy as anyone else (even though the bathroom was down the hall).

Ivan told me about his connections to Jackson and Lowell George, and said he would teach me all he knew about lyrics. He had been a lyricist all his life. Though his armor was a bit squeaky, I could have asked for no better knight when I was a twenty-two-year-old "damsel."

In fact, Sir Ivan knighted me "Twenty-two," and so that was my name for the rest of the year.

Ivan told me stories about the Beats. He knew a few of them ("Gregory Corso, bad guy") and we practiced dance moves from *West Side Story*. We discussed lyrical metaphor and delivering a simple idea without too many complicated threads.

Ivan loved children, he'd spent his life working in preschools. His parents were communists who owned a preschool in the 1950s San Fernando Valley, a sizzling hotbed of anticommunist rural rednecks. Ivan Ulz was a "red diaper baby," and in spite of the ridicule he'd received in school, he was determined to prove that life was an experience to be savored. For Ivan, dignity was not born but created by mastering one's own destiny, all the more poignant because he suffered from manic depression, or bipolar disorder, an illness at that time diagnosed and treated as schizophrenia. Perhaps his animation was due to the little tingling lights of too much serotonin. He was the brightest teacher I could have had, pulling me out of the terrible things that had happened that year, until I was lifted higher than when he met me.

I spent the weekends in San Francisco, walking down Market Street through Chinatown to the Caffe Trieste, feeding my soul on the chilly, ghost-drenched fog and the romantic trolley cars. I heard live jazz on every other corner in Chinatown, the upright bass players dragging their unwieldy instruments off the trolley to play a few standards with other great musicians, sharing the change dropped in a hat. More than once I stood in with those bands, singing "Bye Bye Blackbird," making a good impression. I wrote "The Real Thing Is Back in Town," a finger-snapping, street corner, a cappella song whose lyrics would bleed into "Coolsville" and become the promotional phrase used to launch Rickie Lee Jones before anyone had ever even heard of her.

For just the cost of an elegant cappuccino, my life was elevated to the life of my imagination. I became the old-fashioned girl in the beret, the sexy pinup dame in the gloves, the self-possessed woman I knew I could be. Why not? I was out there alone, no boy to escort me, why not become my own design instead of succumbing to what someone else saw? I *was* those things, all of them and more. Yes. A tough childhood had made me always see the ugly duck in the mirror, but that duck was changing. No swan dives for me! I was an eagle.

In the image of my mom's generation I found a containment and sophistication that I could not see in the Farrah Fawcett world around me. I looked different—*I was different*—and that was alright with me. I could hear fate humming the tune I was writing. She said the only way she had seen me was because I had stood out in a crowd, not blended in the way the rest of the kids did. She said the only reason she even existed, manifested, was because I had made her out of those lonely years. And she was in sight now, fuzzy, a great blue horizon where poverty would be forgotten and everyone in my family would be raised up.

And now everywhere I went I found music, musicians, and windows opening to musical skies. It seemed that the future was inviting me but only if I entered through the door marked "music."

I got a gig of my own, performing at a new place on West Washington called the Skylight. If I could get the musicians, I could have the Saturday night spot. Armed with a few of my own songs like "Easy Money," and "Weasel and the White Boys Cool," as well as some choice standards like Paul Simon's "American Tune" and John Prine's "Angel from Montgomery," I managed to fill two sets, two hours until my bassist Duke McVinnie brought some local musicians. Together, we killed the last set with Ray Charles's version of "Makin' Whoopee," "Louisiana" by Randy Newman, and "The Heart of Saturday Night" by local hero, Tom Waits. Finally, we closed with the song my father wrote back in 1954, "The Moon is Made of Gold." I had done it. An entire Saturday night as Rickie Lee Jones, four sets and a paycheck.

I was able to sublet a furnished apartment on the other side of Montana Avenue—where the rich people had always lived. It was not merely a better side of town, I felt as if I had been invited to the better side of life. I got another job too, and things that were unimaginable when I left Mark a year ago were now presenting themselves to me as if for inspection of possible direction.

Rocky the Gangster

I found my job by pounding the pavement just as my mother told me to do. Hit every door on the street, someone will be looking for an employee. Sometimes it took all day but I always found a job (although I usually couldn't hold onto it.)

Rocky the Gangster hired me on the spot as a receptionist and secretary. I sat in the front office of a small business typing up orders. That typing class back at Elma High School was paying off at last. I didn't get fired, exactly, but it was my last "straight" job.

Rocky was a polyester leisure suit guy whose garters held up his silk stockings. He showed me his money clip early one morning and then showed me more money stuffed into something near his shoes. That's how I saw the garters. He also had a pistol in the drawer. He made sure I saw that, too.

He always wanted me to sit on his lap, and sometimes when I was too tired to insist otherwise, I did. "You want this job or don't you?" Looking at him like he was a creep, I liked to think I shamed him, but he was probably without shame. Then he'd let me get up and go back to my desk.

My main job was managing the shipping. I typed up the forms but more importantly, signed for whatever Rocky was shipping into and out of that office. Sometimes there were ten boxes, sometimes just one per day, so I had hours with nothing to do. I was happy to sit in the reception office by myself, typing away, looking busy. Actually, I was writing lyrics. My songs loved being written on that fantastic new electric IBM typewriter. The clicking of the keys made writing seem so official. I needed that. I worked for maybe two months in Rocky's office. It was exactly what I needed. I got paid and had plenty of time to write lyrics. I enjoyed the self-esteem of being employed. It meant someone valued me for what I could do at a time when I really needed to feel valued. This is where I wrote the lyrics to "Young Blood" and "Company."

Across the street from our office was a row of beautiful old cars parked on the sidewalk, a 1954 Chevy, 1955 Chevy, 1957 Lincoln, 1959

Cadillac, a 1962 Galaxie. I asked about the soft yellow Lincoln. "Eighteen-hundred dollars." I began to imagine what it might take to buy that car. It was that very car that would end up in *Pirates*, that I would cruise around with Tom Waits and Chuck E. Weiss in its sassy driver's seat.

Like in a Greek fable, the job with Rocky the Gangster had one unbreakable condition: I was forbidden from entering the packing room. I ended up breaking this "Follow or Die" rule one day when the knob turned and I accidentally opened the forbidden door. Oops. When it opened, the young guy who worked for us was on his knees taping up a box. I couldn't see the contents but he looked up at me and hissed, "What are you doing, you aren't supposed to be here." He rose threateningly.

"Oh yeah, I'm sorry, I had to"—hmm why did I open that door?—"ask, uh, a question." I felt a hot flash.

"Close the door and don't tell Rocky you opened it. And don't you ever open that door again."

I closed the door and hurried back to my desk where I took out a consolidated shipping form and click-clicked the typewriter keys: "One Box. San Jose." Signed: "Rickie Lee Jones." It was my signature on all those orders. That's what they were paying me for. In their minds, I was a layer of legal protection to shelter everyone in that office. Rocky told me I got my easy job because they couldn't type. Clever gangster.

I returned to my lyrics . . .

> *I and Bragger, we "borrowed" a coupe today*
> *Here comes*

I thought of the nickname Pepe and had a spark: why not give it to a girl? If I had a boy's name, my character could have one too. I was giving this Mexican girl a boy's name.

> *Here comes Pepe—she's got a friend in a Chevrolet*

Uh-huh.

You never know when you're making a memory
They will wish they were here together again, someday

"I and Bragger"—it was like the line from *West Side Story*: "I and Velma ain't dumb." No one used that vernacular. It had atmosphere. If I used that line people would know I came out of *West Side Story*.

One day the sheriff came and stood at the front door telling me that Rocky owed money and he was shutting us down. The sheriff was right, Rocky stiffed me on my last check. I was living paycheck-to-paycheck and Rocky was like all guys who like to show you their wads of money; they are all show, no go.

I applied for unemployment insurance and called my mother: "Mom, I'm thinking about quitting music. I'm just not getting anywhere and if it fails I won't have any skills to fall back on. I can take a course to become a stenographer, it doesn't take very long."

Things had been going better, so when I fell, I fell further. It seemed as if they would never go my way. Getting closer to the mountain had made the mountaintop seem unreachable. What had I been thinking? Who did I think I was?

"You want to be a court reporter?" my mother asked.

"Yeah, it pays pretty well. Sitting in a courtroom."

"I don't see you doing that."

"I don't want to be poor all my life."

I thought my mother would think this was a good idea. I imagined her saying, "Rickie, get yourself a backup job," but that was not what I heard.

"You wanted to be a singer. You've been working so hard at it. It's what you've always wanted to do."

I was worn down, I protested: "I'm going nowhere. Nobody loves me, I've got nobody, I have no job and I'm lonely. I don't know what to do."

She stood strong (she was always so strong!): "I know you feel bad right now, but don't give up on your dream. Maybe you'll be the one who succeeds. Don't you quit now. Don't give up without trying Rickie."

My mother. She was a mom from a long line of determined women who faced incredible adversity and was now reminding her daughter where she came from and where she was going. She kept me going when I wanted to set it all down. I guess it was the dark hour before dawn. For even as I declared myself incapable, the threads of life were braiding all around me.

> *Well they say the city will make you dirty but you look alright*
> *You feel real pretty when he's holding you tight*
> *City will make you mean but darlin that makeup on your face*
> *Love will wash it clean in the night . . .*
>
> "Young Blood"

I had written three new songs while I was sitting in Rocky's with nothing to do. I just had to find a way to write melodies that were better than anything I had done in the past. Enter a young man from stage left, one Alfred Johnson. Alfred would help me do what I could never have done by myself. Together we jump-started our destinies, caught a bus to the Twilight Zone, and came out the other side, all in one night's work, writing "Company."

Alfred Johnson, My First Songwriting Partner

I met Alfred on the boardwalk in Venice Beach. There is a photograph of the moment, Alfred tells me, taken by a passing stranger. To our amazement we shared a love of Laura Nyro and Little Feat, and right away Alfred asked me if I wanted to come over and sing. I did, but it would be risky, driving away with him and his compadre, two men I didn't know. We entered his apartment, a piece of performance art itself, overlooking a parking garage, strewn with doll parts, arms hanging from string and heads, lonely heads, watching his lonely fingers upon the keyboard. It was a test, I was sure. These boys wanted to see if girls ran for their lives or if they took a moment to actually see what was around them.

"Cool apartment," I said. They smiled in approval and I was silently offered membership into the Alfred Johnson club of music-writing.

A young Black man raised in Riverside, California, his appearance on the beach, especially perched on the rolling piano on wheels, was a welcome sight. Little Feat's "Dixie Chicken" was coming from his general direction and I scurried right over. Alfred was playing the music of white kids who loved Black music. He was not playing a song by Taj Mahal or even Marvin Gaye. That bridge I mentioned—the Marvin Gaye bridge of cultural exchange—well, Alfred had crossed a bridge of his own. The Buffalo Springfield bridge.

I like to think this story of him and me was destiny. Alfred's great uncles on his mother's side were the legendary dance team the Nicholas Brothers. Like me, he had history. A light to grow toward. Like me, he adored Laura Nyro, but Buffalo Springfield's music spoke to Alfred like nothing before. I did not understand music theory, but I understood music naturally, intuitively, and could keep up with any music Alfred put down. I had a notebook full of great lyrics, and that was the enticement. Alfred wanted clever, funny, unusual stories. Well, I'm your man. When Alfred heard "Weasel and the White Boys Cool," he wanted to work with me all summer long.

We began writing the day we met.

Alfred and I were excited to collaborate, although I couldn't tell him what chords I wanted. My technique was not so different than my chair in Mr. Ellis's orchestra. Sometimes, I had to describe and sing each note in the chord, a tedious process that Alfred seemed to relish. Our collaboration on "Company" was a visceral, torturous process. It began with me pulling deep emotions out of myself. These were pure feelings as airy and unrooted as a color or a tingle.

Here in Alfred's decapitated doll emporium, I learned the technique of collaboration. Or as Alfred explained it, "the quest to translate emotion into music." I adored Alfred, almost manic in his energy, he was amped up with ideas and exuberant in his appreciation of my lyrics and voice. We lifted each other.

"Is that it?"

"No, it's this," and I sang a substitute note which he reassembled into a new chord.

Sometimes I had to talk about the feeling of the chord to help Alfred find what I sought. He understood me. We shared intuition and heart. In our second songwriting session, I brought him the newest lyrics from Rocky's IBM typewriter, and we transformed all the heartbreak and disappointment of my life into more music and lyrics. We traded off lines, each one singing the next.

Me: "I'll remember you too clearly . . ."

Alfred: "But I'll survive another day."

Me: "I'll see you in another life . . ."

Alfred: "But when I reach across . . ."

Me: "The galaxy . . ."

Alfred: "I will miss your Company."

And so it went that night as we pressed our melodies against each other and wove our lives together. The night of writing "Company" was a lifetime together. We grew up and grew old, and in the morning, our futures had entwined forever.

Our twenty-something-year-old hearts were wrung. I took my notebook home sometime around 1 a.m. but Alfred stayed up with his reel-to-reel, microphones, and doll heads. Separately we were both in deep self-satisfaction knowing that we had just changed something in the world. *We* had written a great song.

When "Company" was completed, we were done writing together. We just did not know it at the time. Alfred and I would always be deeply connected from writing that song.

Alfred Johnson and Rickie Lee Jones got a job under the title "Great Dame" at the Ala Carte on Thursdays in September. By the end of our month, there was a *buzz*. A little buzz, but it was about us and it was in the big city of Los Angeles. There was the feeling that I was rising quickly through the Hollywood music community. It was a time of tests, in the next few months I would pass the songwriter publishing traps and the quicksand of being a local hero. It seemed that each musician I met helped me along. I was being passed up a ladder to escape Hades, that netherworld of poverty that fools your heart into despair when heaven is right at your fingertips. A few people made "demos" of my songs for me for free. A "demo" is a demonstration of what might be done with more money or time . . . Yet a dark winter of depression was threatening to steal me away from this new fortune even as I stood at the threshold.

Alfred had to make a life decision: day job or music. He decided he didn't have the time to devote to music and keep his job as an engineer. He said he had security clearance, and he was very serious about his work, frightened of not having steady money, insurance, a pension. But you have a chance at the brass ring—how can you turn it away? It wasn't that he didn't want to perform anymore or couldn't see the magic in our work. It was, I thought, that he was afraid of failing, of not being essential, of me growing out of him. I was disgusted when he said, "You are going to be a star. You don't need me." To me, it just sounded like one more guy looking for a reason to leave.

We had trudged through our lonely jungles of melody and the myriad mirror of meaning together, creating a permanent refuge there for any who seek it. Still . . . I think he also understood better than I did that my music was deeply personal and ultimately my solitary exploration. I alone would live through my tragedies. I alone was responsible for laying bare my emotions. I alone lived my life into music. My deepest emotions are universal; the further inside myself I go, the closer I am to mankind. When I sing, you can hear your own teardrops falling on my windowsill.

A Distant Adobe

The same summer I met Ivan and Alfred, Tom Waits came into my life. I think of those weeks as the oasis. I would have stayed there forever but I was destined to cross a desert in search of a sea where pirates might bring me home.

By 1978 the legendary Troubadour was a used-to-be club for used-to-be musicians. It had been the premier folk club in L.A. back when folk music was the flag of a new revolution. Not now though. Now it was derelict and disgraced. It was empty every night except once a month when local heavy metal bands drew rowdy crowds.

I remember the first time I saw the joint. Ivan Ulz had a gig there. Why they booked Ivan I cannot imagine except that they didn't seem to care anymore. Ivan did not bring in an audience. I'd seen him spend an entire performance turning the dial of his radio as he explained the real messages being delivered. It was fantastic but only if you watched his audience. It was not great for Ivan, those manic performances, no one wanted to book him anymore and when he did get a show he would become so nervous about performing he might have an "episode."

There was a rumor that Tom Waits hung out at the Troubadour. Ivan's roommate Christina was a huge fan: "He *lives* in a motel in *downtown* L.A.! It's called the Tropicana." Christina was awed. "He lives like one of his characters."

"Really?" I was aloof. I thought of Sal Bernardi and the cum-stained halls of his alma mater. "That's interesting." I actually thought it was maybe pretentious. If you didn't *have* to live there why would you?

"When he is in town, he's always there."

Yet I was intrigued by a man who needed access to the seedy side of life to write. I knew that feeling. I liked those types of people. Characters were what I called friends. In fact Waits's friend Charles Bukowski was still living that way in downtown L.A. No pretense there. Tom Waits had moved up a few stories to the Tropicana in Hollywood. Beverly Hills, actually.

That would be cool if Tom Waits went to Ivan's show. I admit I liked the album about Saturday Night. I was . . . coolly interested. Let Christina suss him out. "Yeah, he looks cool. Something tender about him, eh?" I wasn't sure. I never liked the over-the-top adoration of him. I knew I couldn't be a human being if I adored someone before I even met him.

Christina, however, was ready for him. Yes she was.

Chicken-in-the-Pot

At the Troubadour show, Ivan wanted me to come onstage and sing at some point. The room was empty when we got there and stayed that way all night. Ivan introduced me, I walked up the stairs and took his guitar, sat in his chair, and started playing "Easy Money."

> *There was a Joe*
> *Leaning on the back door*
> *A couple Jills with their eyes on a couple Bills . . .*

With an empty house, I was not really nervous, even when Ivan left the building through the front door. I guess he needed a break. I played my daddy's song now, "The Moon was Made of Gold." Here was my pearl—the introduction, old-school style:

> *Little folks cry when the sun leaves the sky*
> *Well sometimes so do you and I*
> *But if you'll try*
> *Just keep watching the sky,*
> *A new wealth you will find*
> *By and by . . .*

Almost on cue, I saw the kitchen door open and release a halo of light around the shadow of someone, someone watching me. Almost hiding. I felt him. I knew right away, it was Tom Waits's scraggly shadow formed by the kitchen's light. As the story goes, Chuck E. was working as a cook in the kitchen and he called Waits out to listen to the girl onstage.

Don't feel bad because the sun went down
The night has wealth untold
Just keep watching and you soon will see
The moon is made of gold

Well, every ghost in the place was glued to their empty seat. I had 'em in my hands:

One by one your dreams will all come true.
Magic you'll behold.
The night is magic
And the moon is made . . . of gold

I hit my high note with a harmonic ping on the guitar. The song was over. Wow, I *liked* it up there. I felt like I belonged up there.

Where was Ivan? Ah, there he was. Right on time. He closed the show and Ivan, Christina, and I met at the bar to, you know, gloat over our incredible performances. Then we stepped outside onto Santa Monica Boulevard to gather flowers of praise from the faces of strangers. Around us all the young dudes were standing around the parking meter where Waits parked his Cadillac, a '49 maybe. It was there tonight, a spot permanently kept for him. They were waiting for their leader. I remember some of them, Brody, Rick "Bebop" Dubov, Chucky, and Chicken-in-the-Pot.

There he was, Tom Waits. He wore a hat and he held his cigarette like it was a magic wand. An old and short magic wand, worn down from doing too much magic. He was speaking to Chuck Weiss, but what I heard was his body. He leaned on his car, but he was looking at *me*.

I could hear snippets: "She . . ." Mumble, mumble. "Venice . . ." Tom and Chuck were commiserating. As he seemed to with all things, Chuck knew before anyone else who I was.

Ivan and I were leaning against the brick wall by the front door, Christina in her nice clothes facing us. The Waits gang over there by the parking meter. Ivan said the magic words—"It's just like the Jets and the Sharks out here"—and just like that, I started:

> *When you're a Jet,*
> *You're a Jet all the way*
> *From your first cigarette*
> *To your last dying day.*

And through the din I heard a response. It was "Bebop" Dubov singing:

> *When you're a Jet*
> *You're the swingin-est thing.*
> *Little boy, you're a man,*
> *Little man, you're a king.*

Another voice. Was that Chicken-in-the-Pot? (A friend of Chuck's named for his love of a Canter's Deli menu item):

> *You're never alone,*
> *You're never disconnected*

Then Ivan:

> *You're home with your own*
> *When company's expected,*
> *You're well-protected*

Then:

> *Here come the Jets like a bat out of hell.*

Oops, wrong lyrics. That was Tom Waits trying to catch up.

Someone gets in our way, someone don't feel so well.

Then me righting my street-corner bandmate who forgot the lyrics:

Then you are set with a capital J,
Which you'll never forget
Till they cart you away.

Ivan and Christina, Waits and Chuck and me yelling that last line to bring the song to an end:

When you're a Jet, you stay a Jet.

It happened just this way. A bunch of individuals who would become forever linked in the public's mind initially became linked as they sang the "Jet Song" on the sidewalk of Santa Monica Boulevard one summer night in 1977.

Yes, it was magic.

Tom went home with Christina that night and they started seeing each other.

Not long after the Troubadour, Ivan checked into Camarillo Mental Hospital. I kept living with Christina until one day when she told me I had to leave because I had worn her shirt. I went back to Mark Vaughan's and crashed with him and our cat, Yossarian, so sad to visit the living vestige of a life left behind. Back at the Troubadour I mentioned to Chuck Weiss that Christina had kicked me out of her house. He seemed to take it personally and he told Waits. Waits called her up and told her she was a shit for treating me so badly. He was just looking for a reason. She told me I could come back, but the situation was too unstable. I stayed at Mark's, and Waits dumped her that weekend.

After our gig at the Ala Carte, I found a cheap place in Beachwood Canyon. Considering I did not have enough to rent a room in Jizztown, it was a great coup, an idyllic canyon dump with a broken hot plate and a very determined twin bed. This was my year in retreat, the austere season of holy decision when each thing I thought or whispered or cried became a bead on the rosary, a thing worth far more than requests for gas money. Each day was recited out loud, one more bead counted, and with each bead echoed a new face of the Godhead nodding within me as I paced and puked the perfect rhyme or reason. I searched furiously inside myself, where the incense smelled like whiskey and the holy wafers just soaked up the hangovers. I would be ordained into a life of total devotion to my music, where a radical priestess fighting for radical rights might long endure.

With no more Alfred Johnson writing sessions, no job, no boyfriend, no family of strangers in this isolated world far from the beach, a profound loneliness set in. Sometimes I visited a strip club on Gower, trying to understand the seedy life Tom Waits seemed to relish. Why did he portray women the way he did? I knew he preferred straight-looking girls, downtown secretary types, yet he created this idea of the whore with the heart of gold. The reality of hopeless girls selling the bottom of their genie bottles for a buck in the bum cannot be conveyed in a cute metaphor about whiskey-choked incense, I was ashamed that I ever thought it could be hip.

I had driven down to the Troubadour a couple nights, hoping to make friends with the gang there, but they were all guy's guys; suspicious of dames and rude to anyone Waits had thrown out his door. Out here in the big city it was hard to make a family of friends. With friends I could conquer the world, but without someone to say "I love you," all my accomplishments meant little to me.

My illegal basement room immediately lost its charm. I was sleeping right under the Hollywood sign which, up close, was a shabby, broken beacon of glamour. The small twin bed in the corner looked out at the garden and the panorama of Los Angeles's city lights below. Looking out at the big city of lights was overwhelming. How would I fit into that wide world, much less make my mark in it?

I was being swallowed up by my lonely room, and the clock was running on my promise to myself, six months of eighty-five-bucks-a-month unemployment. Eighty-five dollars was just enough to pay rent and a few gigs a month would feed me. Somehow I'd squeeze by. At the end of my unemployment checks I would either have a career in music or the money to pay for my trip back to Olympia.

Ivan told me he knew a publisher, someone he'd once worked with for his own songs. Perhaps he could introduce me. Would he? Could he? Boy if I could have a job writing music—that would be the best job in the world. Sit around and dream. Write words. Get paid!

He brought me to the office of Bud Dain, high up in the Motown building on Sunset Boulevard. I was dressed in my songwriter's best: jeans, wooden platform shoes, and a white Chinese silk jacket. We took a picture just before we went in for a "before and after" record of my life. Bud had been married to the great singer Jackie DeShannon, and he'd been in the music business periphery for a while. I sat down in a chair in front of his desk and played Bud everything I had, "Easy Money," "Weasel," "Young Blood."

When I was finished, as I was leaving, Bud finally offered: "I like that 'Easy Money,' can you write more like that?"

I said, "Sure I can." That one was easy.

His deal was that I would write so many songs per month for eight hundred dollars a month. In my life of 1977, that was like winning the lottery. The day came to sign the contract and enter the fraternity of music professionals. Just a week later, Ivan escorted me back to Bud Dain's office. We got on the elevator that would raise me up to where I was going to have enough money to pay rent and buy clothes. I could even join a spa.

Ivan and I were sitting in Bud's office, and I was reading my new contract. I had the pen in my hand. I was looking at the signature page. Bud was looking at me. A thought, a voice. I was hesitating, looking, looking, looking until I set the contract down. Something in me, that warning voice said, "Don't sign."

"I'm sorry, can I just think about this for a minute?"

Bud stepped out from his desk while Ivan and I collided like a coach and umpire at home plate.

Ivan: "What's going on Twenty-two? Rickie Lee Jones?"

"I'm not sure if I should sign this, Ivan . . . I have this weird feeling. I think . . . if he wants me, someone else with more money will want me too. I'm so sorry."

It was a crucial moment in my life and my career. In just a few months I would have my own publishing company, and those songs and the rights I almost signed away would spectacularly redefine my life. On this day I was broke and I had run out of options, but I made a fundamental decision to have faith in myself and my future. It was a desperately needed paycheck but I opted to remain on the bottom with the chance for everything, instead of climbing up a few stories higher. Respect, money. But . . . I felt a whisper of something greater in the air. The brass ring.

> *Could be . . . who knows?*
> *There's something due any day*
> *I will know right away . . . soon as it shows.*
> (*West Side Story*, "Something's Coming")

I apologized to Ivan and Bud, and said I was going to have to think about it.

Bud didn't need to think about it, he was pissed. "You will never get another chance, this is it, now or nothing."

That hardened my decision. Threatening me with expulsion from a club where I had not yet been granted membership meant I lost nothing. The boy's club of songwriters would have to wait for me. Going down the elevator, I had a feeling of elation. I was now sure about what I had done.

Wait. If he wants you, someone else will too.

It took chutzpah balls to pass up that opportunity and opt for poverty on the belief that something greater was meant for me. I asked Ivan, "You think he'll let me come back later if my music career doesn't work out?" Ivan laughed and said, "Don't worry about it. He's not hurting."

And something great *was* coming.

Chapter 17

The Man
with the Star

Photobooth, Santa Monica Pier

It's only just out of reach, down the block, on a beach . . .
Maybe tonight . . . maybe tonight . . .
                    (*West Side Story*, "Something's Coming")

How do I start the story of Tom Waits and me? Shall I set it up with a lyric, a song? Will you hear me singing? Or shall I offer up some bittersweet fact of life, some optimistic moral about opportunities. Shall I mention that Tom and I were beautiful beyond compare, and so nourished (and inspired) by each other's hearts that for a very short time we nearly consumed each other. Love, they used to call it.

Our disciples rippled out into the world—followers. You can still see them today. Of course I remain the unseen image at the Last Supper. Was I ever there? Scholars disagree. Do women have an impact on men or is it only the other way around? Well, depending on which men you read, I suppose the answer is no, men alone influence women. What a crock of shit.

Tom Waits was from an older musical generation, he'd been around a while, already made his first record six years before mine back in 1973. Waits was singular in his persona but the novelty of his voice was, in 1977, somewhat disregarded by serious musicians. "That guy who sounds like Louis Armstrong?" was the bulk of most reactions, but year after year he was gaining street cred that would surpass all others of his class.

One half-starry night, I had gone down to the Troubadour in my beret and elbow-length fuchsia gloves. Tom Waits came out of the kitchen and stood behind the bar. He greeted the bartender with a "Harumph." He pretended he didn't come out to see me. "Hey," was all he and I said to each other. We were potential lovers growling and scratching out our territory. It felt so good. He sat down by me and ordered a scotch. We drank and talked and laughed until it was closing time.

He walked with me across Doheny Drive to my car, the infamous orange Vega. There, under the streetlight, Tom took me in his arms and we danced. Swaying and singing to each other in the wee foggy hours. Then the song was over. He opened my door, I sat behind the wheel, and he waved me on my way. Down, down Santa Monica Boulevard I floated on a cloud until I found the World gas station, the only thing open between home and the Troubadour. I treated the Vega to a dollar's worth of gas, and floated heavenward, up, up, and out, the soft waltz between girl and Chevrolet. This ride home became the recipe for one of my greatest songs, "The Last Chance Texaco."

All the love in the world was mine that night, for I could imagine what it might be like to be loved by a man who dances with a girl under a lamppost as she sings a song he knows well. Those two still exist as ghosts of that witching hour, the echoes of their heartbeats, the infinite wrangling of lovers, frenzied and smooth, then exhausted, they recover as the sun rises on the freeways, to dream and head west. My ghost, always driving west.

Waits fans were worshippers, girls and boys who would camp out on his lawn (actually, the lawn of Tim Hardin who had a house in front of Tom's) and wait for their prophet to speak. When he did speak, he would say something like, "Get the fuck OUT of here and don't come back."

"You gotta do it," Chuck told me, "or they will never go home. They'll think you are going to marry them." It was a lesson I regarded with some skepticism.

To me, it is a holy bond, the one between song and listener. The obligation by priestess (or priest) to keep it clean and unfettered is a given. I can just go home and take a bath, I don't want to have sex with someone who has mistaken me for my song. For me, real life does not puncture the veneer of people's imaginations. Those people who use their fans for sex have to decide who they want to hurt in the morning.

I was disappointed in how many girls Waits had scratched from his dance card. Great dramatic stories of lovers chasing his cab down the streets of Philadelphia, or most recently, of shame in the Japanese press, the foreign affair—those personal stories he offered as collateral to future lovers. He had a cultlike ability to gather people to him; his inner circle of friends felt privileged and treated newcomers with secret signs and phrases. His charisma, his compelling spirit, for whatever reasons, we all wanted to be a follower of Tom Waits.

But the wounded and dying soldiers outside his kitchen door said otherwise. As characters bled into our real life, maybe I was the one who didn't know where real stopped and began. Maybe I invented a new Tom, who, like Boo Radley, would come out one day with a voice all his own.

It was autumn now. I came to the Troubadour around nine o'clock and sat at the bar. Waits was there. We both knew why we were there at the same time. Tom invited me home with him. We made love amid his dirty sheets and the clothes in piles everywhere. I didn't sleep very well.

The path to Tom's bedroom was scrawled through a living room of miniature skyscrapers of record covers and piles of newspapers and old magazines that had gone to seed where they landed. The bed was the only refuge. There I was safe, worshipped. He was a lion, so much more than his persona could ever contain. I had not expected to be so totally loved for such a brief few hours.

The sun was just coming through the motel curtains. I smelled his Old Spice and the Brylcreem stuck to his sideburns. I turned and touched him. Should I touch him? You never know what you're supposed to do in the morning. They're like sharks or mad dogs, should you look your lover in the eye? Tom sat up. The "we" of last night was no longer there. This morning I was a stranger in his bed and he said, "Time for you to go home. I have a lot of work today."

I inhaled sharply. I must have looked exactly how I felt. Like a broken mirror. I acted cool. How was my acting, anyway? Did he believe me?

I got dressed next to the bed and thought, Oh bed, don't let me go. I grabbed my hat and followed him through the labyrinth of his cluttered belongings. I was still standing on the step when he closed the door and walked away. I could not think. It was hard to breathe. The sun was up and it was already too hot. I was wearing high heels.

I wanted to hide in a bush. I may have hidden behind a bush. I tried to find my car but I was doing the walk of shame that so many others had walked.

I had to face my situation. Was I going to be another ghost, sitting around in Tom Waits's peripheral vision, hoping he looked directly at me? Hoping for a measly "hello"? Now I could see that haunted look all around the Troubadour, the shame and addiction to Tom Waits, his broken soldiers paying their sad homage. How did I get drafted into this misery?

Something Cool

November 7, 1977, the day before my twenty-third birthday, Zachary called from Chicago. "Come and visit, just do it." Meaning, come back to the scene of the crime and fall in love? I must have been very lonely and bored because I agreed to go.

I realized it was a disaster the moment we saw each other and started walking through the airport. What was I thinking? This was the guy who left me with no money, who caused me to get pneumonia, who was cheating on a pregnant me right outside my bedroom door, and who took me to a heroin dealer. But . . . perhaps the impulse to join Zachary really had nothing to do with him, because he was the least important part of my one night in Chicago.

Between arguments at his apartment, a song on the radio caught my ear. A ballad with lyrics that told a fantastic story. I waited through another ten minutes of music for the radio host to back announce the songs. "Something Cool." That must be it! I took the first flight back to L.A. the next morning and bought the sheet music down on Hollywood Boulevard.

I had salvaged something from the disastrous trip. Later that day, my best friend Mary Simon called to wish me Happy Birthday and I said, "I'm so lonely."

She said, "I'm coming over."

An hour later, there was a knock at my door and sweet Mary Simon was there with a happy grin on her face. She kissed me, her breath smelling of red wine. The next morning, we woke up to the sun shining through the open shades and my landlady looking through the window into my room. She was pretending to water a plant but she actually had her head up against the glass.

She saw Mary get out of bed. Beautiful, naked Mary waved to my landlady. She dropped the hose like she'd been stung by a wasp and turned to say something angry to the anorexic model who was lying out sunning herself. The model looked just as horrified, which was kind of ironic since I thought models were immersed in the gay world.

I was also topless when I stood up and walked slowly to the window and looked directly at the landlady as I pulled down the shade. Fuck her, it was none of her business. How did a Peeping Tom get on a high horse of judgement? Maybe we didn't even have sex, maybe my friend was just an extroverted sort of girl. No? Yeah, I don't believe it either.

Mary went home. "Sorry to get you in trouble!" I said. "Fuck her and her crappy apartment."

"No, Rickie, she owns this place. You can't ignore her."

I was very happy that Mary had come. Shameless I remained. I loved my life.

My muse returned. I was twenty-three now. No more time to fuck around. I had to move fast or my chance would become a shade of a ghost that had almost happened. I could feel myself on the knife's edge. My chance was now, right here, my whole future—come on, rise up like the sun! The wait was excruciating because I knew it depended on me being able to write my way out of this place. One good song.

I *would* write a great song, somehow. I was getting out of this shithole for good!

A night or two later, my friend Sandy invited me to see him play in Topanga Canyon, which was a hippie enclave wedged between Santa Monica and Malibu. Sandy was a country songwriter, who wore a white ten-gallon hat that looked a little comical on him since he didn't stand more than five-foot-four in his alligator cowboy boots. Here in Los Angeles's trenches it was all the same. Musicians, actors, comedians—everyone was hustling to make contacts, trying to be seen by someone who could help their career. When people invited you out, you showed up. Sandy had a job writing music for country singers. He was legit, a tier above most musicians I knew. I liked him, he was friendly and he wanted to help me. "Just come," he said, "there'll be real people there," and so I did.

Lowell George lived up in Topanga Canyon. It was Xanadu to us Venice hippies, though few of us had the wheels to get up there and ruin their neighborhood. This little club was Lowell's local joint and sure enough a rumor was circulating that he was in attendance at Sandy's show. I spotted Lowell standing near me in the back of the room. Rather, I felt him. He was a powerful presence. So was I.

I stepped outside and lit a cigarette, then meandered down to the ice cream parlor to play pinball. I didn't want to be another girl in that room hoping Lowell would notice me. Cat and mouse, perhaps. Let's see if he followed me.

Not many girls played pinball and fewer still played well. I had a very good hand with pinball because I practiced at my brother's pool hall. Lowell walked in a minute later and sat there watching me play. Cue the orchestra! I was wearing my little 1940s clothes and my beret and I was a good-looking girl. Yes I was. Lowell just could not resist a good-looking woman. He looked at me with those black laughing eyes, and he asked:

"How did you beat that machine, it's not easy?"

"My brother owned a pool hall," I said.

"I saw you at the club."

"My friend is playing there tonight."

Lowell asked if we could play doubles. Thankfully, he had quarters because I was too broke to play a second game. Then Lowell George and I played game after game of pinball that night in Topanga Canyon, while Sandy's country music whined from the club. This was enough joy and possibility to keep me from falling into despair after being pushed out of Waits's kitchen door. Lowell, he loved women, he had the spark. He made me feel good just to be near him. I was whole again.

I got into my car and drove down 101. I had an idea for a song. Just a feeling was brewing. I turned up Beachwood Canyon to my dump of a home, turned on the one burner of the hot plate that worked enough to heat a cup of soup. This idea, simmering.

The next day, I was in writing mode so I purchased a new notebook. I liked to write in a little coffee shop hardly anyone went to, down the hill from me on Santa Monica Boulevard near La Brea. I ordered a coffee. I had just enough money for the coffee and maybe a fifteen-cent tip. I would stay there for the afternoon. The waitress knew the drill.

I laid out my notebook and took out my pen. The perfect feel of the paper, the pages untouched by half ideas, or my notes about a phone call. A clean notebook only for the best of ideas.

And I started . . .

A long stretch of headlights bend into

Into where? I-10? What rhymed with ten? What about five. Five, alive. Hmm. Nine? I liked nine more than five. Should I do ten or nine?

. . . I-9.
Tiptoe into truck stops . . . and . . .

I lit a Winston and looked up from the page for more inspiration. Into the dark? Into the trucker's cab?

. . . sleepy diesel eyes.

Yes, that was it.
I could see the whole picture now.
Standard. Exxon—the dinosaur, Sinclair? What was the name of that other one? Chevron, hmm . . .

Tried to be Standard, tried to be Mobil
Tried living in a World and in a Shell

All those names had double meanings in this context. Good.

A block-busted blonde . . . free parts and labor
. . . broke down . . . threw all the rods he gave her . . .

It was flowing now . . .

Last chance . . . timing's all wrong
Last chance . . . can't idle this long
Last chance . . .

Like a thing already whole, there was no struggle bringing the vision of this place into existence.

Turn her over and go, pulling out of the last chance Texaco.

Two hours later, I folded up my notebook and drove back up the hill. It was late in the day.

I recalled something I read Paul Simon had said about "the nature" of a key. A key had an inherent nature? There were so many keys to explore. I must play a key I had never played. What was the nature of this key? I played an F-sharp. I didn't know if I'd ever played an F-sharp before. I had to press down hard on the fretboard to make the bar chord. And there it was, waiting for me, the whole song. The moment I played that F-sharp, I felt the entire song.

Now came the painful process of going deep inside myself to find the emotions and sounds to make these lyrics incredible. This highway thing, well, I'm thinking Waylon Jennings or Merle Haggard. Voice of a storyteller for a country song that is not country. Would they sing a song that sounded like this one?

"The Last Chance Texaco" wasn't like anything I'd ever written. It wasn't like anything I'd ever heard. In fact, one year later it received a Grammy nomination for Best Song, even though it was never released as a single. I guess it wasn't like anything anybody else had heard, either. It remains ominous and beautiful, funny and deadly serious. A last chance indeed.

A week later, I returned to the café and wrote the lyrics to "Chuck E's in Love." Same ritual: fresh page in my new notebook, cup of coffee and a cheap tip. The lyrics came in an afternoon and I again went home to find the melody. This one needed to be upbeat. I needed to write songs people would sing. It happened fast, the whole song came in one day.

The clincher was the "E." It was my brilliant stroke. I knew it was a clever twist but I never imagined an entire decade of E's would show up in people's names and even in Chuck E. Cheese pizza. "Chuck E's in Love" would become a hit in ways Billboard could not measure.

I initially thought it was a good song for Bette Midler, and I was after all an aspiring songwriter, so I played it for Chuck and Tom. They did not try to help me place the song. Thank goodness. I would find the exact place the song needed to be one day, a happy lyric that at a slow-to-mid tempo also carried a melancholy, or at least a weight it would never have at the faster tempo Bette Midler would have given it. The breakthrough: I had to get sad to get the music right. I cried as I slowly played the opening figure.

How come he don't come and PLP with me?

Tom was just someone I saw in passing now. He might say hello, he might not. I pretended to be one of the gang but that time had passed. I was never going to be one of those boys.

Champagne and Guitar Strings

I was almost out of time on my six-month-unemployment plan, so I told Ivan I was going back home to Olympia. I'd tried but hadn't gotten anywhere. Ivan said, "Don't go, wait a minute, I'll call you back in an hour." He called his friend Lowell George from a pay phone, saying, "There is a girl you have to hear. She wrote this song"—and then Ivan sang what he remembered of "Easy Money," with the relish and energy reserved for the most sensual of conquests.

> *There was a Joe on the back door and*
> *Jills with bills and stating they were waiting*
> *To get their hands on some Easy Money.*
> *He said Yes!* [I can just see Ivan grinning now] *Oh yes . . .*

Lowell said, "I'm in L.A. working on my new record, how can I meet her?" Ivan called me back and said Lowell was going to call me.
"It's up to you now, Rickie."

Just like that, my future was laid out before me. Just like that. All I had to do was show up or in this case, pick up the phone. I answered the phone. Lowell's voice was full of confidence. All the warm sensual innuendo of when I first met him playing pinball, and his business side was the brisk cold of all those city buses in Chicago. Oh, he had a good voice.

"This is Lowell George. So Ivan says you have a song. He sang some of it to me. Did you write that yourself?"

"Yes I did."

"Alone?"

"Yes."

"I like it. I'd like to come by and hear it if you have time. Do you have a publisher?"

"No."

"Where do you live?"

"Beachwood Canyon."

"I know it well. Can I come tomorrow?"

"Yes you can!" still echoes through the canyons above the old Hollywood sign. I can still hear it late in the day as the sun is setting. Listen:

"YES! yes! yes! . . . YOU-oou-oou CAAAAAN-caaaaan-caaaaan!"

Lowell came to my apartment with his Sony reel-to-reel tape recorder and a good microphone. My room was so proud to have him there. Lowell recorded me singing "Easy Money" and seemed very pleased. I reminded him about the time we played pinball but he was all business. He only stayed an hour, he was on his way to the studio. I felt that all the angels in heaven had cast their gaze at me. John Bonham of Led Zeppelin was counting down before the first chord of my new life and it was going to be a good one. I was being invited into the real rock-'n'-roll hall of fame (the one exclusively among musicians), because today Lowell George recorded my song. Still I did not count one single chicken before it hatched. I told no one except my mother. I kept the magic brewing.

Lowell returned a week later so I could hear his instrumental version of my song. It was nothing like my version. It sounded so big! He said, "I'm doing it kinda like Stagger Lee." His horns were loud, the rhythm thumpin', as sexy a shuffle as ever there was, and his slide solo was as wonderful as always. He also played me his version of the Ann Peebles hit, "I Can't Stand the Rain."

"This was going to be my first single."

Oh, it was good.

"Except that your song is so damn good we're thinking that it might be the first single instead."

You dog!

So much to believe. So much of it was real. He wasn't making a joke? No, no, don't play it that way. Be confident. The Lord loves a joyful noise.

I had just run out of unemployment so Lowell was right on time. What angels, what choreography! A songwriter to the great songwriters! Aim high! Walk tall, act fine.

My confidence was filled and lifted by possibility. The joy that confidence brings, and vice versa, returns to build more. Like a found penny reproducing to make more found pennies. Whatever I had, I was gonna get more of it, so I'd better make sure it wasn't poverty and teardrops. I dared imagine right out loud, I might really get a contract of my own now. So close, so close.

"This is incredible. Wow." This song sounded nothing like my quiet version. I really was a songwriter.

Lowell said, "Let's take a ride in my Range Rover." In California the road and the automobile are the main vehicles of status and seduction. You must get in the car with the boy if you are going anywhere in this life.

"Have you ever had champagne?"

Should I say yes?

"No."

I knew this was a done deal.

"Well, let's go buy some."

I keep saying "this was the moment" or "that was the moment," but perhaps the trip down Beachwood to Liquor Locker with Lowell George was the official beginning of my new life, the one I live today. That ride seemed so right and normal, as if I had always been destined to ride in that Range Rover. Although I was giddy inside, I was cool and, if I may say, beautiful. I knew who I was, the songwriter. The girl in the beret. I *belonged* sipping Moët with Lowell George. I belonged.

We drove back up to my house and drank that bottle. Then we squeezed into my tiny twin bed together. In the morning, Lowell took a shower in my tiny shower that drooled more than it sprayed and he sang, "Fat Man in a Bathtub" loud enough for me to hear.

For a month or two, Lowell and I drove around the Hollywood Hills in his new Range Rover. We drove without direction. We drove just for kicks. We had nowhere to go but we were feeling groovy. His arm was around my shoulder. Every time he drove by Glen Towers he would sadly point at the window on the turret and say, "That's where Linda [Ronstadt] used to live." Driving by the Chateau Marmont, "That's where Vicki and I stayed. You should stay there sometime. It's old but it's got class. No room service. Very private. Ask for room 402—or maybe it was 610."

Like I wanted to sleep where he'd slept with Vicki. Or Bonnie or Linda or . . . and yet I *did* want to sleep in the bed he had slept in and be near him and part of the story he was writing. I liked being in the story of hotels and sweet endless nights and cars that went nowhere and came back home again.

Lowell introduced me to a music manager (and cocaine dealer) who was trying to sign him to a professional contract. It was immediately clear to me that this guy was a real creep. One night Lowell and I drove to this creep's house where he and his girlfriend were cooking cocaine on cookie sheets like satanic homemakers. "Why do you cook it?" I asked. "Oh, it makes it much much stronger. Changes the high and . . ." Blah blah blah. I wished I were anywhere but there. Lowell, he just couldn't stop.

I said, "I think I'd like to go home now."

"Oh come on. What a lightweight you are."

I took my clothes off and swam in the pool, hoping the glamour of a swimming pool would make this seem worthwhile and fun, but the crude scene outside the pool had drained whatever residual glamour Lowell carried. Lowell was overweight and unhealthy. He acted as if we had no right to worry about him, but I did worry. I knew I could not physically keep up with this crowd even though I was ten years younger and over a hundred pounds lighter. I wondered how he could keep it up and why he wanted to die young. I didn't want to die young. I was just getting started.

I put my clothes on, my shoes, my sweater, and I went back into the house. Lowell was sitting in the dark living room on a dining room chair holding his guitar. He was illuminated from behind by the kitchen light, and I sat down on the carpet next to the manager/creep and Lowell started to play. It was church time and no drug could lessen the meaning of what was happening. Lowell was playing "Willin'."

I tried to seal this moment into my cells. Remember, remember, so you can come back any time. Remember Lowell George singing to you here.

But even the greatest moments of life simply slide off our skin with the lightness of fairy dust. They are wonderful but do not have weight. The greatest moments of life don't embed like the hurts of sadness and tragedy.

The spring of 1978, Lowell did not tell anyone at Warner Brothers Records about the girl he had discovered, the writer of his single. When asked, he said, "No she doesn't have anything else."

Lenny Waronker smiled. "He wanted to keep you for himself."

Even though I was meeting important people, no one was going to give me a ticket into the circus. I was in line, but "Polly" would still have to buy her own way in.

Lowell George died just one year later. He had sung "Easy Money" at Lisner Auditorium in Washington, D.C., on a tour promoting his album *Thanks, I'll Eat it Here*, a terribly ominous title. That night after the show, he finally lay down to sleep next to his wife, but his thirty-four-year-old heart simply stopped beating. His obituary was on a banner at the bottom of my first *Rolling Stone* cover.

Now, looking through a cynical window at my happy-ever-after took the place of the pure awe that had illuminated my path. The loss of my friend, Lowell, one of those who had made this possible, made me wary of each bit of good fortune that would come my way. Could it be that the only way in was to get some skin from the devil? Are we instantly transformed into a thing that cannot perceive happiness the moment that happiness comes our way? Is there some fucking virus that causes this kind of thing? Is it cynicism? Is there a cure?

> *Wanna get to heaven, let me tell you how to do it*
> *Just grease your hands in mutton suet*
> *Reach right out and take the devil by the hand*
> *And slide right into the promised land*
> (traditional blues song my daddy taught me)

My old neighbor from 21 Westminster, Nick Mathe, had seen me play at the Ala Carte and asked if he could be my manager. It took him a month or two, but sometime near Christmas he was booking some shows. He was talking to lawyers he wanted me to meet. Owen Sloane was the second showbiz lawyer I interviewed. We had no money, Owen represented me on spec. "For a song." Speculation, gratis, for free, to be paid if and when I made money.

Working on spec, you met 'em all. A deejay who was heavily into S and M was the first person to mention my name on the air:

"Miss Rickie Lee Jones, the Mae West of rock 'n' roll, is down at the Skylight." He added, "She is ready to eclipse Bette Midler."

Oh no! Don't say that! Bette was the most likely singer for my kind of songwriting. This deejay was a one-man Department of Sales Prevention.

I liked Owen. So I began my career with one of the most powerful attorneys in music. I did not have a contract or even a real demo so there was nothing but my name and talk, but there was a contagion in the air and everyone seemed to catch it. *Rickie Lee is going somewhere.* Nick Mathe and Owen Sloane were creating the momentum.

Nick introduced me to his friend Phil Erinberg, whose parents owned the entire building on the corner of Hollywood Boulevard and Cahuenga. Phil said I could use his office to work on my songs at night after he left the building. In the couple of months I was there, I wrote "Danny's All-Star Joint," inspired by the gay ex-con from Alabama who manned the counter at the hamburger joint. I changed the name but other than that it was pretty much straight reporting. That month, working up there in the darkened halls of that 1930s leftover from a Raymond Chandler murder mystery, I discovered it was much more difficult for me to write in a place designated for writing. I needed to catch the song by surprise. Once I got my advance, I stopped by the burger place to tell Cecil I had money to buy myself a burger. He said, "It's on the house," and thus the song was born—if you're broke you can't get a free anything, but if you've got money, people give you everything for free.

> *Come on Cecil, take a dollar!*
> *Come on Cecil, take a ten!*
> *I finally geared up to a whole bunch of big ones*
> *And you're acting like I'm down-shiftin'.*

More automotive metaphors, but instead of lowriders I liked under-riders . . .

Imagine Bugs Bunny and Daffy Duck singing the Looney Tunes theme. That's how Nick and I felt.

Overture! Curtains! Lights!

> *This is it, the night of nights . . .*
> *This is it, we'll hit the heights*
> *And oh what heights we'll hit*
> *On with the show this is it!*
>   ("This Is It," from the *Bugs Bunny Show*)

With the New Year, Nick had hit the ground running. With Owen's guidance and their behind-the-scenes plans, phone calls, and appointments, Nick and Owen completed the work of seasoned managers combined with the enthusiasm of real fans. Their energy made people feel good when they left the lunch or hung up the phone. Nick was such a sweet guy. I was awed at how my next-door neighbor could do this stuff. To say it was already written, that it was fate, would subtract from the day-to-day work that created a groundswell of interest in me. And yes, it was fate too.

Remember, I could barely pay rent but I suddenly had a business team whose work and payment was foreign to me. I saw people talking and talking and shaking hands. It was as if Nick and the business people spoke a secret coded language. It was the language of success, we needed each other.

I didn't even have a publicity photo, much less the money to pay for a shoot. Nick arranged for a photographer but not just any photographer. He was so proud, he'd been going by A&M record studios flirting with Bonnie Schiffman, talking me up. Bonnie was a staff photographer.

I showed up at A&M after working hours for an "under the radar" photo session. I brought some outfits, some music, and a bottle of cognac. I knew how I wanted to be seen and, although I had never done a photo shoot, I fell right into the spirit of the thing. I was acting but I was representing *my* family, *my* imagination, and most of all how I wanted to present myself. I was not going to compete with the record bins of competitors with their fluffy hair. I wore a 1940s bathing suit with mirrored sunglasses.

In one photograph I had Nick place ten bucks in my bosom. In another, I simply held my glove in my hand and looked into the lens. That picture was the first that Warner Brothers received and it remained on Lenny Waronker's desk for many years.

Nick generated three showcases where he would invite the "artist and repertoire" guys from the record companies. A and R guys scout for new talent and songs for record companies. A showcase made their lives easier, presenting the best of a new talent in a short twenty or thirty minutes instead of the standard forty-five-minute music club set. The idea was to knock 'em dead. Like vaudeville, there would be other short acts before and after me. No one would be a headliner. The A and R guys came looking for a hit but also for something they could mold into their own image. They needed to see a full house with an enthusiastic audience. These guys were in business, numbers meant money, and that elusive satisfaction that fame brings.

Warner Brothers was different, though. They were the label of conscientious professionals, and the people who worked there put the artists first. They wanted a long-term project where artists grew and thrived. Once headed by the "Chairman of the Board" himself, Frank Sinatra, Warner Brothers sent its company heads on frequent pilgrimages to Sinatra's home in Palm Springs to get his take on matters. The president of Warner Brothers, Mo Ostin, had been the accountant during Sinatra's tenure as chairman of Reprise. Sinatra had set the mood for a musician-friendly company and it had flourished. The year 1978 was a golden one in rock music, and Warner Brothers Records was Asgard.

The Big Night

Few people experience careers where one single hour makes or breaks the entire enchilada. Showcases were the deciding moment of a music career. The now or never, the do or die. It was my moment, I seized the living daylights out of it. The showcase at the Troubadour was last-minute, but Nick got me tagged on a Wendy Waldman concert there. I would sing between the opener and the closer, but I had a full thirty minutes. Most important, it would be in my home court. There was a buzz about me that centered on the Troubadour. The joint was packed to the gills.

I still remember the long black dress I wore with a large ruffle and an embroidered shawl. I was a Spanish lady. Anyway, it was the only nice dress I had that wasn't forty years old. That night I played "Young Blood" and "Weasel and the White Boys Cool, and brought my friends up for an a capella version of "The Real Thing Is Back in Town." Sharing the stage was payback for the people who had supported me that year: Yusef Rahman from Venice, Bebop Dubov from the sidewalk in front of the bar, and Amy Lofgrin and Joe Turano (my friends from Great American Food and Beverage Company). Four voices to grease it up for me to do my thing. Finally "Easy Money" and a rousing "Chuck E's in Love," in the upbeat swing tempo I'd envisioned for Bette.

For the closer there was only one possible song, an acknowledgment of God, a chance to wink at past and future angels. "Thank you." From a life of no prospects to this moment of possibility—I could see my impossible dream! Just getting this far was a grave accomplishment. But from this vantage point I could see everything, past and future, every possibility. Suddenly where I went in life was my choice, not my fault. The song I chose was very sentimental, and it was perfect. Young Amy played the opening notes of "Somewhere Over the Rainbow," and then I began:

When you wish upon a star

It was an open metaphysical invitation, an evocation. I was telling the producers, directors, and the presidents to make a dream come true tonight: by the end of the show, I just knew they would.

I was singing my dream into existence, as if by the time the song was over a new future would appear on the horizon. Like a bolt out of the blue.

fate steps in and sees you through . . .

It was almost over now, this night I had waited for all my life.

I thought of Lenny and the record company boys out in the audience:

When you wish upon a star.

I was tapping on the shoulder of my future and boldly.

your dream . . . comes . . .

It already happened, didn't it? I sang it perfectly, didn't I? Yes, my dream came

true . . .

When I woke up in the morning, I woke into a new life. I knew it, I could feel it. I had won what could be won—and never by street urchins like me.

The very next day a bidding war broke out for my signature on a record company contract. Owen Sloane was happy to report that so-and-so offered this much and the other guy was offering that much. This part was no fuzzy dream, no spiritual negotiation for redemption, this part was *business*.

I knew the ones who offered the most money would have the biggest investment in me and would work hardest for my success. There were three labels. Tommy LiPuma's and Dr. John's label was the first to drop out. I wanted Lenny Waronker but Warner Brothers was still low so we told them they had to meet the other offer. They did.

Vision of Lenny

I stipulated Lenny Waronker must be my producer. Lenny accepted my provision. He liked the music and he loved my songwriting. It would be up to Russ Titelman, Lenny's partner, to show the world what a great singer he thought I was. "Like Roberta Flack," he cried when he heard "Company." Great praise indeed. Warner Brothers accepted my terms. Warner Brothers would become my family for the next five years, longer if they picked up the options.

I got what I wanted, my vision from way back at the sailors' house was fulfilled. The long, long journey was completed. The Warner

Brothers lawyer brought a nice touch to the contract signing in May: a feathered pink pen. I was embarrassed at the silly emblem for such a serious occasion. Before the ink dried, I felt the gap between how I saw myself and how others saw me and my music. I'd have to do something about that. The "Mae West of rock 'n' roll" was going to be more than a boa and a pink novelty pen.

Warner Brothers gave me a check for fifty thousand dollars as an advance against my future earnings. An unimaginably huge check, but while standing in Lenny's office I sheepishly asked to borrow money from Lenny and Russ. Yes, I had a check worth fifty grand, but I had no cash, no bank account for the check, and I was low on gas and lower on rent. I think I won a special place in their hearts that day. I had something they couldn't buy. I was baked by the sun of hard knocks, and my "streetwise" moniker was about to become the coolest of the decade.

Nick found me a bungalow on Ninth Street in Santa Monica, and we took another advance he had wrangled from ASCAP (the American Society of Composers and Producers) to pay rent for six months. That would impress the landlord enough to let me have the place, because I had no rent history and no legitimate papers of any kind; that is, except the most legitimate paper—money. After being more than broke my entire life, it felt good to push that dough around. People fell right over, and that was the first unhealthy lesson.

Nick threw down the "just got signed" card everywhere we went. It felt a little funny, since I had learned from my mom to hide good things so nobody could take them. I was thinking, Wait till we've done it, till we prove it. I knew it was the only way in the invisible world to store up enough magic to get through the fun house. Music success is a labyrinth that confounds more than a few young artists into failure before they even begin. Nick and I were getting to know each other from opposite sides of the mountain.

Santa Monica was still a town left over from the glory days of the 1930s when movie stars peopled its bars and sunned on its sandy beach and where barkers called for marks on the pier. Nothing had been knocked down or rebuilt. Its charming wartime bungalows were fighting a losing battle against the tide of ugly four-story apartment buildings that would quadruple the landlords' profits. I personally loved the disrepair, the broken clock, the leftover or left out. It made me feel like I alone had found a treasure before anyone else.

I bought a bed, my first bed, and a beautiful 1950s stove. I found a couch on the street, the one featured in photographs by Norman Seeff from one of his three attempts at my first album cover. No more sleeping on couches or floors secured by an hour-by-hour unwritten lease. I had an address. Now if only the phone company would get that phone installed . . .

Inexplicably, things started warming up again with Tom Waits. I would call Tom from a pay phone to talk about what was going on with my career, standing outside for an hour or more. This lent a certain sweetness to our conversations. Each time I put a dime in the phone, Tom and I got a little closer inside. He answered the phone with, "WHAT," but when he heard my voice he'd grow littler and sweeter. "Ahh, hey you." Sometimes he'd run over to visit before I hung up the phone. He was responding to me now, giving me some reins, some trust, not too much, just a little. By the time my phone was installed we had become lovers again.

Now we were religions, we converted to each other, we inspired each other and we spoke in tongues. He growled, I cooed. He softened, I growled. Our natures similar, both of us apparently lacked the ability to hang onto our core identity. We wanted to be parts of stories because without a story, who were we?

We stayed in character for our entire romance and our characters were sometimes cruel and often selfish. We needed those characters to love from our "real" selves but maybe our real selves were too damaged to trust. I knew Waits was dangerous to trust and perhaps so was I. But we were trusting each other, we could not help it.

So we lay in bed brooding like newborns into each other's eyes. We inhabited black holes where we floated upward and down again. We were jellyfish, floating from day to night. Only poetry evokes the long undulating time of our lying in each other's arms. We had drifted out to the open sea. One day we both wrote the exact same melody though separated by ten miles. Tom wrote a song about a person who had been defeated by the blues, and I wrote one about a mother who had been chased by the devil from a social services office. Our shared melodies born there in "hang on to my rainbow" and "blue horizon," our little children born in melody.

Soft-Bodied Sea

Santa Monica was the perfect vacation spot for jellyfish. A floater like me could bask in Tom's stories, hiding in the back of a protective cave. What does a jellyfish possess? A transparent bulbous city in which all things pass through?

We liked to stay in motels, which became our own little home, our private fiction, so we would drive around Los Angeles and land in some motel where we could continue our film noir together. I loved riding shotgun with Tom, before I met Mac and lost my way.

It was vastly different when Tom and I slept on his home court. The Tropicana meant people saw him with me, he had to deal with how that made him feel or how it made him look. He was very protective of his career and his privacy.

We were in his bed now, with the leaves and the dappled light sparkling against a wooden balcony. Overgrown and fragrant jasmine pressed its fingers through the French doors like a crazy fan trying to get inside. Tom still loved to walk over to Duke's in the morning, but now he dressed me in his clothes. Anyone could see we only wanted to return to the bedroom where creatures like us could belong—to each other.

But like the snake in the garden, our hearts were imperfect with love.

I loved Tom but he always played a game where I had to act like I didn't need him. That hurt me, I had no ability to not need the thing I loved. Tom felt like he could come and go as he pleased. He did not want to be a couple.

The only way I could do an on-again, off-again thing was to pretend to be stronger than I really was. Men liked women who could take them or leave them. Yes, perhaps I could find a way to pretend that I didn't need anyone, pretend to be tougher than I was. I was with someone so stimulating, someone I so adored that I was willing to remake myself. That meant staying in character.

I did just that, and we stayed together until the summer. Then while we were broken up I met Dr. John.

Dr. John

The fairy dust that fell on me when I first listened to Dr. John's album that night back in Chatham, Ontario, eventually pulled me into the real Mac Rebennack orbit.

Mac was a dubious figure in my life, a creator and destroyer, one whom I would work with right up until the last months of his life.

I first heard Dr. John's real name, Mac Rebennack, from Chuck E. Weiss, who knew everything about anything musical. I tried to tell Chuck how I knew about Dr. John in my spiritual way but, as always, Chuck had real information, the real lowdown, and it was more amazing than my mythical Dr. John.

Mac switched from guitar to piano after he lost part of a finger when he intervened to save fellow musician Ronnie Barron from a pistol whipping and the gun went off. The finger was reattached but didn't work as well so Mac switched to piano. He brought his technique to Hollywood and became a session player. His stage name, "Dr. John," was already known among hoodoo circles and Mac was deeply into the practices. Like most musicians, he probably did not see the problem with becoming that which he admired.

Tommy LiPuma, legendary jazz producer of Miles Davis and so many others, was now the head of Horizon, the new jazz arm of A&M Records. Dr. John was his A and R man, a brilliant choice because Dr. John had played so many roles in the music business, including A and R man, studio musician, performer, songwriter (with Doc Pomus), and producer. LiPuma trusted Mac's ear, so he asked Mac to check me out for Horizon. Mac and I met one sunny afternoon before I signed with

Warner Brothers. I parked the famous orange Chevy Vega on La Brea Avenue in front of the gate to A&M Records (which was housed in Charlie Chaplin's former Tudor-style movie studio).

I saw Dr. John advancing from the south end of La Brea, walking toward me in his beret, holding his snake-head cane with his mojos, gris-gris bags hanging from his belt, and other animal parts attached to him. I was in my red beret, my high heel wedges, gloves, and a little white suit from the 1950s. I could smell his patchouli oil well before he reached me. He regarded me, smiling, but watching. He was tall. We were two planets circling a black hole that history could fall through.

We walked through the front gates and over to Tommy's office. Tommy was a small man with a bit of a limp. He looked like he could be Martin Scorsese's cousin. Dr. John announced:

"I was going to carry her over to the bungalow and try some songs."

"Great."

We drove around the block to a little house one street over from the corporate studios. Mac sat down at the piano and began to musically frisk me, to see what I had on me.

"You know 'Since I Fell for You'?"

Mac began playing piano. I didn't know what was coming at me. He was playing some weird improvisations but I kept singing the song. Then we did "My Funny Valentine," in B-flat, of course.

Mac drove us back to A&M where we met with Tommy LiPuma. Seems he had been checking out my musical vocabulary and my most fundamental musical sensibilities. He told LiPuma that he was playing the root of the fifth, or the inversion of the primary, tonic of the gin, some type of hoodoo music language terms I still do not know. He was testing me to see if I could keep my ground. Did I have innate musicality? I did.

"So it was a test?" I asked.

"And you did great, girl."

I was very pleased with myself, I had passed a thorough musical exam administered by Dr. John. Here I thought we were just playing songs together. Mac seemed genuinely happy.

I liked and respected Tommy and Mac but ultimately I made the decision to go with Warner Brothers. Even so, for the first half of the summer, Mac and I drove around in his station wagon. He fed me headcheese and po'boys. I was learning about Dr. John's lifestyle and that made every word, every mile, every bite, and every note an initiation into a historical figure in music. It was going to be an unusual gourmet summer.

Mac and I took a trip to San Francisco for a few days for some events he had to attend. He was writing songs on pieces of paper in the Holiday Inn, where he would do his own kind of disassembling and reassembling of syllables into new words. I was delighted to begin to understand his dialect. Like there, dialect might have become "dime-ametric" or "sign-alectic." He played with syllables and meanings. He was a twenty-four-hour-a-day songwriter.

I remember walking into a dry goods and clothing shop in Chinatown where there was an old man sleeping in a chair. Mac said, "They got dope here, I can smell it." I bought a little white three-dollar beret. He said, "Good, white is for purity. You are a sweet and innocent girl. You should wear the white beret, not the red one."

And so I did, on the cover of *Rolling Stone*, one year later.

Chippyin' your little kiss

One day I asked him about heroin, if he still took it. He had scars on his arms. He was evasive. I asked him if he could get some . . . for *me*. And so into the wonderful garden that I had finally created, I invited the snake.

Now junkies usually have a code: never induct a new soul into hell. Dr. John asked, "Have you ever taken it before?"

"Yes, I did."

I left off, "Once, seven years ago." With my answer, I was one of his secret krewe and he was off the hook as far as karma was concerned.

Here was some kind of test that I would not pass. Mac went and copped some dope, and shot me up in a motel room on La Cienega.

He left me there that night and all the next day. I wonder if he thought I was going to die because I sure thought I was. I know that I did not wake up for hours, and when I did, I threw up and threw up again and again until I could not throw up anymore. Then I stepped outside and stood on the balcony looking at the traffic going by.

Mac came back that afternoon and drove me home. All that summer I "chippied," taking dope for just a few days at a time. That is how "Junior," the dealer, and all the junk-o lingo, found its way through the gates of my Eden, even before I had a chance to tell the Lord how beautiful I thought the garden was.

I would end up using for the next year, taking dope for a week or a month and then stopping. At first I had the willpower, no problem, but it wasn't me, it was my angel who pulled me from the mire. Each time, a little bit of my skin was taken away. My angel would tire. Junkies think chippyin' is worse than just staying on dope the whole time. That's just junkie reasoning.

The dope I was smoking in Los Angeles was "Mexican Brown," a thick and tarry substance, "unshootable," which was a lucky thing. I had no intention of ever shooting drugs again. It helped my angel that shooting Mexican Brown was not possible.

The dope fiends devised a way to smoke it on tinfoil sheets they called "chasing the dragon." It became my nightly ritual. I lit a match under the heroin and watched as it turned to liquid and smoke. I chased that smoke trail with a rolled-paper tube. One single puff, and all the world was right. All things were possible. Everything was even. Loneliness did not hurt anymore.

I didn't feel heroin was taking from me, I thought it was giving so much that I was becoming a new and improved Rickie. If Tom Waits wanted me to show that I did not need him, I did him three better, I didn't *need* anyone, anymore, anytime. Heroin flattens all the sharp edges and makes a junkie think they're a better version of themselves. Maybe they are—for a while. A little confidence breeds confidence, a little soothing keeps the anxiety away. Junkie talk. Excuses.

Some Witches in Arkansas

One night after smoking dope, I nodded off and into a heroin "waking dream." This was my first and most terrifying waking dream. I had dreamed of a witch doctor, and during the dream I realized I was dreaming but could not wake up. Since there was a kind of voodoo about the dream, I called Dr. John: "This witch doctor was going to kill me and I could not get back into my body." He listened quietly and then said, "Sounds like you got in the way of some witches in Arkansas. There's some witches in Arkansas who're trying to do some curses or some hoodoo on me."

Dr. John made a house call. He came over to my Santa Monica home with some incense, dirt, and dragon's blood. He lit the incense, said some prayers, and did a voodoo "four-corners ceremony" by anointing the corners of my apartment with the dirt and dragon's blood. He banished the demon, I never saw it again. So far . . .

Mac and I played together many times through the years. *In a Sentimental Mood*, the big band record he made with Tommy LiPuma in 1989, had Mac and me on it singing "Makin' Whoopee!" It won a Grammy for Best Jazz Vocal Performance, Duo or Group. It made it to No. 8 on Billboard, and had a VH1 video that was very popular. We also appeared on Johnny Carson together promoting the record. The song only took two takes and it was good. That year would be a great musical year for me: duets with Rob Wasserman ("Autumn Leaves," which garnered a Grammy nod) and Dr. John on "Whoopee," which won a Grammy, as well as working with Walter Becker for *Flying Cowboys*.

"Blue Valentines"

Tom had asked me to come to the recording of "Somewhere." He wanted me to know it was for me, my *West Side Story* influence and my gentle nudging him to sing with his own voice. Tom and Chuck then invited me to the cover photo shoot for Tom's *Blue Valentine*. I was excited to be there. The invitation made me feel like I was part of their circle, maybe even something more than just a third wheel. Chuck was acting his role as ambassador, always the Svengali for Waits. I was to be a romantic lead in this movie.

My friend Mary Simon painted "Blue Valentine" across the fender of Waits's brand-new T-Bird. He could have gone to any chop shop on East Sunset Boulevard but had thrown her the job and she had overcharged him. My first lesson in the complex ways money hammers friendship.

I'd bought two shirts at a secondhand store, presents for my boys, Tom and Chuck, and I brought them with me to the shoot. Chuck wore the polyester one that Tom thought looked like it was soaked with blood ("Romeo is Bleeding"). Waits wore the little green kid's shirt I had bought him for the cover, a gesture that made me feel like I might really matter to him. Certainly it signified Tom's leaving behind the white shirt and tie. He was changing. I knew that I was drawing him out.

Chuck was playing the role of Tom's fix-it-man on the shoot: "Tom is nervous, he's not getting the shot. Go talk to him, he needs you. You can relax him." Me? Near Tom *now*?

Sure, sure, I'll go pet the lion.

Tom was standing by the gas pumps. I stepped out from the sidelines and approached him. He looked anxious. He was not himself. But he growled his sweeter growl when he saw me, and I hunkered down on the ground and started talking to him. "Just you and me here now, bub. Look at *me*." Kind of reminded me of talking to my brother in the hospital. Then I got out of the shot and kept on whispering.

Tom was kind of turned on. He closed his eyes.

The photographer saw what was happening and asked me to be *in* the shot. Tom said, "Come closer." I leaned myself against him, I slid down his body, and he raised his arms. There is the enigma of our very private love and passion, caught in that photo. Even that moment showed up in the culture. I saw it in *Dracula*, Gary Oldman's very sexual vampire doing his own Tom Waits with Rickie Lee Jones.

We fed a craving so sharp that we wanted to become each other. We had an attraction so potent we were in danger of eating one another. "Here bub, climb into my skin, then you'll always know where I am." And then he would disappear. It was as if he had never been there, as if he'd never heard my sighs and never whispered how he needed me so.

> *Goodbye boys, you buddy boys, you sad-eyed Sinatras*
> *It's a cold globe around the seas*
> *Keep the shirt that I bought ya . . .*
> *I know you'll get a chance to make it*
> *Nothing's going to stop you*
> *Reach right out and take it*
> *You say, "So Long Lonely Avenue"*
>
> ("Pirates [So Long Lonely Avenue]")

Santa Monica

My father showed up unexpectedly that summer. He felt like he was entitled to a little bit of what I was about to receive. He came to my home and planted himself in the spare room, waiting to write a song with me, singing me his compositions. It was painful. His music was not the vision I had for myself. My mother was furious that he showed up after all these years now that fortune had come my way, but I could not totally blame him. He wanted that success long before I was even born; the best I could do was pretend I didn't care.

I wasn't Father Flanagan and I couldn't send him back to his father so I avoided my house by driving around with Dr. John. One late night my father waited up for me like I was in high school. When I came in, Dad said, "Now sit down here with me. I have been here all month, and you have not spent time with me." He couldn't seem to see that I was in trouble and needed help. I picked up my guitar and sat down next to him. "Okay, Dad, I have been having a hard time with this song," and I sang:

> *All the gang has gone home*
> *Standing on the corner all alone*
> *You and me, streetlight,*
> *We paint the town grey.*

Without missing a beat, my father replied:

> *O, we are so many lambs who have lost our way.*

Sweet. I liked it. I was writing with my dad. He was so happy that he would be a co-writer with me on my upcoming record. Somehow a lifetime of being the black sheep with the old man Peg was redeemed. Peg, Bea, all the showbiz Joneses, they were with me now, showing me the way to go.

I changed "so many lambs" to "so many lamps who have lost our way," because I was speaking to a streetlight, after all, and it would mix metaphors to bring in lambs. Ivan Ulz lesson number one.

> *All the gang has gone home*
> *Standing on the corner all alone*
> *You and me, streetlight*
> *We'll paint the town grey*
> *Oh we are so many lamps*
> *Who have lost our way*
> *Say good night, America,*
> *The world still loves a dreamer*
> *And all the gang has gone home*
> *And I'm standing on the corner*
> *All alone.*
>
>   ("After Hours")

Finally in September, my dad left me to go back to his own life in Arizona. It was time for me to start recording. Dad had found a good romance in his second wife, Jean, and he needed to be with her, not me. Unfortunately, Dad was chasing my success. He and Jean soon moved to L.A. and he was serious enough about making music that he eventually recorded his own with the help of the guy who owned that building over Danny's All-Star Joint. Phil Erinberg, I believe. Richard finally claimed his place on his own merit. I guess.

Chapter 18

Rickie Lee Jones

At home in Santa Monica after
the cover shoot for *Rickie Lee Jones*

Nick Mathe rented a large, abandoned café near Amigo Studios for me to write. About 8 p.m., after the recording day was finished, I'd drive over to my café studio and work all night. I would sit there and suffer, like I was cutting those songs from inside of me. In one night I wrote "On Saturday Afternoons in 1963." The next week I wrote "Coolsville." It was very painful, lots of tears and despair went into those songs.

You stick it here
You stick it there
But it never fits

Lenny and Russ recorded my first album between September and December 1978. Two weeks of tracking with the greatest people in the business—I'd never heard of any of them.

It was a big challenge for me, hearing my songs for the first time interpreted by other people. Up until then I heard my songs more like expressions of their original feelings than as completed recordings. I knew and cared little about bass drums and keyboard parts. So I learned a lot that fall, about the recording board and musicians and about myself. I was really very mature given my inexperience. A fine musician. I knew, musically anyway, who I was.

There are two sessions that stand out in my memory. Drummer Stephen Gadd had played with singer-songwriters like Paul Simon and super-literate musicians like Steely Dan—he knew how to play stories. I was working with *the* premier drummer for singer-songwriters. I recall as we listened back to "The Last Chance Texaco," Steve laughed: "This was like driving down a road; we went uphill, we came downhill." Until then I had no idea I had sped up or slowed down. I was following the natural storytelling cadence instead of my music tempo. He was the ultimate drummer, teaching me a lesson about myself.

Victor Feldman, the British percussionist who had recorded with Miles Davis, also offered me a lesson in music. Victor was a musical genius who had that youthful energy of all great players. I was having trouble landing "Coolsville" and its sublime subtlety. I didn't want it to be cliché. We'd already recorded it a couple of times, once with the great Randy Brecker playing trumpet, à la *Mean Streets* (Warner Brothers had screened it privately for me), but it made me sound like I was . . . trying. I knew what I wanted, I just didn't know how to say it. Six hours into the session, it was now ten o'clock at night when Victor said, "I think I know what she wants. No more talking. Just record us."

He put his sticks and brushes away and played the snare with his hands as I sang. I called the control room, "Turn down the lights," and we recorded the song twice. I listened, still sitting at the piano, Victor still at the drum, and I wept. I was overcome with emotion. Russ came out and patted me and smiled.

"Come back now. We have work to do."

My inability to convey what I wanted was simply inexperience. I had no real musical vocabulary, nor music education, so I had to rely on the empathy of great musicians. They were professionals and they were artists. Just as Alfred Johnson had been able to do when we created "Company," they could feel my descriptions and create the musical dialogue to meet my muse.

From the very beginning I was surrounded by the very best people in music, the best musicians, the best engineers, the great Amigo Studios. Russ and Lenny were the perfect people to connect me, a young singer who hadn't ever recorded or worked with veteran studio musicians, with the incredible resources of Warner Brothers. I was accepted as a peer and treated with the respect of a seasoned musician because I was giving it my all to release that something inside me that was "my music." I think the musicians, Lenny, Russ, and all the people at the company recognized the magic I was trying so hard to create, so they cheered me on and respected and even loved my effort.

I don't think Warner Brothers had any idea I would be as big a success as I was. There was no time to build a stable home. I was launched like a rocket and the rocket went much further than the expected trajectory.

The Orchestra

Christmas Eve would be the last day of recording. I was to sing on the huge movie soundstage with a sixty-four-piece orchestra under the great conductor Ralph Burns. We would put strings on "Company," "On Saturday Afternoons in 1963," "Night Train," and "After Hours" (twelve bars past good night).

I was to sing live in front of the whole orchestra. Me, in front of the same orchestra as Frank Sinatra (Frankie Machine!), Randy Newman, all those old cats. I admit I was kind of nervous and very thrilled as I entered the sound booth. The pianist, Randy Kerber, began, elegantly playing Alfred's line, the one he wrote that night just over a year ago.

> *I'll remember you too clearly,*
> *But I'll survive another day,*
> *Conversations to share,*
> *When there's no one there,*
> *I'll imagine what you'd say.*

I thought, Alfred, can you believe it? Here I am a year later singing our song! Can you hear me?

> *Well I'll see you in another life now, baby.*
> *See you in my dreams,*
> *But when I reach across the galaxy,*
> *I will miss your company.*

Nick DeCaro was so overcome by the song that he walked up to me in the control booth and gave me a big fat kiss. I think he stuck his tongue in my mouth. Russ Titelman entered the room at that moment with Lenny and asked, "What's going on?" Lenny said, "I think Nick likes our girl's singing."

We giggled like kids. It was bizarre but I suspect a sensitive musician like Nick must have felt the energy of the night.

We were running up against Christmas Eve union rules, three minutes left until we reached *triple golden time pay* for the sixty-four musicians and staff. That's Jesus's union time, overtime on a holiday. Triple it and then double that. I knew the folly of pushing any further. Wow, O union! We needed to decide if we had "Night Train."

I paused, not wanting to rush into a bad take, but no, it was good. I whispered into the microphone:

"We are done."

"It's a wrap." Ralph corrected me.

I walked out of the recording booth and the orchestra applauded, slapping their bows and clapping their hands. They had remained the extra minutes to offer me, a newcomer, that respect. My producers smiled like proud fathers.

It was a bittersweet drive back to Santa Monica. I had not yet learned that every single moment, every accomplishment, deserves a hallelujah and a smile to celebrate the here and now of it (that is like nowhere else). But when it's over, well, it's done. (I didn't want it to ever be over.)

I called my mother. "Ma, I finished my record."

"What are you going to call it?" she asked.

"Rickie Lee Jones."

"Good." She said she was proud of me, and her voice was enough lullaby to allow me to sleep. I woke to the greatest Christmas gift imaginable. My dream had come true. I had completed my record. From now on and forever, this would be true.

Lee Herschberg began mixing the album as I poured over photographs for the cover. I'd done three sessions with Norman Seeff but I didn't like any of the photos because he had shot the kind of thing I saw everywhere—glamour-puss stuff. I wasn't sure what I wanted but I felt it deeply so I would know it when I saw it. We would have to shoot again, maybe find a new photographer. Every detail had to be right. The font, the back photo with barefoot Rickie as a child in her braids with her arms around a couple boys. Like me now with my producers. It had to be perfect. Let's print all the lyrics, it's the story of me.

Norman came to my house on a winter's day to try for some pictures in my element. We shot in my living room where I wore my sweater and my bathing suit. (Just like that dreadful day when my dad beat me.) I changed into my old 1940s coat, my delicate knitted white scarf, my beret, and my brown Shermans, and we hurried to the beach to get those few minutes of golden light.

"If we hurry we can shoot the sun going down behind you. Stand over here, maybe let your hair . . ."

"No. Just shoot me like this." I was almost irritated.

I lit a cigarette and Norman shot away. It didn't take long, he caught the iconic shot with the colors of sunset behind me. The golden light had set and we were done. We all gasped when we saw the pictures a few days later. They were stunning, unlike anything we'd seen on an album cover.

We took home our "test pressings" and listened carefully to the precious vinyl, which could only be listened to a couple of times before it lost its quality. Russ and I agreed on the sequence—my choice to open with "Chuck E" being a controversial one. Musicians usually save their first single for number two. We had been trying different orders for days. Each time we changed it, the studio had to press a new vinyl.

Then Russ called me: "Rickie, I think we have a winner here. You made a masterpiece." Lenny called and more succinctly declared, "We are going to reap teen coin with this one, kid." I could see his grin through the telephone wire.

Everything was lining up. Even the album cover photograph was the same pose as my grandfather's publicity shot from fifty years ago. Frank Jones had lit a cigarette and bent toward the fire, his hat upon his head just so. Like I said, destiny. Magic.

In March my record was released to little fanfare. The very first notice for my work came from an industry magazine reviewing new releases. The writer gave me one line: "Jill Clayburgh meets Raymond Chandler and there's a bad connection." Ouch. The second mention came from the *Los Angeles Times*, the most important music paper at the time. Music critic Robert Hilburn quoted me saying, "We live the jazz side of life." This became an idea associated with me for the rest of my career.

"Say something they can quote," said Chuck E. Weiss, sage advisor to the young and unquotable. "They like simple phrases, that makes it easy on them." At that time, nobody else in American music seemed interested in "the jazz side of life." I knew it was unique. In 1979 the world was disco or maybe punk, even Miles Davis had abandoned the jazz roads he himself had dug. The jazz side of life would be home to me from now on.

In a world in a shell

Warner Brothers took a budding, highly innovative marketing approach. They were experimenting with creating "a movie" as the launching pad to get my music to my potential audience.

Bob Regehr spearheaded my promotion, hiring photographer Ethan Russell to direct my video. Ethan had gained prominence shooting *Abbey Road* and the Beatles. Warner Brothers had already filmed Emmylou Harris and Leon Redbone in two separate Western-themed pieces of no particular consequence, at least as far as promoting the artists or the genre. But I was different. I was new and I had some kind of fire about me, a real-life fire that was highly marketable. Warner Brothers pulled out all the stops.

Ethan created a storyboard of a fictionalized Rickie Lee Jones, built around the romantic "street" images I continue to be associated with. I chose "Young Blood," "Coolsville," and "Chuck E's in Love" as the music for our film. There was no dialogue, just me acting in my songs. Ethan used my personal trinkets and photo booth friends to create background imagery authentic to me. The story would be of me as the girl next door, on her own in the big, big city. I had not yet learned to protect what was private, no matter how sellable it might be. As far as I was concerned, my life was no different than my music. If I was selling a song I was selling *me*.

The video worked; it was fun, iconic, compelling. I was a beautiful creature on film. The songs, the sound, I exploded all over the whole dang radio format. Warner Brothers had another trick up their sleeve: the image, whole and intact, that took promotion to a whole other level.

Warner Brothers installed the new technology of video players and television monitors in record stores nationwide. They put me and my music video right next to the music buyer. I had prime placement in the window displays; sometimes I was singing right over buyers' heads as they flipped through records. This was spectacular new technology rewriting all the rules. Eventually I walked into a record store to see myself up there, tossing my cigarette as I walked off the soundstage onto the real stage. It was mind-bending. There I was standing in the world that actor walked away into. Was I real or was I Memorex? Eventually even *Second City Television* (the comedy show that launched many of the great eighties comedians) got the joke—and included a skit of Tom Waits and me inventing ourselves inventing ourselves. Waits growling, of course, but what of me, their impression of me? Just a great big smile! That was how people saw Rickie Lee Jones that first year: a huge smile. Well, I had a lot to smile about.

In the fall of 1979, I had dinner with Ethan Russell as we watched *20/20*, a serious news show created to challenge *60 Minutes*. The idea of a "music video" was so impactful that they devoted a segment on how video would be the new direction for music and how it was *possible* that future videos might reach the caliber of the work of this newcomer Rickie Lee Jones.

"Who is Rickie Lee Jones?" Both the question and the answer were broadcast nationwide before I ever even set foot on the performance stage. My first tour was not the traditional outreach to create myself, but to prove a *fait accompli*. I was already a successful realization in the audience's mind, I simply had to sing the songs. I was launched into the public as a fully-developed rock icon.

Instead of a marketing process that would take many years, many concerts, and perfect reviews, people knew who I was immediately. And they knew me not by word of mouth or from profiles, they knew me because they saw and felt me in the video. I had one of the best head starts in all of music history before I hit the stage. I was indeed the first video sensation because I was the first video.

More than just giving listeners an image of who was singing, my video persona brought a depth to the recordings. I had charisma, emotion, I had chops; all the terrible and wonderful life I had lived up to now was in the very soil of my voice. My persona already had deep roots before I stepped onstage. The marketing was not a ruse—I really was something to believe in.

People are always hungry for a new and young, sophisticated musician. The fact that the person fitting this bill was a *woman*, well, that was refreshing.

This also flipped the sequence on the critics who usually functioned as early-warning systems to define new music for a mass audience. This time the critics had to catch up to the audience. Some critics simply ignored me. Others compared me to Joni Mitchell for the superficial reason that we were both blonde women with guitars. (Critics didn't cite blond-haired Stephen Stills to introduce the blond-haired singer of A Flock of Seagulls.) There is still a long-standing sexist attitude about women's appearance.

It was sloppy thinking and writing to automatically group Joni and me together, and that sexism diluted both of our unique musics and personalities. This wasn't a cakewalk—there was only one chair left for the woman musician at the big table, whereas the boys-only room had plenty of empty chairs. Comparisons insinuate that neither party is unique or can create unique work.

I had proclaimed the virtues of my mentors from the get-go. I shouted "Laura Nyro, Taj Mahal, Van Morrison," but many of the lesser critics could only see how Joni and I appeared to them, as "blondes with guitars."

I wanted to have staying power. I was aware before I even made a record of the danger of being used up too fast. There is a frenzy that happens in the pop music world and I was in the thick of it. I planned to stay around for a lifetime while frenzies were fleeting. I knew I would have to make my records interesting enough to withstand a fall from the top. I needed many more hats than the Rickie Lee Jones brand of raspberry-beret-wearing, streetwise, jazz-side-of-life-living girl next door.

So there I was with my song blasting out of car radios. So cool!

> *What's her name?*
> *Is that her there?*
> *Christ I think he even combed his hair.*

But I never said a word. If I was quiet and used my powers of invisibility, then maybe they couldn't see me to take my dream away from me.

Just one year before, I was getting ready to do my showcase. Now here I was, greedy to do my first tour. A year ago, my dream was modest but still beyond my grasp; I only wanted to be a professional singer. It was well beyond even my overamped imagination to be the subject of someone's high-minded talk about recreating America's musical standards, or to be so famous that people everywhere saw themselves in me.

I had a record, we knew it was good, we had a plan, and everything was going our way. But still, there was no guarantee that the snake wouldn't come into my garden. Instead of living my musical dreams, I could end up as a stenographer with a head full of daydreamy music fantasies, transcribing depositions about feuding neighbors. I was lucky that Heaven and Earth had finally cooperated with me. They had tested me with decades of pain, then gave me a lifetime of glory compressed in a summer of impossible success.

THE WAY BACK SEAT

Chapter 19

Saturday Night Live

At *SNL* rehearsal

I got the word that I would be doing *Saturday Night Live* as we were finishing production on the *Rickie Lee Jones* record. Lorne Michaels had seen the video and was very keen to have me debut on his show the very week my record was released. Warner Brothers and NBC were getting together to make the debut a success. *Saturday Night Live* would even design the stage to look like the video. This was so far beyond my expectations that I was actually confused at first—why were there garbage cans on my set?

There was a buzz in Warner Brothers. I did my best to stay cool and collected. Which meant being straight, being ready, being thin, and looking good. My job was to walk right up like I belonged there.

Did I belong there? My mind was a storm but I kept the winds at bay by concentrating on what I needed to do.

I designed a dress and had it made for me. In the era of tight disco polyester clothes, I would look like no one else. My 1940s-style dress had three-quarter-length sleeves and went down to midcalf. My seamstress even found fabric left over from the forties. When she was there measuring me I felt like a throwback magazine character, like Damon Runyon's Apple Annie. Tom Waits had given me *The Damon Runyon Omnibus* as a birthday gift so that I could explore the American vernacular and its metaphors. Damon Runyon and Tom Waits were teaching me the literary side of what I did naturally. Anyway, I felt like Apple Annie.

I wanted to know how to do makeup 1940s style, so I called my mother. She told me to go to the dime store and buy "pancake makeup." She said that's all they used when she was a kid. Dampen the sponge and wet the powder, apply liberally. I applied liberally alright, on my face, on my arms, on my shoulders, everywhere. She was right, it covered everything. I didn't have any shoes for the show. Surely I could find the right shoes in New York City. But the closest thing I found to 1940s style on Madison Avenue had metal stiletto heels. They ended up on the cover of *Rolling Stone*.

Bob Regehr hired Susan McGonigle as my tour manager for the show. McGonigle was an inspired pick even beyond the fact that she had been living in a tent in Ojai. She was soft-spoken but a stickler for details and getting things done. For five days Susan and I sweated out every detail of rehearsal for the big show.

This would be my first real rehearsal with an entire band. It was only two songs but it was a good idea to rehearse all week, not so much for the music but so that I could wring out all that anxiety and be relaxed enough to click my ruby slippers when the time came.

Sound Check

I came early to the sound check. The union guys had to set up the entire stage, and since I was early I sat around with the crew, the union boys, drinking coffee and telling them dirty jokes. I knew instinctively that I wanted to be remembered by them. They were the regular folks I was reaching for: "I am one of you" was my banner. Decades later I met one of those crew guys and he reminded me about the risqué joke I told to that roomful of union men. He said, "After that joke, we all loved you." That's the way to stay in show business. To remember that the people behind the curtain or the camera matter every bit as much as the people in front of it.

The musicians arrived and set up their equipment. I was allowed two run-throughs for my sound check. The crew would do their sound and camera blocking. My set was looking rather "streetwise"; those garbage cans were bothering me. I knew this was like the video, but I didn't want to be associated with garbage. Charlie Lorre, my product manager at Warner Brothers, re-explained that *Saturday Night Live* was recreating the *video*. Yes, but other than Lorne Michaels and a handful of others, nobody else had seen it yet! I accepted the set, and the thoughtfulness of *Saturday Night Live*, although in my heart I thought it was kind of over-the-top. I know now that this was a concerted effort to create an image right out the gate.

Originally Lorne Michaels wanted to choose which songs I performed. He wanted "Danny's All-Star Joint" and "Chuck E's in Love." Get outta here! I felt strongly that I had to retain control over my music. I was encouraged by Chuck and Tom. Although they had not experienced this kind of success, their principles were sound: keep control of your music, don't let them change you. Lorne relented.

One thing though, Lorne did not want "Coolsville" as my second song. There was a meeting to decide but it didn't happen until the day of the show, at four o'clock in the afternoon, not long before the show started. I argued that "Chuck E's in Love" was too upbeat and unusual so it needed a counterweight. Showing the dark, somber side of my work by doing "Coolsville" as my second number would show the range of my music. Anything else would be a misrepresentation. It mattered to me that I be accurately presented from the very start, or not presented at all.

"Coolsville" was probably the last song they expected to air on a comedy show. They wanted up, up, up! But I *knew* the contrast of

"Coolsville" was the way to make a much bigger impact. It would be good for everyone. They said they would put "Coolsville" on at the end of the show, though there was a small chance that time would run over.

That sounded like bullshit, but I said to Lorne, "Well let's see what happens." I believed somehow that it was going to work out but with all my inexperience and bravado, I confidentially announced to Charlie Lorre that I would not do the show if I could not do "Coolsville." Charlie agreed.

Charlie Lorre was a good choice as my product manager because he was a jazz guy and he liked the jazz evocation of my style. He understood my determination to not be corrupted straight out of the gate. I didn't need to shout "I am a jazz singer" to Charlie, he had already heard it in my music so he was on my side. That may have cost him his job later on but on that Saturday, between my saucy stage fright and his determination to protect me, I almost didn't do the show.

The Performance

Now it was time to get ready. My hair was in curlers. I was putting on my mom's dime store pancake makeup. Lookin' good! Two hours now. I felt very much at ease. The music part felt as if it had already taken place. We were so prepared we could do it in our sleep. I could feel everyone else was nervous but not me. Susan came in. I could feel her heart racing with excitement and nerves. Someone else came in. Then another person and another. Roles were being reversed, I was managing everyone else's nerves and emotions. I said, "You guys, can you leave me alone?"

It helped them to know I had this, it was gonna be alright. Whatever it was, it was gonna be okay. I was trying to stay very calm, very still.

Then in came Charlie Lorre who said:

"They're going to cut 'Coolsville.'"

"Huh?"

"I just overheard them talking. You need to know. I can't lie to you. It's your music, kid. Your decision."

"But they said—"

"I know what they said, but . . ."

Then a very agitated Lorne Michael was standing in my doorway. "What did you tell her?"

"I told her the truth. You are planning to cut 'Coolsville.'"

"That's *not* the truth. That's *not* what we said. We are not going to cut 'Coolsville.' Why did you say that?"

Lorne was passionate but firm: "I said if we ran out of time, we might have to drop the song. I didn't say we were going to."

Everyone was looking at me now—so what was it going to be, Rickie Lee?

I silently started taking out my curlers and preparing to look good. There, I thought, that's my answer.

I came here with my big dream which was now as real and immutable as the walls in this room. If I compromised on this, where would I be a year from now? What did principles mean if you dropped them when the pressure was on? But I *wanted* to do this. I *had* to do this. Would I be the girl who could have done it all and left on a technicality?

Nick zipped his lips as if to say, it's up to you but I really want you to do it. I knew I had to go on now or not ever. All eyes were on me, but I was silent.

My answer was to walk into the hallway to wait with the band while the comedians before me finished their bit. It was like waiting on the gangplank to board the Apollo. At some point everyone just has to wait before they take off.

My people were there, too. Charlie Lorre looking sheepish and amped up at the same time. Susan McGonigle, smiling and quietly checking every detail. Nick Mathe, keeping his distance so as not to bug me. His buttons were about to burst. "I'm gonna go sit in the audience," he giggled, "or I'm gonna lose my mind." He was like a little boy. "Break a leg!"

Now they cut to a commercial and we had a few minutes to walk quickly and quietly out from backstage and onto the set. The audience was not facing us, they were to my left. We quickly took our places: the drummer and bass player, guitar player, the percussionist, the singers, the *Saturday Night Live* horn players, and me, out front and center. Surrounded by everyone and also so alone.

I was holding my guitar and smiling, nodding, talking to the musicians around me like a band leader, "It's nothing. Just a song. This is what we do."

I was basing my self-confidence on my faith that I was meant to be there. Faith that I could do this. Faith that I was destined to be "Rickie Lee Jones, happy-ever-after."

It was my natural inclination to sing to the audience, but the audience faced a different stage than the one I stood on. Tonight I would have to settle for the millions of people watching through that little lens.

Now the moments were counted in seconds, and I went inside myself. Just one more effort and I'd cross over to happy-ever-after. One of the singers, Arno Lucas whispered, "You'll be great." Or maybe the whisper was from Chuck E. Weiss. Or my mom. Or that union guy. Maybe it was from me. I know I heard it.

"You're already a star, girl," Leslie Smith said, and Matthew Weiner smiled in agreement. My singers were ready.

"Ladies and Gentlemen. Sixty seconds. Sixty seconds everyone."

This was the moment before the battle. The moment before the rising of the sun. The moment before all was changed. An ink was about to touch the paper that would color the meaning of my past and future. We were seconds before nothing ever being the same.

My brain was moving fast. Was I still holding my guitar? The hat still on? I touched the hat, it was there. A stillness came over me. I was okay, so I half-wondered, Why am I okay? I answered myself:

"I like it here, at the gate, at the beginning of all things. I came here to sing."

At the speed of light, thoughts shot across my sky. The audience was to my left so they weren't looking at me. Oh no, those people weren't looking at me. Why weren't they looking at me? Please don't let my mouth get dry now. I smiled. Was I smiling? Yes, I was still smiling.

"When you see the red light go on, that's when you are live."

And then, like being lifted on a tidal wave, I was taken up out of my head and then placed back on stage. The cameraman, counting down with his fingers now, gave me a smile and said:

"Say hello to America. Five . . . four . . . three . . . two . . ."

Bump, badabada bump, doyeeoeeo bump . . .

I did not play the opening of my song. I started as if I were bringing my band, my crew, my theater into your home. My back was turned and I was playing with my hat. I knew just who to be. I was walking into America's house.

Badabada bump bump ba-bada-bada . . .

Were my fingers working? Yes! Was I playing the right notes? Yes I was! I heard my voice:

> *How come he don't come and PLP with me?*

(Let 'em figure out what that meant . . . surely someone would remember Public Leaning Posts.)

By the second verse I was at ease. I had it. The music fit like my skin. The show fit like I'd lived in it for years. Hey look, here comes my chorus! Hi, chorus! I was so happy. Hey Mom, look at me!

Okay folks, here's a rhyme you have never heard before:

> *Tell you what, I saw him down at the Pantages*
> *And whatever it is that he's got up his . . . uh . . . sleeve . . .*
> *I hope it is not contagious . . .*

The cameraman pulled back and looked around his camera. I reached him. He smiled at me.

I looked into the lens and thought, For a dragon you are not really so scary after all. I loved the camera. I loved the audience.

Is he here?
Look in the pool hall.

People had to lean in now. I had America in the palm of my hand.

Is he here?
Look in the drugstore.
Is he here?
No, he don't come here no more.

The end was coming. The song was almost over. The last line of the last chorus:

Chuck E's in love . . . He's in love
With me . . .

My three minutes and eighteen seconds in front of millions of people had come and gone. It was over. Millions and millions.

Back in my dressing room, everyone was celebrating. "Congratulations kid, you did it," Charlie Lorre said, smiling, like he'd seen it all before.

Nick was so happy I was picking up his burst buttons everywhere I looked. He was a very white-skinned guy, with white hair and pale blue eyes, but he turned pink when he was happy. He was tinting the air pink with his joy.

"Oh Rickie, you were incredible," as Nick sat down and got all teary-eyed.

"Look how far we came from 21 Westminster! *Saturday Night Live*! I can't believe it! Oh my God. You did that—you knocked it out of the ballpark."

More Nick-tears.

"Now I have to do my part. And I *will*."

I was not yet speaking. I was nodding. I was still at work, still waiting for the call for "Coolsville." Charlie Lorre was working too, waiting there in my corner. We still had the impossible job of standing up for musical principles. We were watching the clock, wondering if they would call me for the last song as they promised they would. Why did I care so much? Why couldn't I just accept that I had nailed it and that happy-ever-after was coming my way? It was me, it was my music. I had walked out of Bud Dain's instead of compromising when I was starving and near homeless. My parents and I had walked out on Lew King's television show when they insisted we needed an insurance policy for me, the fourth-grader, to sing.

With only six minutes left in the show, Charlie and I were ready for the letdown from the Man and his lies. A knock on the door and a head appeared: "Come on, you're back on."

Someone was saying, "I told you we would do it if we had time. Didn't I tell you?" No time to rejoice, I had to get ready to show the world "Coolsville," the dark side of town, where nothing would ever be the same again.

I hurried to the set that was a scene from *On the Waterfront*. See the rats in the alleyway? Can you see the junkies and the hookers down there? Only five of us were on the stage: a drummer, bass player, guitar player, and a piano player. I would stand and sing now, no guitar in my hand. Let them see me, all of me, in the 1940s dress I'd had made, my hair, my hat. Let them see that I was not like the others. "Ladies and Gentlemen, I have a scar. Would you like to hear it?"

They heard me. To imaginary people who felt the deep loneliness of the song, the junkies and the lonely girls, the old women and night porters—to people like me, the song meant more than just a television appearance. I would have done the song if no one was watching because I was introducing myself, and "Coolsville" represented who I was. But I was lucky, I got to perform "Coolsville," and I was fully introduced to millions of people watching live from New York City on April 7, 1979. The die was cast, I had invited the world to listen to my story.

Walk Tall, Act Fine

But after all
There are such things
And these are the things
That turn your memories
Back into dreams again

I went back onstage and stood there for the *Saturday Night Live* closing with everyone from the show sharing the stage. What if no one said hello, like back in school? Hey beautiful goofus, goof unto me. Go out there and say good night! It was as if we walked on the stage in one dimension and came off in another. I was taking care of business. Then I jumped offstage and went back to my dressing room. Susan had packed up my curlers and dress. I grabbed my suitcase for something fundamental to me—a quick escape. Oh oh, where was Nick? Susan was looking for him. I was bewildered that he wasn't by my side to finish the job.

Then Nick appeared and said, "Oh man incredible things are happening, I just met the most beautiful woman, we're going out." He leaned in close and whispered, "Her dad runs the network." I heard the kid from 21 Westminster looking forward to a girl. I did not hear my manager making sure we finished the job.

"You're leaving me? At this moment?"

"I'll see you tomorrow! You did it!"

Well, Nick was always a fool for love.

Susan and I went to the hotel on our own. There was a definite sorrow about Nick leaving us. He never came back, not the next day when we had to leave our hotel, or the day after that. Susan talked to him but he said he was not going back with us to Los Angeles. When Nick finally got the nerve to speak to me, I pleaded, threatened, pleaded again but he couldn't stop whatever he was doing. I gave him an ultimatum: "If you don't come right back now Nick, you are fired." He did not come back.

Susan and I flew home alone. First class. That goddamn snake had followed me into the garden. Susan said, "I know this is horrible for you, but I have you covered. I'll take care of everything." She did stay close, for the next six months, Susan stayed close.

I came back to my Santa Monica bungalow and could not understand why things had taken such a terrible turn. What was Nick thinking? I told Lenny, "I lost my manager somewhere in New York City." Bob Regehr said, "I never trusted that guy anyway."

Regehr would take on my in-house manager role. No one could have been better than Bob. No one. He spent a lot of my money but he made me a lot of money. It would be hard, the rest of my career, when I did not have Bob Regehr to do it right, first-class, no-holds-barred.

After *Saturday Night Live*, the radio went nuts with requests for "the new song by that girl with the beret." I was selling twenty thousand records a day for the first couple of weeks and it just kept going for months. I had front-window photographs displayed in every record store and this was before summer, when video monitors were installed in Tower Records and other record chains, playing my video in constant rotation.

In the following couple of years, I was voted Best Rock, Best Pop, and Best Jazz Singer in polls from *Playboy* to *Rolling Stone*. I was nominated for five Grammy awards including Best Album, Best Song, Best Rock Vocal and Best Pop Vocal, and Best New Artist, which I won. I am proudest of my Best Song nomination for "The Last Chance Texaco" because it was an album track, not a single. Acknowledgment of this sort was rare because only singles were nominated for this category. "Texaco," the elegant child who did not fit in, was still offered a seat at the banquet. I felt that I was storming the gates by my very presence. For those months and years that followed, my public image was as fresh as spring water is clear. Things were going my way and even Tom Waits and I were back on.

I had to pay Nick fifty thousand dollars to end our contract. So be it. I was learning that it didn't work when friends tried to storm the gates of my happy-ever-after. There was a cover charge, a drink minimum, and a long line to get in. Nick cried in court. All he wanted was to come back to me. It was heartbreaking to have to be so cold to him. He had done well up until he made a terrible mistake, but it was a mistake of professionalism and trust.

We were all inexperienced and we were all going to learn how difficult it was to be an overnight success, but we needed to be able to trust each other. In my profession it's absolutely necessary to resist the succubus hangers-on who use drugs, fame, sex, and other distractions to entice you into trusting them. It only gets worse with more success.

Tom and Chuck E. watched *Saturday Night Live* from the Tropicana office because they didn't own televisions. When I returned from New York they picked me up at the airport. I was part of them now. Suddenly the world took on a new shape. I was loved, I was liked, I was making money, and I was famous. So what was the problem kid? What was not to like?

I can tell you that fame brings no solace, no love, and no warmth. I can tell you also that money isolates. You may say, "So what?" and "I'll take it if you don't want it." I *do* want it, fame and money and all that goes with it. It's just that they weren't what I thought they would be.

Shooting my Rolling Stone Cover with Annie Leibovitz

Annie rented a studio in L.A., and I arrived with my own clothes and my own makeup. About thirty minutes into the shoot I took off my lacey top and tied in around my waist. I hunkered down on the ground and invited Annie to come down with me. Not with words, but with energy—that is what a photo shoot is all about: energy. We were down there about fifteen minutes. She got the shot, and said:

"You are the sexiest person I have ever photographed next to Mick Jagger."

I remember thinking, I am way sexier than Jagger.

I drove home alone and the high of the shoot had nowhere to go but the little spoon I kept on the kitchen sink.

Annie and I shot two *Rolling Stone* covers, and one of them was important. Being photographed by Annie Leibovitz was more akin to acting for a director than shooting for a photographer. She indicated what she wanted by clicking sounds—the camera—the more clicks the more she was digging what I was putting down. If the clicks slowed down, I knew we had the shot and moved effortlessly to a new pose, a new idea.

I suspected that this photo shoot was more about Annie's performance than mine, I was just the song, the vehicle to express herself through. Annie was the one who would see gold in the frame—human vulnerability or sexuality. Many people's careers were boosted by Annie's golden eye and a lot was at stake.

For many years, my debut cover eventually became one of the highest-selling issues in *Rolling Stone* history—I was told this by Bob Regehr one afternoon, sitting in his New York office as he pronounced statistics and accomplishments.

She and I did a couple shoots afterwards. One was with a scorpion in the California desert, and the last one was at my house in Ojai, California. It was some time around 1990. I don't think I ever met Annie again.

It seemed to me when my career began to falter in the 1990s, my professional friendships faltered as well. People seemed to be, well, ashamed somehow. Some of them treated me like I was an embarrassment. A few photographers, a couple of musicians and journalists, they treated me as if my career had never mattered to them. Annie was one of those people.

The thrill of seeing my picture on the cover of the magazine didn't really hit until I was driving down the street in New York City. I got out of the limo and walked over to a row of *Rolling Stone* covers just standing there, wondering if anyone was making the connection. I took a magazine out of the rack. Did anyone see? I had come such a long way for this moment and now it had already passed. Kind of anti-climatic. I put the magazine back and crawled back into my limo.

That big-shot high note was tempered by the fact that I felt a little guilty about having all this good fortune. I promised myself to keep my "feet in the street." Seemed as if I was always "representing." From 1979 to 1982, Annie and I documented my part of the greatest time in rock's history. Me, Rickie Lee Jones, non-folk singer with an acoustic guitar, jazz singer who is as sexy as Mick Jagger, expanding the view of women in music. The women who came after me would have a much wider palette from which to draw their colors, they'd be more than a guest in some guy's band. They could roll around in their bras or dance around with their acoustic guitars and no one would say they weren't serious musicians, simply because they were dancing. I did that. That was me. The girl in the red beret.

Chapter 20

The Bus Stop Blues

Le chat and I, Chateau Marmont

Tickets for the first tour had gone on sale even before *Saturday Night Live*. I kept my prices at the pre–*Saturday Night Live* level (three bucks a shot) and sold out every show in every town. By summertime I had a set and lights and monitors guys, the whole shebang. I thought the record company was footing the bill, so no expense was spared to make my set fabulous. I designed a rooftop scene like the one in *West Side Story* and my video. Marc Brickman, the genius set designer, made the sky behind me transform from dark night to daylight as if the sun were rising throughout the show. Eventually I got a bill from Warner Brothers, but it didn't matter, the show was everything. I grossed a million and came home with fifty thousand. What did I care, I was selling so many records I would never run out of money, would I?

My First European Tour

I left for Europe in the summer after my second round of U.S. tour dates, but in Europe it was harder to set up our stage. In some places we just couldn't do it. I was by nature rather shy, I had never been to Europe and this touring thing was still new. Everywhere I looked, I faced my own image in giant proportions, ten-foot-tall posters that lined the streets with my cigarette-smoking, beret-wearing self.

You may remember the Baader-Meinhof people were very active in those days with kidnapping and terror activities targeting Western imperialism, including the U.S. Here I was, a giant poster girl for "The new voice of America." Oh great, put the crosshairs on me so I can hold water for America too. We were selling tickets just fine but Warner Brothers, were you trying to get me killed?

I was to perform at a university in Hamburg in a smallish auditorium with folding chairs. I remember the room seemed too bright and the piano was too close to the edge of the stage but the sound check went well.

I got through the first three or four songs and the show was going fine. The audience seemed distant but I figured they would come along as I opened up my heart at the piano. Language differences seem obvious now but remember, everyone spoke English to me, and touring musicians often forget which city's (and country's) stage they're gracing. It never occurred to me that the audience could not understand me. I sat down at the piano and began a spoken-word introduction of the very personal "We Belong Together." Or maybe it was "On Saturday Afternoons in 1963."

Rickie Takes on the Germans with One Hand Tied Behind Her

I heard something from the audience. What was that? What were they doing? They were *whistling*. I looked over at Buzzy on guitar. Was whistling good or bad? He shook his head. Arno helped, "I think it's bad." I took my hands off the keyboard and looked out at the audience.

Are you really whistling at *me*? Do you think you can bully *me*? Okay, let's see who's tougher.

I sat back on my piano bench and waited but the whistling got louder. They were not stopping. Didn't they want to hear the music? I was getting scared but my ego (my main tool of protection) was swelling up to overwhelm the confusion. I will fight you to the death with my ego! I didn't want to lose control over the audience, and the tour (or my life). I turned back to the piano and wondered how to save the show.

I took out a cigarette and looked for a match somewhere but nobody had rehearsed this skit. I was almost blind with fear but I kept my cool. I stood up and said, "Anybody got a match?" That quieted them. Someone rose from the back and came forward. He reached up to light my cigarette. He was Scottish like the great audience of a few days earlier. He quietly smiled at me and said, "They can't understand you. That's why they're whistling. They just want you to play. They like you."

Okay. They liked me? Okay. On with the show!

I inhaled that Winston, smiled, and turned back to the piano. Out of the corner of my eye I saw two security guards briskly approach the Scottish guy and beat the crap out of him with batons. Right there, right where he had just lit my cigarette and tried to save me and the show. Right next to the stage where the piano was too close to the audience and I could hear the sickening sound of baton on bone. I mean, obviously I had *asked* him to come up. What was *wrong* with these security guards?

I cried out, "Hey, what are you doing? Stop it! Stop that!" Now the show was rapidly slipping away. It was blasphemous for me to lose control over my show, it was the one thing my ancestors would not tolerate, but nobody beat my protector and friend. The whistling was back with an anger, and the show was passing from "slipping away" into "total anarchy" without any subtle gradients.

The crowd seemed to rise as one as their folding chairs toppled over. A wave of fury hit the stage and the musicians ran for cover out of a very real fear of a charging mob. One of the musicians remembered me and came back, not onto the stage (that was too dangerous) but to shout at me still sitting at the piano trying to wait it out and impose my quiet will. "Get off the stage. Get off the stage *now* Rickie!" He was Elmer Gantry and I was Sister Sharon. My whole world was suddenly on fire.

Regehr pulled me behind the curtain backstage. The audience was now throwing the folding chairs. Someone pointed at me and said, "Get her to a safe place." They took me down the stairs to a small basement room and locked Bob Regehr and me in there together. I could see people running by me through a small window overhead.

Bob brought the storm with him. He was furious but not at them, he was furious at me. "What did you do? Why didn't you just fucking sing? You had them in your hand. Why did you do that?"

"Well, they started whistling at me."

"Why didn't you just sing? You had them. You had them!" He kept repeating that.

"You blew it."

Poor Regehr had a lot on the line. He was going to learn the hard way that I was no pop star, no rock star, I was Rickie-star. *Frank fucking Sinatra.* I was gonna do it my way, even if I had to learn the hard way. Bravado is sometimes the only compass we have when times are unfathomably dangerous.

"What I need right now is you not yelling at me. Do not yell at me," I spat back at him. "I have never done any of this before. I'm hiding in a basement in Germany because people want to hurt me over my performance and you're yelling at me?"

I surprised myself.

"You are way too personal, we're in business together Bob. I am not your girlfriend. I think you better go back home right now. *Bob.*"

Talking like that to someone who could make or break your career was a sign of my insistence on professionalism. I had to keep our business relationship firm or I would never be an equal in his eyes and then never be worthy of his commitment. I knew instinctively that

I was making "Rickie Lee Jones" every minute of every day. It was exhausting and I was bound to make mistakes. There in that basement, I raised the bar; Bob and I would conduct ourselves from then on with professionalism no matter the circumstances.

My words took him by surprise. I was worried that I had hurt him and would lose his care of my career. But damn, do you think I *wanted* a riot? I didn't need another insurgent in the room, I needed a manager worldly and professional enough to avoid these messes. Regehr was a PR guy trying to create a buzz across the whole wide world.

And so, my second show in Europe was a riot, literally.

I was in despair when I called Tom Waits. He offered consolation with his personal touches: "Run the bath, you love the sound of water." Tom knew how to soothe me. We had spoken for ninety minutes after Hamburg. It cost me a thousand dollars.

The next day we were back on the phone. "I'm quitting. I want to come home. I hate it out here. They don't even have pancakes." Pancakes suddenly became very important.

"Don't come home. You've come too far to quit and you aren't a quitter."

And finally, "What if I was there with you? Do you want me to come there, baby? Hang on. I'll call you later with my flight number. Everything is going to be okay."

Tom arrived two days later for my Amsterdam show. I met him at the airport, just me. As always they had strip-searched him. They didn't like his greasy hair and pointy shoes. Didn't they know? Couldn't they see that he was an artist?

We lay in each other's arms all day, then he came with me to my show. "Something Cool" was always the opening number that year. It's the story of an older woman who comes into a bar on a hot day. She talks about a "so long ago." Her grand former life, a big house, jewels, and someone she loved. Then someone asks what she wants to drink and she snaps out of her fever dream. She remembers herself and him:

He's just a guy who stopped to buy me something . . . cool.

The Amsterdam show went well and then Bob Regehr returned to the tour for the London Odeon show. I was relieved, I thought I had lost him after that riot. The British audience seemed very different from the German one. When they rushed the stage at the end of the show it was just to be close to us. No flying chairs, angry whistling, or baton beatings of the kindest man in the audience. "You're like a fucking Beatle!" cried Buzzy. I felt like a Beatle with the kids rushing the stage. They were doing it to me!

Backstage, sweaty and tired, Bob had one more guy for me to talk to, one more European president of Warner Brothers. I had to meet them all. All these men were working on my record. While I had no interest in meeting anyone after a show, Regehr knew that personal relationships were the difference between gold and platinum, between a lifelong career and a five-year swirl.

I sat down to talk to the British head of Warner Brothers backstage with my boyfriend at my side. Although Tom had his own fan club and he knew this fame business better than I, he also shied away from the camera. He wanted no part of my celebrity just as he did not want to share his own. Tom felt the business of *Tom Waits* must stay uncorrupted by our affection.

There is a photo of Tom holding my foot; his affection was constant and very physical. We always needed to touch each other. I cannot remember anyone else holding me so completely so that I felt safe to go outward. Now that I had love I just wanted to go home and be loved. My tour, this whole thing, did not compare to being touched by my baby.

Finally I felt like I didn't have to maintain him every moment. He was there for me now and when I went back to America, he would still be there. I could not conceive that this could ever end, and yet I *had* conceived of it with "Coolsville." I knew very well that it was likely one day "I and Bragger and Junior Lee" would be past tense.

My first gig in Paris was at the Casino de Paris. Tom walked around the crowd shushing people. My boyfriend. (Still makes me smile to remember.)

The next day everybody took a flight home to America. Tom and I were in first class which was still new for us both. We ate steaks and got ready for the movie. It was *Superman*! In the film Lex Luthor causes the death of Lois Lane, and Superman turns back time to save her life. I was imagining how long I could hold my breath if rocks came down on my car and smothered me; when I glanced at Tom, I saw that tears were falling down his face as he watched Superman desperately turn back time, making the whole world go backwards so he could save his girl. It was as if he knew the end of us was coming and he could not stop it. I thought then he was overwrought, but we both knew something unnamed was stirring within us.

"So Long, Lonely Avenue"

My last performance for that triumphant year was at Perkins Palace in Los Angeles. It was a downtown theater where Tom, Chuck, and I had seen some Chinese acrobats or Russian folk dancers. I was really high so I don't remember. No one had ever done a rock show there so I knew it would be a unique venue to meet a unique act (me) and everyone would have a unique time. I would be viewed as an *experience*, not just another pop act.

By now all the audience had probably read about Waits in a recent *Rolling Stone* cover story. Those who didn't know who he was would want to know. Those who already knew were either jealous of me or thought, "What a perfect couple!" That was hard on us already, we felt the pressure of the bankability of just being ourselves. Tom used to call me "trendsetter" and I think he loved it and made fun of it at the same time, but that dubiousness followed everything we did.

I wore a skintight spandex pantsuit. I wanted to look sexy. Why not? If Tina Turner could do it, so could I. I wanted to defy what was expected of singer-songwriters. I pretty much looked the same as I did with Little Caesar and the Romans. I wore it with elbow-length gloves I'd bought at Lili St. Cyr (a store named after the famous stripper mentioned in the song "Don't Dream It, Be It" from *The Rocky Horror Picture Show*). Red pumps and the Fredericks of Hollywood bra. I was playing one of Tom's sexiest characters. In fact, his entire record, *Blue Valentine*, seemed to be inspired by his relationship with me.

Between shows Waits came to the dressing room, my amorous suitor (what was it they were doing in there?), then it was time for me to go out. I was already late for the second show, I didn't want to leave him. I just wanted to be his girl. I knew somehow that all this fortune was emanating from a heart that beat for love, for family. The family I always wanted seemed so close in Tom. That was when he said, "Go on out and getcha some glory" in his daddy's Texas drawl. Glory it would be then.

My show began with me and the band bursting through the pretend rooftop stairway onto the stage calling, "MARIA!" the way Tony did when he thought she was dead. Neil made it to the keyboard and we began the set with "Something Cool." Open with a ballad? Dangerous. If it worked, brilliant. And it worked. The crowd went wild.

Tom and I got out of the theater and loaded up his T-Bird. "Goodbye Susan. Goodbye Reggie! Goodbye Art Rodriguez and Buzz and Neil!" At last my tour was over, I was released back into my life.

Tom wanted to make a stop at a humble little house he'd seen for rent in Echo Park, a Hispanic neighborhood with lots of gang members. He kind of liked that gang member thingy. We got out and looked in the windows, then sat on the front porch floor. We watched the lights of the city and dreamed about a life together in that house with our kids. ("You kids knock it off back there.") I would make dinner and he'd mow the lawn. He was laughing and joking about crabgrass and I wished we would never leave, just stay there. Tom and Rickie on the porch.

That porch, that night, was our crossing-over place. There, in each other's arms, dreaming of a life we'd never have together. He went back the next day and rented the house, a place where he would take care of me and I'd always know where he'd be. See, he liked knowing where I was and he wanted me to feel safe. Now he would finally emerge from his longtime cave at the Tropicana and claim a woman as his own.

It was August when we moved into the house. Maybe we should have stayed in the Tropicana Motel and let ourselves recover and grow together. We could return to our routine of rolling out of bed for breakfast at Duke's and not look back on the changes in our lives. But we ran ahead, got a house, and could not keep up our masks.

I know now that coming off a tour is a very difficult thing; it takes years to develop the muscle to slip back into normal life again, and this was coming off the biggest ride of my life. I was pacing, nervous.

For the past six months I had been caught in an engine constructed around me. Every person, every day was focused on me, my performance, my every whim. All the motion and thrill was absent now and a large empty elephant took its place. This transition back from all that was unsettling, to say the least, our little house too quiet, too "normal."

The girl who sat on the porch with Tom that night was fresh off the stage, still sweating through the tears of the big finale. I really wanted to be the character who would be happy living there with Tom. But we belonged elsewhere. Tom had left the Tropicana and I had left the beach. We may as well have been in the closed quarters of a rocket ship to nowhere.

"Hey, Bub"

I would call him, Hey Bub
He had a little place he kept for me
He would tell me, shh, he was so in love
He moved us to a home there
A place where he'd take care of me
And I'd always know where he'd be
I don't know, it happened so fast . . .
Sometimes, all I see is lonely.

It was a particularly hot, hot day in late August. We had just moved into the house on Sanborn with Tom's piano, his boxes, my stove, and my guitar. Our new home didn't have air-conditioning so as hot as it was outside, it was unbearably hot inside.

We weren't on tour anymore where people would take care of any problem. Now everyone guarded their air-conditioned homes from us. We could lie in a pool of our own sweat but not in their guest rooms. In spite of our star power none of the rich folks we knew wanted two stinky beatniks hanging around. We went looking for a hotel.

I was feeling desperate—mostly because I was quitting dope (as I did every few weeks) but also because people died in heat waves and I had that in my mind. When I quit, I would go through withdrawal but no one ever seemed to notice and I didn't expect this time to be any different.

Tom and I headed north in his T-Bird, looking for a motel with air-conditioning. Not even his car offered relief. We would see a hotel sign, pull off the freeway, and wait in line at the front desk.

"Do you have a room with air-conditioning?"

"No, we're full."

Over and over and over again; drive, wait, rejection, get back into the hot car, repeat. How did I go from the glory of the Variety Arts Theatre to this "no can do" in a few short weeks? We did this all day and even crossed into Ventura County. There, a mile or two from the fairgrounds where I once snuck in to see Jimi Hendrix, we finally found a small air-conditioned motel room that was too close to the noisy railroad track. I turned on that little air conditioner and stood in front of the cool wind. Finally relief, but they only had one night of vacancy. One night out of the hellfire and chaos of our new life together. We were sustained by our love. It was a good love but we were exhausted. We slept restlessly.

In the morning I woke up first and got dressed, went for a walk, and found a little park. I felt loved and whole: on the other side of begging, on the other side of "I hope he doesn't leave me." I thought, It's gonna be hot today but we're in each other's arms, it's gonna be okay. Yet I was a storm, and my emotions seemed to change without warning. One moment I was content and the next I was brooding. Was that me or the drugs? Did it matter?

A voice inside me said: "Tom adores you Rickie, anyone can see that." I walked around the park thinking about us:

If he loves me, then I can tell him.

I think I can tell him.

I need to tell him. Now. About the dope.

I walked back to the motel and he was standing outside the door. His body was taut:

"Where did you go?"

"Well I went for a walk."

"I thought you left me. I thought you weren't coming back."

Uh-oh, what was happening to Tom Waits? I couldn't take a walk? I loved that he wanted to possess me, didn't I? Then again, I didn't really like it at all.

"I woke up, I couldn't find you anywhere."

Was that old ghost of mine whispering in my boyfriend's ear? Did some part of me want to get out of this life together and he detected it? Inside the room we sat down on the bed. Tom started:

"I thought you left. I thought you left me here and—"

"Why would you think that?" I touched him for reassurance.

"I don't know. I love you."

I hugged him.

"What a thing to think. I just went for a walk bub."

But some part of me *was* disconnected, perhaps I had a premonition of what was about to happen to us, the survivor part of me saying, "You could just go. *Now.* Hitchhike somewhere. Don't go back to that motel." Or maybe I just needed some goddamn space.

Tom wanted to live with me, he said, so I would always know where he was. I would feel safe then, and he could take care of me. The room he offered was the room of the beloved, the weakling, the troubled. It was a room I would not be able to sleep in.

The next day we went back home to Echo Park to tough it out. Tom said he needed to go to his rehearsal space, for writing and getting ready for his tour. That was good, we both needed separation. He drove away but came back an hour later. "I can't do anything. I can't work, I can't write, I can't think about anything but you. Baby I don't know what to do."

So the tables had been turned, it was *he* who needed to know where *I* was. He had trouble going to work. He was suspicious and jealous and losing his power. I knew that he would strike back and I wanted to let him know I was true, I was not going to take advantage of his vulnerability. I was going to make myself even more vulnerable than him.

I held him tight. He was falling too much in love. For the first time in my life, I was the more rational thinker. I knew why he kept coming back to see if I was still there—he found no strength in loving me now.

A month ago we could not stop kissing, but now we circled each other round and round. These roles we wanted to play—wife, mom, dad—were like bit parts in our public drama. They were not true to our identities as real live girl and boy. We needed to grow toward a real sun, not the sun of our imaginings.

Cheerily I said, "I'll make dinner." That was exciting, right? I was the wife. He'd eat my food. We would be right again.

> *But after all there are such things*
> *And these are the things*
> *That turn your memories back into dreams again*
> *Oh, it's all flying and waiting for you to keep trying*
> *You're so close, so close*
> *And all The Returns one of these days*
>
> ("The Returns")

Tom was in the backyard in his sleeveless T-shirt and his pointed shoes, hand-watering the weeds. I was stirring my spaghetti sauce. How could we possibly make this pretend idea a real one? Oh, I wanted "us" to work. Oh, it just had to work! Over dinner, we'd hold hands. If we believed, it would work. Hold on Tom.

Then there was the argument. The pretend half-baked versions of us were punching out of our shells. I threw my plate of spaghetti on the wall. I frightened myself. Why did I do that? We were in full fighting mode now. No more Tom and Rickie doing the Ozzie and Harriet show. He liked us better this way—passionate. This was a language he understood and so did I. But I liked us better a week ago, passionate and hopeful and kind. So kind.

After this hot argument we went into the couple's cold war. Now we were brooding, tense, and separate. It has always been hard for me to wait out anger. The unresolved is painful. This comes from my upbringing, where my mother could shut me out and not speak to me for days. She did not hit, she did something far more damaging. She rejected. It is a thing I still cannot bear.

I thought, I can end this tension, maybe this will help:

"Tom, I have to tell you something."

That always sets up a good conversation. People get nervous, then I say something good and we work our way back. He looked at me. He was still looking. He was waiting for me to tell him my something. Okay. I'll tell you something.

"I have been . . ."

"Mmmmm . . . ?"

"Taking . . ." (Say it fast.)

"I've-been-taking-junk and I . . ."—Uh-oh, he did not look well—"quit a few days ago."

Uh-oh, uh-oh. This was a big mistake.

"And I'm kind of sick now." (My apology for throwing the spaghetti against the wall of our new kitchen the first time we cooked in it.)

Indeed. It had been thirty hours since I got high.

I felt bad, I was sweating, I was deep in the plak tow of pon farr, except unlike with Spock, there was nothing sexy about it. As bad as my body felt, the worst part of withdrawal was the feeling that something was wrong in the universe, a spasm of human connection. In this urban, polluted, 102-degree heat where no one spoke English and all my tinfoils of dope burnt away, something in me began to panic.

Tom was looking at me differently now. There was no going back. I was appealing for sympathy, but there would be none.

"You take dope?"

This was like when Tony told Maria he had killed Bernardo. I was already dead to him.

I raised my eyebrows. Yes?

"Junk?"

"Heroin."

He almost buckled like he had been hit in the stomach. I tried to soften the impact:

"Off and on."

"At the Tropicana?"

"No, I didn't get high there." That much was true.

"For how long?"

"For almost a year."

The outer edges of my safe space were closing in. My stomach collapsed and it was cold. So cold. Tom had stopped responding. My eyes would not see. He was vanishing before me. My invisibility—reversed. I scrambled:

"No, I mean, now . . . just for the . . . a few days . . . since I got back I was getting high. It's been four months or so."

Oh, what the hell. Let's get this out:

"And then last spring I quit. Then I took some in New York City."

"That time I came to meet you on Avenue B?"

I should really lie. "Yes."

"When we went to the carnival in Little Italy?"

He was deconstructing our romance and building something else. A darker, unloving relationship where dope had tricked him.

"Yes."

I was thinking, Why did you think your lover suddenly left you at the St. Regis and urgently took a cab to Avenue B, Tom? And, Didn't I look different when I was high? And, How come no one knew? I heard my other self saying:

"But I quit."
Silence.

Run for the shadows . . .

I really wanted to run and get out of there, get high and come back and work it out. With drugs, I had courage. Or the confident apathy of "I don't care what you do." See Tom, you love the heroin me because the real me has no confidence. The real me is speaking now and you don't seem to like the real me much. You prefer that heroin woman; strong, sexy, and a liar. Well, meet the real me; frightened, stupid, honest Rickie Lee Jones.

(Of course that wasn't the real me, that was the dope-sick me. Meet Rickie Lee . . . jonesing!)

I stood there in that house because I wanted Tom, and I wanted our love. I wanted him to water the weeds again and make jokes about Budweiser. Come on. Let me back in the club!

"Baby. Hey bub?"

No response. He had stopped talking. I was alone now watching my baby fall because of me, because of *me*. He seemed so weak and unmade by disappointment. It had also switched our roles back to where they were before I signed the Warner Brothers contract. He was back on top as the powerful one and I was another sad-eyed Waits girl begging for his attention.

I could not find a path forward. My mind and my options were closed. No area was safe. I went to backpedaling, trying to undo the inevitable. I wished so badly that I had drugs now. Anything not to feel this horror. Drugs would make me feel sure again and act like I knew where I was going and like nothing could unseat me. I needed to be drug-strong again. Our make-believe personas were fueled by the heroin I was ingesting. I regretted telling him. I wished I had not told him.

Tom's rejection of my holler for help precipitated a complete and utter break from him. Right there in my creepy, painful opiate withdrawal, I had a terrible vision. I could feel we were past-tense, as phony as this stifling house in the suburbs. This future us was happy but fake, and disrespected. Something had shifted in our future. These characters that we were, they were not going to endure. Not together.

Tom and Rickie, "the Steve and Eydie of hipsters." Now to me, Steve and Eydie were about as pretend as a famous couple could be. They were great jazz singers, and they looked sweet together, but no one took them seriously. We would be stuffed into that box by the press. A world that seemed infatuated with us would throw us away like yesterday's whatever. This thought had now invaded my most sacred inner sanctum: "Tom and me." Our future.

It may seem too self-sacrificing today but I could not let that happen, even in my withdrawal hell. Perhaps this weird horror was just a splinter, a cut of that withdrawal knife, but I would not let my fame cost Tom Waits his cool crown. Fame was hard to manage. I could suffer it, but not him. Maybe it was just an excuse. Maybe I wanted to be Steve and not Eydie. I don't know anymore. Tom had replaced his love with contempt, the pat reaction of strangers toward heroin addicts. Not what I might expect from a friend or family, really. He saw me as a stereotype, just another lying junkie.

All night long Tom cried. He cried like a baby. I began to recede to a faraway place, for I knew there was no going back. In the morning he rose, picked up his wallet and keys, and drove away. I gave up trying to kick and I went and got high. I cannot assign more despair to the past so I will not say I might have killed myself, because I didn't. But without drugs to sleep with all night long, I don't know what would have happened to me by morning.

A day later I went to see Tom at his studio, where he was rehearsing for his tour. I was thinking, Okay we had a fight and that's enough of that. Right? Instead, a doppelgänger had taken Tom's place, and my boyfriend was not there anymore.

Back at the house, there were three bags of fan mail and the sad old piano. Among those headstones of our brief family, I wrote "Skeletons."

The desolate afterlife of tragedy is what I grew up with. I created the characters out of the mire of my hopelessness. I felt there was no getting off this stage. My desolation was like the Sisyphus band which almost finishes the set list and then starts again at the first song. The world would want Tom and I just as it met us, forever.

"Skeletons"

I had heard about so many acts of violence by the LAPD against unarmed Black men, but this story in particular really caught my attention. An unarmed man was pulled over—"a waltz of red moonbeams." He went for his driver's license and was shot dead. When I heard this, the unbearable memory that at any moment life can be swept away overwhelmed me. I picked up a pencil and, sitting there in that tomb of a home, I made a snapshot of the slow-motion fall I was in.

> *She was pregnant in May*
> *Now they're on their way*
> *Dashing through the snow*
> *To St. John's, here we go . . .*
>
> *When he turned off the road*
> *Steps in a waltz of red moonbeams*
> *Said he fit an APB*
> *For a robbery nearby*
>
> *And he goes for his wallet*
> *And they thought he was going for a gun*
> *And the cops blew Bird away.*
>
> *Some kids like watching Saturday cartoons*
> *Some girls listen to records all day in their rooms*
> *But what do birds leave behind*
> *Of the wings that they came with—*
> *If a son's in a tree building model planes?*
> *Skeletons*
> *Skeletons.*

I caught a plane back home. Mama met me at the airport, she brought all the kids with her. I was home with my family again. In Olympia I lay in bed for two nights not eating. The children came into the room to sit by the bed and feed me milk toast. They made child noises. I think my mother had them come to "wake up Rickie." She was wise, she knew how my heartbreaks crippled me but also how I didn't want the children to see me in pain. The next day I got out of bed and took a shower. The children must not see me like that. I came out of my stupor.

A Ride on the Blooming Green

My old high school buddy Julie was playing piano and singing at a country club bar. I ordered a scotch and then another. At her break, she joined me and we ordered another drink. We'd had so many adventures and fun but we had never had a drink together.

Her gig was over and although it was barely noon, I was drunk when I walked out of the bar. My buddy, my pal. Julie said, "Don't drive now, I'll call your mom to come getcha. Come and drive around in the golf cart with me!"

"I hate golf."

We got in the cart and she floored the accelerator. We tore around the golf course with Julie's boyfriend running after us screaming, "Not on the greens!" For the first time in so long, I began to smile.

"Don't drive on the greens Julie!"

She looked at him and then looked at me, pursed her lips and floored that golf cart like the race car driver I knew her to be. My smile broke into laughter and then she was laughing, which led us both to laugh at our laughing, just like when we had our sleepovers and her father shushed us all night long. I laughed all the horror and sorrow away.

We laughed so hard, so deep, and so long that all the pain I had stuffed into my body broke away. The pain moved out of my head and disappeared into the air or sank into the putting green. I stood there by my friend, drunk, laughing, and exhausted. Julie had defied her boyfriend one more time for her old best friend. That's what friends do.

My mom showed up and took me home, the day still bright. She would always show up hard-nosed, but she always took action when no other parent would. Like that time eight years before when Tom Jacobs and I went to see Elton John up in Seattle. His brand-new motorcycle was stolen and his parents said we had to hitchhike or take a Greyhound home at 3 a.m. Mom drove up to retrieve us in thick and cold fog, then took Tom to his house. We still had a long drive home. It felt like that when she retrieved me from the country club. She was bringing her daughter home again. This time I had a daytime headful of fog.

A Place to Play Piano

The next day Julie arranged a place I could write with a piano. She introduced me to the head of the music department at St. Martin's College and he gave me the keys to the music room. I could go there alone after school hours and stay as long as I liked. This would be where I wrote "Pirates," "We Belong Together," and some of "Living It Up." The monks in robes walking through the autumn leaves and an empty room with a piano was all the healing I could endure. I was whole again.

Singing was as difficult as lifting dead weight off the floor, but I sang, and singing uncovered Rickie Lee Jones and lifted her back up again. My cells were stitching themselves back together. Every leap of faith, every writing ritual mattered. The first mark on the paper would be the direction in which my life would proceed:

> *I say this was no game of chicken*
> *You were aiming at your best friend . . .*

My mourning was the process of rebuilding my heart. It took a while and I was not sure that I would ever return to being that light, bright girl who had appeared on *Saturday Night Live*. Something in me grew just a little bit darker after Tom drove away.

> *The only angel who sees us now*
> *Watches through each other's eyes . . .*
> ("We Belong Together")

In 1980, I was nominated for five Grammys. I had told Bob Regehr I would not attend because the pretense and self-congratulation was not my style, etc., etc. Then at the last minute, I rushed to the award show wearing my leather jacket, a feathered boa, and my cashmere beret. I accepted my Best New Artist award. The press were calling out to me, "Where is Tom Waits?" Funny, I thought they knew, so I looked pretty—and pissed.

At the after-party, Bob Dylan found me and he said, "Don't ever quit. You are a real poet." Russ Titelman poked me like a big brother and giggled: "Bob Dylan just called you a real poet!"

Quite by chance, by some bold stroke of kismet, I ran into Sal Bernardi a week before the Grammys, in a bar in North Beach, San Francisco. Six months later Sal and I moved to Greenwich Village, where we lived together on Ninth Street around the corner from the one-hundred-fifty-year-old Bigelow's Apothecary. I celebrated my twenty-fifth and twenty-sixth birthdays at Jerry Wexler's home, the man who recorded Aretha Franklin, and who with the great Ahmet Ertegun had helped define soul music.

These would be some of the worst years of my life and some of the greatest. Worst for my becoming an addict and greatest for creating *Pirates*, the album that is generally considered my most important work. I was featured on the cover of *Rolling Stone* twice in less than two years. I am pretty sure that had never happened before.

My music caught a greater fire than anyone imagined. I caught a greater fire. I hit like Marlon Brando. There were low-slung berets in all kinds of movies, suddenly "street" was the thing to be. And that "E" phenomenon was everywhere. Suddenly, young musicians used the "E" I used in place of the "y" or "ie" in "Chuck E." This gag showed up in names for the next decade, "Tone E," that kind of thing. People loved that spelling as much as they loved the song.

I remember Warner Brothers being furious that certain industry magazines would not count "Chuck E's in Love" in the top three positions of radio spins because the formula was "radio spins" *plus* "how many singles sold." "Chuck E's" was a track on an album, not a separately released single; I was missing something the disco songs had—singles. I would always remain an album artist.

I would meet and hang with many famous American icons through the years. Lou Reed, John Prine, Robin Williams, Bob Dylan, and many others. Still, my favorite story remains the night I met—wait for it—Eddie Money!

I was walking down Broadway near Seventy-Second Street when I heard someone call my name. I turned and saw a white guy standing in front of a bar. "It's Eddie Money, Rickie. Come in and have a drink with me and my brother."

I went in and met Eddie's brother who was a detective with the narcotics squad. They bought me a scotch. I bought them one. He and Eddie and I drank until the bar closed. The detective knew of some after-hours joints, so we climbed in his plainclothes car and he put the blue light up on the roof, turned on the siren, and we roared down Broadway. Even the red lights were green for us and all the cars pulled out of our way. We were going to have an adventure on this glorious night of abandon as we tore through the streets of Manhattan. That thrill remains one of the greatest memories of my life. Eddie's brother and that car were our two tickets to paradise indeed. The adventure and the glory seeped into my lyrics, so whenever I sing these lines I remember the night all the traffic and the traffic lights of Manhattan bowed down to me and the boys.

> *You might meet me tomorrow*
> *As all the lights are blooming green . . .*
> *Feeling a little lonely, a little sad, a little mean*
> *Remember a place inside of this hotel*
> *Where you can do anything you want to do*
> *And you can never tell*
>
> ("Pirates")

Chapter 21

Jazz Side of Life

With Sal on *Pirates* tour

I t was Valentine's Day, 1982, when my second album was released and by summer it had a five-star review in *Rolling Stone*. All the journalists were ga-ga over this woman who could kill a jazz ballad, and gyrate in a spandex suit while imitating the sound of a passing semi-truck. The thing was, I was much more complicated than I wished I were. There was no way I was going to make it easy on myself.

Pirates achieved a status that is hard to translate to people forty years later. It had to do with the sophistication of the record coming from a woman. This might seem embarrassing now but it was true then. On *Pirates*, I reintroduced characters from the first record and developed far more serious themes of racism, of domestic violence, of addiction, loss, love, and the strength to keep going. I had no single unless it were "Woody and Dutch," the finger-snappin' good-time song that would become so imitated, when people heard it, they thought I was imitating the imitators.

I wanted to continue the story I had begun with the first record, the gang, the friends, the fellowship and the tragedy that befalls them. It was as if the kids on the first record grew up. Having lost my gang, I had to dig some new characters out of my own imagination. I found them down down down at the bottom of a well. Their stories were rougher than Chuck E or Bragger. Zero and Johnny the King might not even survive. In fact, I killed Bird the third song in. *Pirates* was considered a masterpiece. The Grammys, though, ignored this record all the way down the line, and all my records for the next twenty years. There was no money to be made off a woman who was going to die from drugs soon, and my reputation was making acknowledgment of my work unnecessary. There was a sense of disgrace, the kind reserved exclusively for women who take heroin.

With my first album, I had made the case for myself as a legitimate pop songwriter, and now I knew that I could stand on the stage with any man and hold my own. *Pirates* took over a year to make and cost a quarter of a million dollars. Because I was given free rein to write in the studio, taking as long as I needed, the bills piled up. Producers stayed in four-star hotels. Many musicians charged $1,000 a day.

My boyfriend Sal Bernardi would join my *Pirates* band. We had written together and I felt he was an integral part of my life and music. It would be a challenge to fold him into the respect the musicians already had for one another, musicians who had all auditioned and won their chairs while Sal came through the bedroom door.

The *Pirates* tour was another story. I had expanded my personnel to what would be an unmanageable number. I recall the movie *On the Waterfront* being my inspiration, and now our backstage passes were photos of Marlon Brando, saying "It was you Charlie." My new backdrop was a waterfront, and it changed from twilight to dawn as the two-hour show progressed.

The tour started off as a sober flotilla of ex-addicts but soon everyone had slipped except me. I started drinking to hold back the tide of compulsion and then I got sloppy. I recall a review that said I was "an ugly woman." The reviewer might have hated my music or performance but he took his license in a very personal direction. He attacked my sexuality and my appearance. He was appalled by my lingerie and seemed to suggest I lacked the moral character to even be onstage . . . he was livid. I recalled a Canadian border guard looking at braless me in my miniskirt and little hat, then arresting me for *being in danger of leading a lewd and lascivious life*. Men have been corralling me all my life. I've had enough.

Sure, I was wearing a black slip onstage. Vintage, it was neither too short nor too revealing. But yes, it was a satin slip.

In a few years everyone would be wearing slips—they would be haute couture!

It wasn't just the slut-shaming. I was also saddled with being expected to play the female role of deference and sweetness, when the essence of rock 'n' roll music was in-your-face. Testosterone rebellion was fine but add a goddamn slip to the mix and people are foaming at the mouth. The violence and self-destruction among male musicians was a badge of manliness. Keith Richards and Ginger Baker are winked at, even admired for their longevity in drug use.

The sloppy performances of the late sixties did not ruin anyone's career, the men and the solos and the crappy musical ideas. But the sloppy performances of Rickie Lee Jones very nearly destroyed hers. It seems to me that people really wanted me to be perfect. Rock women were being shamed for the same behavior men were being hailed for.

As the tour evolved, I stopped drinking. Still the theme of the *Pirates* tour was "Ain't nothing but a party," inspired by my saxophonist, New Orleans native, Jerry Jumonville. Every evening before the show we would share a cocktail and the band and I would sing The Stylistics. By the time we got to the Roxy Club in L.A., we had added Jackson 5 and Marvin Gaye songs, and Arno Lucas and I were dancing the jitterbug. Our favorite dance tune was ironically "I Won't Dance," an old tune I would record with the actor Robert Mitchum for Bruce Weber's film on his life.

There are outstanding drums on every record—like the fill in "Chuck E's in Love," or Jim Keltner's timing on "Jolie Jolie" in "Flying Cowboys," and on *Pirates*, Steve Gadd playing a tape box on "Woody and Dutch." The sound was so unique, it was picked up and edified by the culture in general. I know that I heard what sounded like "Woody and Dutch" in many commercials for many years.

For the next ten years of touring, I worked with many new artists who would become stars in their own right. When not touring I lived in two cities for the next few years: Greenwich Village in New York and New Orleans, where I rented a loft on Decatur Street, overlooking the Mississippi River. Dr. John had hooked me up with people he thought I should know. James Booker and I hung out many nights, singing "My Funny Valentine" to each other. I also had the privilege of watching Professor Longhair's last recording session. At one point during this time, I was renting three apartments and often still staying in hotels. My mother stepped in and packed up my New Orleans apartment for me, and while salvaging an antique string of pearls I had carelessly left on the floor, she realized her daughter was not taking care of her belongings—or herself. I lived like I just didn't care. I guess I thought the money would never end.

Quitting Dope

> *E.A. Poe or Johnny Johnson*
> *If you dial in they call from the Western Slope*
> *Who's a thin thread of light keeps you stranded in the scenery?*
> *Can you hear me?*
> *Follow my voice*
>
> ("Traces of the Western Slopes")

Pirates was written at the end of my addiction when I lived on Ninth Street in Manhattan with Sal Bernardi. That was where Sal and I lost our way together. We stayed up all night and slept until 4 p.m. and rose half-dead to get high and feel half-alive again. We wrote music and read Edgar Allan Poe. We lived in the strange twilight, the slow motion fluid that fed our memories. We were junkies.

For two solid years I couldn't see any way out of my addiction. There was no memory of light in the dark compressed days of my addiction. I had a frank discussion with my doctor, who said, "I have no doubt that you will quit drugs. It is not a question of *if*, it is a question of *when*."

That was my light at the end of my tunnel. My way out. The words I walked toward every day. It was as if I had already quit drugs because he knew I would. I just didn't have the date on hand. Faith was my program. Faith in myself, and I also prayed to God. Faith in the invisible world would light my way. Divine intervention was *my* program.

I started drugs alone and would leave drugs alone. Socially I could not share my journey so there was no rehab and no meetings. Rehab was not yet invented anyway. People didn't understand opioid addiction then.

I had to replace my former bad habits, so I replaced the physical ritual of going out to get drugs with other rituals. The main thing was to stay busy and find new habits, better obsessions. First I ate a lot. Then I fasted for a few months—a liquid diet. Then I exercised like crazy, exercised to exhaustion, but I was in great shape. I needed extreme things to counter the extreme I had become. As I got back on my feet, I carefully removed myself from all the places and people who were associated with drugs. I was going to start new and clean as I built myself back up.

For me heroin was like a carnival ride I couldn't exit until the ride was over. Then I must take my cue and hurry out. One day I knew it was time to get off the ride. It was now or never. Maybe I would relapse for a day or two here or there, but I would begin the journey out and never return. I would get to my destination: that refrigerator magnet. Today, months go by when I forget I was an addict. The dark is gone, the shadows faded. I am recovered and whole.

*　　*　　*

The songs I wrote were dredged up from a cacophony of feelings from long ago and from the very moment I was writing. The songs were healing invocations. *The Magazine* was written at a time when I was trying to ward off drugs, as if drugs were a person or a place. In my weird vision was also the mythological cousin who had tormented me all those years before. I did not realize until this moment that the song had less to do with drugs and everything to do with forgiving and overcoming the wounds she left.

A Desert Girl on the Street of the Invalids

> *Wild girl, you must have been a terror when*
> * you were young . . .*
> *Your momma must have let you run free*
> *But it wasn't very nice all that sugar and spice*
> *What "they" want a girl to be*
>
> ("Wild Girl")

My life in Europe made me feel part of a larger world. That was just what I needed, a broader context to catch up with the ride of my life. I had exited the drug life. I would show everyone how well I was.

For many years, this would be part of my agenda. Who, I wonder, was I trying to convince? That journalist who hated me so much?

In Europe I learned that being American was just another habit of mine. There was more to life than what food I ate and where I ate it. "Mon dieu" as opposed to "Yo, Adrian!" I loved being a part of a world that did not know my secrets.

I met Alain Bashung in Paris in the spring of 1983 through Boris Bergman, his lyricist. I met Boris while I was in Paris because he had been hired by my French publisher to interpret and translate my lyrics into French. In fact, my lawyer, Owen Sloane, had made lucrative music publishing deals for me around the world. Boris spoke five or six languages fluently and had volunteered to translate my lines but he didn't have a lot of knowledge about American colloquialisms. Oh yeah, my own personal use of double entendre, metaphor, and portmanteau made his job very difficult. I must have helped him where I could, but even I was unsure whether my use of, say, "easy mark" should be interpreted to mean "sucker" or "Capital M for Mark." This "slow, easy Mark" was a play on words very difficult to interpret.

In my months in Paris I walked along the Seine, studied Toulouse-Lautrec at the Orangerie, and drank enough otherworldly good wines until I understood the meaning of "spirits." There was more than one soul at the bottom of those bottles.

I learned one very valuable lesson about being an American, one I could never realize had I never stepped out of the mirror and looked back in. Living in America, we are often preoccupied with how different we think we are from one another, how divided, how antagonistic. One afternoon, I was watching CNN and saw my Americans talking about something or other and I had a revelation. Look at the bravado and confidence, the Wild West, the iconic persona. Those are Americans and I am one of them. I will always be one of the brown and white, male and female, old and not-so-old children of adventurers and immigrants; it wasn't that I loved them, it was that I understood them. I wished they knew how unified they seemed to the rest of the world. We are a formidable force. I called Lenny Waronker up that month, and said, I don't know what I'm doing here. Lenny said, "Come home." I was so moved. "Come home" meant that I had a home. It meant that I was a part of someone: him, Russ, the whole record company, the whole city. So I began to plan my return to Hollywood.

It was July and there was a terrible heatwave in Paris. I had to get out of town. I traveled to Ireland to see Van Morrison. This is an amazing and impossible story of magic and destiny. This was a journey long-planned by some invisible drummer, perhaps the real purpose to my time in Paris. While there have been many such counterpoints since, this is the only one with a leprechaun.

I first heard Van Morrison's *Astral Weeks* in 1970 when I traveled from Sky River Festival outside of Olympia to some hippie house in Eugene, Oregon. From the moment I heard him singing about gardens all wet with rain, where I would never, ever, ever, ever grow so old again, I wanted to be in that garden with him. And you know what? I did land right smack in the middle of that garden, just thirteen years to the month after Eugene, Oregon.

Astral Weeks was like nothing I had ever heard, or would ever hear. It took a while to seep in, like a new language, and it wasn't until the third or fourth time I heard, "I shall drive my chariot down your streets and cry" echoing against the grooves of the vinyl, that I sat up and took notice. The upright bass was a rare instrument in the hippie world of 1970, and vibraphones were about as in-fashion as a baritone saxophone. Van Morrison made me realize no instrument is out of fashion if it's played with innovation and dedication.

Van's poetry is probably derived from something like Keats or Shelley, but the source of his poetry is Irish and wild. He could sing all the blues he wanted, but he had transcended the genre long ago, and it would never be his home. Van Morrison's music gave me maps to use when I found myself in midair. His voice heals me still when nothing else can.

"Visions of fairies flying through the sky . . ."

I arrived in Ireland, a trip I had been secretly planning since I was sixteen years old. I was finally there. I arrived a week early to see Belfast, the home of Van Morrison's youth. On the train to Belfast I met a young boy who invited me to be part of some kind of civil disturbance the Catholics and Protestants engaged in each year. I called my ma and told her I was thinking of joining the battle. Bettye said, "Don't you dare go with that boy. Rubber bullets kill just like real ones."

The Lisdoonvarna Festival in County Clare is as far from Dublin and Belfast as the other end of the rainbow, but on July 31, 1983, I took a taxi from Dublin across Ireland all the way to where the highway ended. From the east coast to almost the western coast. Across the rocky green Ireland of sheep farms, meadows, small towns, and smaller taverns. It took much longer than I thought so the sun was low in the sky when the driver said, "Dis is as far as I go, no more cars allowed from here. It's a mile or so from the town here, just walk straight down that road."

I stopped in a bar to buy cigarettes and every single patron poked fun at me. Irish pub behavior. I lit a cigarette and started walking with the people, lots of people, along a country road in the direction of the festival.

From out of nowhere, a little Volkswagen appeared. Odd, I thought no cars were allowed. It was an old VW right out of 1969 and it stopped, you guessed it, right by me. A long, lean man looked out the window.

"Dyawantaride?"

"Who me?"

There were lots of people walking around. Why ask me?

I really did not want to walk a mile or two, so I got in and he began to speak but I could not understand one word. It was a thick, Irish accent spoken through a mouthful of clover. It was a different kind of Irish accent than I'd heard, and he was a different kind of man. He was creepy with long, spindly fingers. A spidery man. He made a quick, furtive glance from the lane to me. He pointed at my body.

"Excuse me?"

He repeated, "And where are ya from?"

"America. I am from Cal-i-fornia. Where are you from?"

He cackled. "Far, far from here."

What? Far, far from here? What did that mean?

"No really, where are you from?"

There was something wrong about this guy. He was in a VW on a road with no cars, and he picked me up out of all the people, and he kept alluding to weird things but I could not understand what he was saying. Was he speaking Gaelic?

He looked over and sized me up. Then he placed those spindly, spidery fingers around my kneecap. An amorous gesture except he clasped it like a many-legged insect. It was wrong. All wrong. He wanted to drive with his hand on my knee.

"You don't want to do that," I said with all the badass American Rickie bravado I'd earned through too many rides with too many creeps. I took his hand off my knee. Or I tried to. It wouldn't budge. He wouldn't let go. He squeezed harder. Harder! I thought, Okay sure, leave your hand there. Whatever.

We drove along the lane with his hand on my knee. My instincts said, Don't fight. If he does not back down, I can jump out somewhere. I felt safe enough because there were people on both sides of the road walking to the festival.

My driver was picking up speed and there were fewer people on the road. Wow, a long walk and now empty fields, shouldn't it be getting more crowded? I was thinking, How am I gonna get out of the car? He was going twenty-five, thirty miles per hour. I did not come to Ireland to get killed.

I was looking for a place to jump out and calculating my injuries when we came upon a cluster of young people walking in the middle of the road. My driver slowed down at just the perfect moment for me to leap out of the car. Actually, he hit one of the people walking to the festival. Just bumped him but he stopped the car as the pedestrian turned and started yelling. I opened the door and ran for my life. This was another of my moments of divine timing. As the VW took off, I shouted back to the pedestrian, "I don't know him, I was just trying to get away from him. He wouldn't stop." I hurried away only looking back to make sure the Cosmic Volkswagen didn't come back for me. When I felt safe, I stopped running and took stock of my situation. Where was I? Directly in front of the *artist's entrance* to the festival. I mean, right there at the gate.

I shyly approached the backstage guard: "I wonder if I might come in? I am Rickie Lee Jones." He nodded as if he knew the name and said, "Well let me ask." A few minutes later I was welcomed into the festival and just in time to see Van Morrison. There were no stage lights, only the sun which was beginning its exit. I winked at an imaginary camera and whispered, "Thank you."

Listen! Ireland was cheering for its own son. The man who inspired all the other boys to write about boogie-woogie boys playing saxophone. Van was the source of so many disciples who became sources themselves. People like Bruce Springsteen, and Adam Duritz. An entire artery was derived from a couple Van Morrison songs that continues to feed the great poets of rock 'n' roll. We owe a great debt of culture to all musicians, but especially to Van Morrison.

I knew this would be the greatest Van Morrison concert I would ever see. Van Morrison can be nervous or shy, stage fright maybe, and he masks it with anger. At least, that is my take on him, but this night he was, as Lowell George would say, *willing*. Yes, and he was playful, and even dancing. When a mohawked punk-rocker jumped on stage and started hopping around with him, he smiled at her! It was a great, great reward for the magnitude of the journey I had taken to see him, to be a part of this world.

There he was with his shock of eyebrows and his red, red hair. His blue eyes made bluer by the contrast with his white skin. His poor taste in clothes too. All of it made him the sexiest man I'd ever imagined. The fairies were out and the people were singing. And Van Morrison was actually smiling!

There were no stage lights so Van's concert ended as the sun set and the world turned grey and cold. I didn't have a warm coat or a plan. Shall I just sleep here in this field? I had reserved a roadside motel but it was so far away and I doubted I could find my way back to it even if I did have a ride. I just knew somehow it would work out. I thought. I hoped.

I was standing in the green grass behind the stage, near the refreshment tent where Van was talking to some people. I knew Van saw me. I stood there, well, looking like I was just standing there. It was all so seventh grade, "Will he make eye contact?" sort of stuff. Mark Isham, Van's trumpet player, came up to me and introduced himself. As we spoke, I peered over Mark's shoulder to see Van Morrison was looking at me. Suddenly, he walked over and stood next to me. Oh my heart,

I couldn't breathe. He introduced himself and we stood in the pocket of each other's very spirit.

Van said, "I was just going to get a coffee. Would you like a coffee?"

"Yes, I would."

"I'll get it for you. What do you take?"

"Uh. I take . . ."

"Black, then." He finished the sentence for me.

Was this happening?

I felt I was at the dance in the gym in *West Side Story*, and "Brown Eyed Girl" was playing. "Behind the stadium with you . . ." *I want you to meet me!* I was Maria! "My, how you have grown . . ."

He brought two cups and I thought, How can I save this cup? For one brave moment I saw Maria and Tony, they had all made it onto that bus out of town, the one they borrowed money from Doc for. They were laughing. They were alive! Look! Here on the New Jersey turnpike, everyone singing, "All come to look for America." That car I stole, with Ricci Cretti and me in it. Look! We are driving right next to them! Suddenly everything was healed and even old sad endings unmade themselves and were remade for the better. Everything was possible because I was standing next to Van Morrison and he was looking into my eyes and talking to me.

Wow, those eyes. Look at those eyes. Blue eyes made of blue fire. Bluer than Ol' Blue Eyes, Frank Sinatra. I met Frank once. You have some eyebrows on you, too. Where is your hair? Can you be mine? Will you be my neighbor? What are you anyway? Oh my mind was racing.

"I met your dad and mom, you know," I said.

"Oh, yeah?"

"At their record store in Northern California. Sal Bernardi and I went there hoping to meet you."

"They've always owned a record store."

Van thought for a moment. "*Pirates*. That is a great record. I mean"—indecipherable Belfast accent—"beautiful, great music."

"Thank you."

Just like that, there was nothing left to say. He turned and walked away to talk to someone else. It was over. That's okay. I did it! I *found* Van Morrison. I could go home now . . . except I didn't have a ride.

Mark Isham noticed me among the crew's exodus from backstage. The band was loading onto their bus. I was standing by myself, in the middle of a Randy Newman song. Mark thoughtfully read my situation and came up to me, "Hey, do you need a ride? We can take you to our hotel. You'll never get a cab now."

"Oh, thank you."

"You can go back to your hotel in the morning."

Thank God and Mark Isham. As I was moving toward the bus, Van's limo cruised by. I smiled at the darkened window, then the car stopped and the window rolled down. Van Morrison's head pressed against the air where the window had just been. He had heard Mark ask me if I needed a ride. I saw him watching me.

"Hey, uh . . . You want to ride with me? Might be faster."

Why was I hesitating?

"Come on."

I think I walked on my toes to the other side of the car. I was twelve years old. I climbed into the back seat with Van Morrison and we slowly began to converse. Gaps.

"You know, I had a very weird ride that dropped me off in front of the artist's entrance."

"I thought no cars were allowed on the road."

"Yeah exactly."

I told Van about the spidery man in the Volkswagen, how he showed up right next to me, out of the blue, on this road with no other cars and no cars allowed. How he said he lived "far, far from here" and grabbed my knee and wouldn't let me out. How I jumped out right in front of the festival.

"Ah, well. You met a leprechaun."

"Ah! . . . Ah? . . . Oh?"

"You're lucky you got away."

A leprechaun! I checked Van's face to see if he was kidding me. He was not, he was deadly serious.

Now it all made sense! That spindly and sinister thing that had picked me up was a mischievous, magical Irish leprechaun. My half-Irish father had told me about the fairies and how the Irish (including the Irish Joneses) believe in magical beings. Here in Ireland, they weren't fooling around. Dad was exactly on the money with that and now I was experiencing it.

"Of course!" Van said, "Ireland is full of magic. Be careful."

We drove along in our limo and I looked out the window at cold, dark Ireland with its crazy leprechauns. I was safe in the car with the greatest songwriter of his generation and so proud that he regarded me as a peer. We spoke of Dr. John, New Orleans, folks we knew or knew of together. Levon Helm and all the rest. We talked about San Francisco. He had a daughter there, he said, she was with her mother. Then we were quiet. The overwhelming perfection of this night with Van, who had told me, "A fairy got ya!"

Suddenly during the ride, Van lost his temper and started yelling at me. It was as if he blanked out on who I was or how I got in his limo, because he was angry about some journalist and what journalists take for granted or some such thing. I just happened to be there to yell at. Suddenly I was utterly rejected. So high, and now so low, I was crushed, shaken to my core.

I was still in the limo and we weren't to the hotel yet. What could I say to fix this? It felt to me like having made love and then being thrown out the back door like it never happened.

Finally, the one lovely little hotel in the woods. Van got out, slammed the limo door, and stormed into the hotel with me following behind. He did not speak another word, not even a "good night." I was lucky to get a room. I came out and sat with the band at the bar. Mark Isham said:

"He's just like that. He does that to everybody, it's not personal."

It sure felt personal. Yet, I glimpsed a man driven by a storm he could not control. A storm of feelings and emotions, the very things that glowed in the dark for all these years for so many listeners. It was his raw emotion that made everything he did so magically delicious. We wanted to be warmed by that fire, all of us. I had come too close.

I felt wretched and only half slept for a few hours. Then I just "happened" to be in the lobby at seven in the morning when the band was checking out. Van was there with them, but he did not speak to me. Mark Isham saw it all now, me there early in the morning looking for . . . what? Van was famous for the bullshit he was pulling with me. Mark approached me and wrote down his phone number. He said, "When you come back to L.A., give me a call." I smiled, "Yes I will." That felt good.

Van was watching Mark when he handed me the note. Maybe Van needed clues on how to act civil or on "what people do when . . ." but something clicked. He hurried up to me at the front desk. He too scribbled something on a piece of paper and handed it to me, then said in his ferociously Belfast-fast brogue, "If you ever come to London, give us a call." Then he rushed to the bus and was gone. That nasty schoolboy Van had met the sultry teenager Rickie Lee and it was good.

I saved that number for many years. Do you wonder if I called him? Me too!

Chapter 22

It Must Be Love

Mary Simon regards my wedding ring.
Bisbee, Arizona, October 1985

September 1983. I returned from France to record *The Magazine,* my first project without my producers Lenny and Russ. *The Magazine* was a new direction for me, a new producer, a new classically framed idea. This was probably the influence of all that classical music I heard playing back in Europe. Whereas in America, pop music dominates commercials and playlists, Europeans heard Stravinsky and Bach pumping out of every café and hotel radio. I recognized there was a terrible gap in my education, and I wondered how I would ever learn this instrumental music well enough to become familiar with it the way I was familiar with Lennon/McCartney or Neil Young. I wanted to recognize Beethoven the moment his music began. It would take many years. My own instrumental themes, nocturnes, and preludes, began with "Prelude to Gravity" as if the opening frames of the movie were revealing a poignant and dangerous moment from childhood. And indeed, that is the picture I saw. Without lyrics I had to trust that the music itself would tell the story.

Long instrumental passages were meant to illustrate an invisible movie: the story of my recovery from drugs. Rorschachs (The Unsigned Painting / The Weird Beasts) was a collage of disjointed poetry, the broken places that perhaps led up to the emotional collapse of addiction. I went with the original demo for the song on the record because I determined even in 1984 that it was about the feeling, not the perfection of the notes.

What begins as a recitation *"On Sunday the ladies took off their wirey old hats and made donuts in the back of the church. I could always smell them cooking in the middle of mass"* is joined with a melody *"I brought the Weird Beast here from Van Nuys Boulevard. so I would not be without him when the Tar Tars reign covered the empty streets of Paris. And on one of those passing boats I thought I saw the Weird Beast speaking in the Russian. Will he kill the czar? Will he kill the czar?"*

Like I said, a collage. This music was created and produced by my new producer James Newton Howard, who would go on to score all of M. Night Shyamalan's movies. He hired the great Ralph Burns to score my piano parts—thus the flutes and harps, some of them far too precious for my taste but I stand by it. *The Magazine* brought new fans who had not particularly responded to the first record because of the massive hit, nor the second, again, because of "Chuck E's in Love" and what they thought I was about.

The Magazine tour included interpretive performances of the songs, with staged vignettes, even choreographed dancing. I was determined to take my career, and pop music if possible, in a new direction. I thought I had the power to do that, being the bankable Rickie Lee Jones, whatever that was. The singers wore microphones, freeing them to dance, and I choreographed a lot of dancing for this tour. This was theater. Unfortunately, I was booked in large concert venues. Location is everything, and for the first time, I let agents and managers rule over my better sense.

But what I think really went wrong was the death of my mentor Bob Regehr, followed by the long dying of my father. I was venturing out into a new direction without the producers I had known since I began working, and the company that had been my home through all these changes of the past few years. I simply feared every step I took and every day I awoke. Would I relapse today? So what happened on stage, it was going to happen sooner or later, I guess.

This half concert was confusing for most audiences. Success seemed to depend entirely on the venue. Our first show at the University of Illinois was a huge success. (I think that was where John Malkovich saw me, as he told me when he came to discuss making a video for "Satellites" some years later.) I saved the review for many years. After this first performance, it seemed like I was going to be able to change my image as I forged ahead with innovative ideas. But my manager had insisted on booking me in secondary markets—a huge amphitheater in Spokane, then a strip mall in Eugene. By the time we reached L.A., the mismanagement of this crucial step in my career had put me in a highly emotional state. In spite of great receptions in San Francisco and Seattle, I could see the writing on the wall.

Perhaps because it was my hometown, Los Angeles was my judgmental father, my frowning mother, my dangerous home. Musicians rarely enjoy playing hometowns where we are forever trying to prove something. Me, I had too many hometowns. This show at the Universal Amphitheatre would be my final American show. I was too young to know that one should never book an important media city on the last night. The musicians are already half-gone.

Even though I'd sold out five thousand seats pretty quickly, I was worried and discontent. Something in me was still trying to apologize to the people for having been an addict. That critic—the one you keep in your heart—he would never forgive me for who he thought I was.

This theater piece was an attempt to explain myself, and so it was, in a way, as much therapy as theater. I used Father's war stories in a segment called "The Scorpion" and a metaphor for my drug use was called "Gloria in the Kitchen." Drawing parallels with songs like

"Gravity" would bring together the entire performance. It was going alright, at first. All the lighting cues, the dance moves, everything perfect. I remember actually sighing as I approached the audience and stood at the microphone. Then, some guy yelled out:

"Play 'My Funny Valentine.'"

I should've smiled, grateful that he loved my rendition of this tired old standard. I interpreted his request as a rejection of all that I had offered. If he was yelling at me, and everyone could hear him, it meant this work I created did not captivate him. If he was not captivated, maybe the rest of them weren't either. Suddenly, I felt that I had failed. The new life I had envisioned melted before my eyes and in the hyper state I was in, I just . . . collapsed inside. I turned and left the stage.

I recently received a letter from a person in attendance that day, who wrote something like, "It was a great show and we all cheered and cheered for you to return. We were so happy when you came back and you sang. 'Have Yourself a Merry Little Christmas.' We were on your side." But the Rickie that I was could not feel anyone on her side.

Next day, Rickie Lee Jones's Universal Amphitheatre show received not one but *three* reviews, two of them hailing the end of a great career, but one of them highlighting an essential clause in the contract between artist and audience. The clause that says, "Artists sometimes act like artists."

The review said something like, *We have these great artists among us who do not always act the way we think they should. They act up, let us down. Judy Garland was one, Van Morrison, and . . . Rickie Lee Jones. These artists are driven by muses we do not understand. Their art is great and so is their suffering. Their genius takes them high, and sometimes, we witness their fall. Last night we saw Rickie Lee Jones fall.*

The critic offered respect where all the rest felt they had the right to admonish and ridicule. My heart was broken after that show. The writer's admiration lifted me, gave me the strength to continue touring, and I did so with great determination. I left America a few months later to finish up *The Magazine* tour. I broke up with my boyfriend/director, and I was looking for love with a capital S—ex.

I headed to Australia for my first tour down under. It was an amended version of *The Magazine* play and it was very successful, on stage anyway. My crew, my band, not so much. The tour manager stole my American Express card and took his family on vacation. He said it was severance pay for how much he hated working with me.

Upon my return I stopped in Tahiti, where I met some French surfers who were making a movie about the reef around Papeete. The director sent a young man, Pascal, to my hotel to give me a lift to the Museum of Gauguin. He seemed nice enough but terribly sad. True love had let me down so why not just try a stranger instead? Pascal spoke no English, but I was only looking for company. I would marry him. We would get to know each other as the years went by. And that is just what I did.

Three months later we married in Bisbee, Arizona, where my father was living with his Jean, the love of his life. My father was dying of cancer and I wanted to get married before he passed away. I wanted Daddy to have this one happy day of being my father, and I wanted for him to "give me away," so I married Pascal on October 4, 1984. I wanted to show my father that I was going to be alright. I had someone. I am sure he saw through it all. There was a little conversation between us, sitting on the back steps eating a bowl of Pascal's creamed vegetable soup. Liquids were all my dad could eat now.

"Good soup," Daddy said.

"Yours is better."

He smiled at me and leaned in close. "And I don't dirty every pot in the kitchen."

I knew that he understood what I was doing by that one remark. And somehow, we were at peace, he and I. Our little secret about the soup, I kept it close to my heart all these years.

The day after my wedding, Dad and I were desperately trying to say something that mattered. We knew we would probably never meet again in this world. Father, who had judged every effort I made so severely, "You can swim faster, dance harder, sing better," was now unable to speak without drooling, the cancer had claimed the back of his throat. He still smoked though.

"It's all I have," he told me.

I knew I had to accept this old man as he was, not condemn him for not being the dad I wished he could have been.

My father took my hand in his and said "Rickie Lee, I can't have been a failure, if I had you as a daughter." It was a moment both elegant and awkward. I was duly dumb and undone. I looked him in the eye. "Know that I hear you, Daddy," I said silently.

A few minutes later, my husband and I climbed into our rented car and drove north to Tucson, and then made our way back to France.

Father's votive of words was an acknowledgement of sins, a lantern lit at just the right moment, meant to illuminate the path of one lost child. Rehearsed, yes, probably for years. That was what made it unbearable in its beauty. He had finally decided that I would be able to use this candle to forgive him and so before he died, Richard Loris Jones and I were father and daughter again. Rodeo riders, gold prospectors, exchanging falling stars, enough golden moondust to write a thousand songs. That day I drove away feeling like my father was finally proud of me.

Daddy died three months later, in January. I was living on Île Saint-Louis in Paris, and I got the news on a cold winter night, a phone call from Jean. I got dressed and I walked by the river Seine, trying to find my father in my heart, but I could not find him anywhere.

I flew back for the funeral. Only my cousins came to honor their surrogate father, none of my own family, except Janet. The wake could have been fraught with unseemly drama—there was my older sister wearing the black dress she had stolen from me after seeing me crawl in the window of my house in that first *Rolling Stone* article. She just crawled into my house herself and stole my guitar and my dress—and now she was wearing it! I did what my father would have wished. I hugged her and consoled her. After sitting there on the folded chairs a while, I stood up and read a poem from Dylan Thomas, "After the Fair."

When I came home, a letter from my father was waiting for me. I was exhausted, overwhelmed, and overjoyed. Thank you! One last very private moment with my father, after his death. A line from heaven's own screenwriter. In his letter my father wrote of all the great things still left for me to do, acting for one, and he mentioned his plans for the café he would open soon.

He closed with:

I am still waiting for your letter, it must be stuck in the mail. I am sure it will arrive any day.

Love Always,

Father

The Albatross

The Albatross is a seabird who sometimes has a very difficult time getting up off the ground. His extraordinary wingspan makes him clumsy to the landlubbers. Once aflight, the bird is a beautiful sight to behold, brushing the clouds, its call heard by the other side of the sea. Seen from the sea by sailor and pirate alike, the Albatross is good luck to any whose feet are not wholly on terra firma.

"The Albatross" is the only song I wrote about my family. It was included on Geffen Records' *Traffic from Paradise* which would be my final work with Warner Brothers Records. As well, "The Albatross" would be the final song of the seafaring theme. The poetic vessels which came before it, like "Pirates" and "We Belong Together," had long waited dockside for "The Albatross" to be christened "Her Majesty" and for me to return her captain to the pirates one final time. Once I wrote the last verse about my ancestors, I knew I had no more to say about one-legged men. So I burnt the ship and rowed to shore.

> *There, there is my ship finally come in*
> *I see the mast running down stairs*
> *Over the garden wall I hear the sailor's call*
> *I see The Albatross.*

Oh now I can go home.
Home to my children I left behind long ago.
With my mother, the Moon,
That's where my father is,
This broken heart is his . . .
Archipelago
Here, here's where we live
Here is a sea—My Family
We'll always be
As young as we've ever been

Death will not part us again
Nearer to heaven now then
10,000 ancestors
Who dream of me.

("The Albatross")

I would keep making music. I had to. In 1989, there was a beautiful record with Walter Becker, *Flying Cowboys*, maybe too beautiful. We had a number-one hit on adult radio with "Satellites," and I made another video at last—but too long after my debut eleven-minute video had paved the way for anyone to notice. Then I made a jazz record with an Argentinian flavor. Put that in your jazz standard, Mr. Feather! He panned it, but my friends in Argentina loved it. It was 1990. It seemed as if so much of what I did for that decade was met with suspicion. Still, I could not stop singing. I was getting better at it. In 2000 I received the Tenco Award in San Remo, Italy. It is given to musicians whose work has uniquely impacted music, especially those who take the road less traveled and light the way for others of the same ilk. Few recipients are American. I was honored.

It was 2010, and I had not been to Australia since 1995 when I toured as a duet with Rob Wasserman. Finally, I was invited by Lou Reed to play a festival he was curating called Vivid Sydney. Then I was invited to also perform at the Melbourne Festival. I checked into my suite, there was a bouquet of flowers. Nice. As I ate the little chocolate treats the hotel sent up, I took in the view of the park and flicked through the television channels until something caught my attention. It was a horse race and in the middle of the stadium was a singer. He seemed familiar—and I heard a song I knew well. That was the moment I discovered that my song, "The Horses," had become the unofficial Australian national anthem. The entire stadium was singing my song! It was awesome! Dude!

> *That's the way it's gonna be, little darlin'*
> *You'll be riding on the horses ya ya,*
> *Way up in the sky, little darlin'*
> *If you fall I'll pick you up, pick you up*
> ("The Horses")

He was singing the song I'd written for my only child, my daughter Charlotte Rose, the year she was born. 1988. That was the day I discovered that my song had a life of its own far beyond me. I wished my daughter could experience what I was experiencing. She was having so much trouble navigating her way in this life, she must have felt alone. If only she knew, if only these voices could lift her up and sail her away. It seemed as if the words, no, the hopes I had when I wrote "The Horses" were manifest. Surely the world itself would lift her up because here was a stadium on the other side of the world singing Charlotte's song. Her journey was every bit a Jones tale, every mile hard-won. I felt my mother was with me too on that day in Melbourne. Yes, yes, she was gone, but I felt her there watching me, laughing at the magic of it all. You see, magic never left my life.

Family will break your heart either way. Yes, they'll come to your dad's funeral wearing your stolen dress, but they'll also drive to the bus station in the middle of the night to pick you up when someone steals your buddy's new motorcycle, and you two got no way home. It is family who leave the flock just to save one little lamb—you—and sing as they do it. Finally, you will suspect someone was up there watching this whole the time. Human or divine, family sings a song no one else can hear, and if you will only listen, they will sing it each night until you are fast asleep.

My brother Danny lived his life in Olympia. He got a real estate license and joined a health club. The manager of the club told him patrons were uncomfortable seeing his stump. He had to remove the cumbersome plastic leg when he sat at the bench to lift weights. He felt so humiliated, he never went back. I bought a house from him. Handicapped people are not very popular in the real estate business so he gave up trying to sell stuff and joined a pool tournament crew. They won a few games. After my mother died, Dan and I lost track of each other. He ended up in a bottom ring nursing home in Eastern Washington and it took a great deal of money to get him out of there. For some reason the little legal echelon of Spokane wanted my hide, kept talking about my concert there back in the 1980s as they pressed my attorney to take custody of my brother. I kept hearing my mother say, *Don't you let them take him.* How was it possible after all that we had been through that he should end up in the custody of the state just like my mother so long ago?

Turned out there were good folks up there trying to look after my brother. Danny's brain injury was finally getting the best of him, he was having trouble staying in the here and now. Hey, it's hard for any of us to stay in the here and now when so much of our life is unseen, an iceberg, the past frozen beneath us. I will not cry over the past, and it was a pretty glorious past, wasn't it, Dan? Baseball mitts and BB guns, a baby stallion and an old guitar. Mama's blue, blue eyes.

Danny is doing okay. I sent him some new T-shirts. He asks how my record is doing. My career makes him happy.

Motherhood had come to me late. I was thirty-three, the year I began *Flying Cowboys*. In fact, I was still nursing when I began pre-production. The birth of my Charlotte Rose gave me a reason to live, and to keep living. I saw my duty as a mother come before all other duties. I sidelined my career—happily—and devoted myself to the incredible miracle of a new human being in the world. Motherhood suited me, I became the better version of myself. I guess I was perhaps a better mother than daughter. Year by year, hour by hour, we never stop learning, not if we don't want to. That is the certain grace of aging. We keep changing.

My mother had a stroke in 2006, and since her stroke, she and I communicated much the same as we always had except for one thing. My mother could not really speak anymore, so I had to rely on a lot of telepathy and common sense.

I would watch mom's sentence traveling down a road but the intersection was blocked. She knew what she wanted to say. There had been an accident and her idea could not get around it. Mom and I had to find new ways of getting her thoughts across. This was my greatest year with Bettye, for even in her dying she taught me lessons, and I served her, quite literally, in a way I had never before. Sometimes it took minutes to say the simplest thing. I could hear myself being gentle with my mother. She was teaching me patience, and I was learning that mom had an unlimited reservoir of humor in her. She never pouted and always laughed out loud at her mistakes and foibles. She became the better version of herself at last.

I resolved that the most important thing was whatever she had to say, period. This moment, right now, is why we live. And I am here to listen to you, Mom. We live with powerful heartaches at the end of our parents' lives. Mother and I grew close again. I really enjoyed being with her, imagining that all that she was—humble, kind, innocent, vulnerable, tenacious, unstoppable, and unlimited in her potential—was because she refused to feel sorry for herself. All that must be inside of me too. And, for the first time since I was six years old, I was proud to be made from Bettye Jones.

I was standing there in the barn trying to feed my horses. It was 2006, I came home late, had no one to help me. In my dress clothes I ran to the stables and started throwing flakes of hay into the stalls. I looked up and my mother was there, just like she would be if I were ten, or if she were not crippled from the stroke, there she was trying to help me. Mom was trying to lift the hose and put it to the water trough. And she did it somehow, she helped me with my work. Turning my head away from her so she would not see my tears, I gathered myself, opened the stall door for Ella to get her rations.

Mom was my greatest champion from the very beginning. Except for drugs, I shared every event with her. Boyfriends, famous friends, triumph, and regret. My mother subscribed to *Rolling Stone* for an entire decade, complaining that I was not on the cover again. Watching me fade from the limelight seemed harder on her than it was for me. She didn't understand that careers must be pliable. If an act insists on not changing and making the music audience come to them they can end up an oldies act. I did not want to be an oldies act. I always wanted my music to be a place un-aging. The real danger of early success is that our parents, our children, our friends also reap what we sow. I had watched the trajectory of every member of my family change as they chased the fairy light of my success.

I weathered the storms of humility, the people who did not offer backstage passes anymore, or the people who did not even know my name anymore, and I kept on working. Mom told me I should just quit. Finally, I asked:

"And do what, Mom? This . . . . this is what I am."

The horses watered, Mom and I held hands as we walked back to the house. We held each other up in different ways that night. We spoke in silence, our hearts content, that contentment only Mother could bring to me. The old nest, I guess, my mother was my old nest. I made us some hot tea with milk, and we sat in front of the television listening for a car in the distance. Mom went to bed. I sat by the window waiting for my daughter to come home. I drank in those last visions of my mother as if I knew one day I would thirst for her, and there she would be. But I am always thirsty now. I miss her terribly.

Rickie Lee at the fair

EPILOGUE

T he fact is careers breathe like everything else. There are good years and bad, great decades and evil ones. Show business is the business of showing your life to the whole wide world. It is the finest tempering of one's mettle and one's friendships, for friends mostly fall by the wayside and the ones that last are the kind that the great lines are written for. It is a hard road but a great one. I'm glad I lived long enough to say this and believe it. I have had the greatest opportunities. I did not try to be a billionaire, the money was bewildering to me. I lived a life of destiny and chance. I chose a different road from the "Big" wealth and fame, and it must have been the one on which I was most likely to find happiness. I am glad I can introduce myself to a new audience of young people and know I am being heard for who I truly am now.

Fame is a tincture made for the brightest and deepest souls among us. We have what it takes to withstand it. Fame was never meant for the fifteen-minute brand. This troubadour life is only for the fiercest hearts, only for those vessels that can be broken to smithereens and still keep beating out the rhythm for a new song.

ACKNOWLEDGMENTS

Gratitude is not worth the paper it is spilled upon
Unless it has been hard-won.
But once you use it, you will keep coming back for more.

My thanks,
    For praise and direction

From friends, who read pages, found photographs,
listened to entire chapters
as I cut and expanded and rewrote and returned
to the original . . .

    For devotion, tears and joy

Ron Stone, Gwen Thompkins, Lexie Montgomery,
Carla Parisi, Teresa Tudary, Kim Gillingham, Mike Dillion,
Russ Titleman, and Della Puckett

    For patience

Which is, rather than a virtue, a muscle.
You can grow a big one if you have the time to wait.

To the following, thank you for hanging in there. Who could imagine
It would take seven years for me to get through that tunnel?

Andrew Blauner, Morgan Entrekin, Katie Raissian, and Yvonne Cha
at Grove Press,
And especially Elisabeth Schmitz
Who watched me nail myself to the cross
Get down climb back up get down and
who waited
For nearly seven years for me to finally say
"It is finished."

For showing me the way
With humility and perseverance

Jamie Dell'Apa
When I had nearly given,
Jamie spent a year organizing,
Stroking and gentling the pages
Of my wild horse of a story.
It reared back on its reckless abundance of pages—

"I'm going in!" he cried.
He confirmed dates and locations for his own satisfaction,
Prepared a glossary of songs, and quietly
Became a believer in magic.
That was when the battle turned around.
"Good stuff in there," he promised.
"Right back at ya," I mused.

For still being Willin'

The Glens of Ohio (especially Heidi) for pictures and stories of our
Grandmother Peggy.

Lee Cantelon,
And the photographers and music producers who granted licenses,
Especially Bob Dylan,
Who set the pace with kindness and a low fee.

To my brother, Danny, my champion,
And my daughter, Charlotte,
I am in your corner always

Thank you.

GLOSSARY OF SONGS

"America"

Words and Music by Paul Simon
Copyright © 1968 by Paul Simon Music (BMI) Copyright
Renewed International Copyright Secured All Rights Reserved
Reprinted by Permission
Reprinted by Permission of Hal Leonard LLC

"For Emily, Whenever I May Find Her"

Words and Music by Paul Simon
Copyright © 1966, 1967 Paul Simon (BMI) International Copyright Secured All Rights Reserved Used by Permission
Reprinted by Permission of Hal Leonard LLC

"I Can Never Go Home Anymore"

Words and Music by George Morton
Copyright © 1965 Screen Gems-EMI Music Inc., Tender Tunes
Inc. and Trio Music Company Copyright Renewed All Rights on
behalf of Screen Gems-EMI Music Inc. and Tender Tunes Inc.
Administered by Sony/ATV Music Publishing LLC
All Rights on behalf of Trio Music Company Administered by
BMG Rights Management (US) LLC International Copyright
Secured All Rights Reserved
Reprinted by Permission of Hal Leonard LLC

"Infinity"

Written by Rickie Lee Jones
Published by The Other Side Of Desire Music (ASCAP)
Licensed courtesy of Blue Raincoat Songs (PRS).
All rights reserved. Used by permission.

"Jet Song"

by Leonard Bernstein and Stephen Sondheim
© 1956, 1957, 1958, 1959 by Amberson Holdings LLC and
Stephen Sondheim. Copyright renewed. Leonard Bernstein Music
Publishing Company LLC, publisher. Boosey & Hawkes, A
Concord Company International copyright secured.
All Rights Reserved. Used With Permission.

"Just Like a Woman"

Written by Bob Dylan
Copyright © 1966 by Dwarf Music; renewed 1994 by Dwarf Music.
All Rights Reserved. Used With Permission.

"Like a Rolling Stone"

Written by Bob Dylan
Copyright © 1965 by Warner Bros. Inc.; renewed 1993 by Special
Rider Music.
All Rights Reserved. Used With Permission.

"A Lover's Concerto"

Words and Music by Sandy Linzer and Denny Randell
Copyright © 1965 Screen Gems-EMI Music Inc. Copyright
Renewed All Rights Administered by Sony/ATV Music Publishing
LLC, International Copyright Secured All Rights Reserved
Reprinted by Permission of Hal Leonard LLC

"The Moon Is Made of Gold"

Written by Richard Jones
Published by The Other Side Of Desire Music (ASCAP)
Licensed courtesy of Blue Raincoat Songs (PRS).
All rights reserved. Used by permission.

"The Needle And the Damage Done"

Words and Music by Neil Young
Copyright © 1971 by Broken Fiddle Music Copyright Renewed
All Rights Reserved Used by Permission
Reprinted by Permission of Hal Leonard LLC

"Sugar Mountain"

Words and Music by Neil Young
Copyright © 1968 by Broken Arrow Music Corporation
Copyright Renewed All Rights Reserved Used by Permission
Reprinted by Permission of Hal Leonard LLC

"What's Going On"

Words and Music by Renaldo Benson, Alfred Cleveland and
Marvin Gaye
Copyright © 1970 Jobete Music Co., Inc., MGIII Music, NMG
Music and FCG Music
Copyright Renewed All Rights Administered by Sony/ATV Music
Publishing LLC on behalf of Stone Agate Music (A Division of
Jobete Music Co., Inc.), International Copyright Secured All Rights
Reserved
Reprinted by Permission of Hal Leonard LLC

"Where Is Love?"

From the Columbia Pictures — Romulus Film *Oliver!*
Words and Music by Lionel Bart
© Copyright 1960 (Renewed) 1968 (Renewed) Lakeview Music
Co., Ltd., London, England TRO – Hollis Music, Inc., New York.
All Rights Reserved. Used With Permission.

"Wooden Ships"

Words and Music by David Crosby, Stephen Stills and Paul Kantner
Copyright © 1969 Stay Straight Music, Gold Hill Music, Inc.
and Icebag Music Corp. Copyright Renewed All Rights for Stay
Straight Music Administered by BMG Rights Management (US)
LLC All Rights for Gold Hill Music, Inc. and Icebag Music Corp.
Administered by Wixen Music Publishing, Inc. All Rights Reserved
Used by Permission
Reprinted by Permission of Hal Leonard LLC

"Yesterday"

Words and Music by John Lennon and Paul McCartney
Copyright © 1965 Sony/ATV Music Publishing LLC Copyright
Renewed All Rights Administered by Sony/ATV Music Publishing
LLC, International Copyright Secured All Rights Reserved
Reprinted by Permission of Hal Leonard LLC

"You Don't Love Me When I Cry"

Words and Music by Laura Nyro
Copyright © 1969, 1972 EMI Blackwood Music Inc. Copyright
Renewed All Rights Administered by Sony/ATV Music Publishing
LLC, International Copyright Secured All Rights Reserved
Reprinted by Permission of Hal Leonard LLC

All Rickie Lee Jones lyrics licensed courtesy of Blue Raincoat Songs
(PRS). All rights reserved. Used by permission.